ADVANCE PRAISE

Although a lot has been written on the topic since the 2018 revelations by Tanushree Dutta, Vinta Nanda and several others, non-fiction books on the topic are hard to find. More importantly, this book goes beyond MeToo and deep into gender today in India. Through an apt mix of interviews, articles and references to Indian culture, delineating the nuances of a woman's status in the Indian society and the patriarchal system, the book delivers excellent scholarship in a narrative tone which is easy to grasp and hard to put down. Each chapter takes up an important, relevant piece of the puzzle while the chapters, conceptualized in an orderly manner, deliver a seamless denouement. It is one of the most comprehensive and contemporary reads on women's issues that are out there.

Dr Reicha Tanwar, *Director, Centre for Women's Studies and Development, Kurukshetra University, and Gender Rights Activist*

Tanushree Ghosh has given us a remarkable book. At one level, it is a reasoned analysis of how the MeToo moment that grew into a movement has worked out (or not) in India. We see so clearly from her book how all the ways people have created to make themselves different in India—religion, class, caste and tradition (read patriarchy) have made it easy for violence against women to flourish. How difficult it then becomes for women just to be recognized as human beings! At another level, *Beyond #MeToo* pinpoints the similarities and differences between Indian and worldwide #MeToo movements. The book brings to life a social movement for justice through its gripping stories of courageous women.

Roald Hoffmann, *Noble Laureate; Poet; and Chemist*

The issue of gender has been ever-pertinent and becomes more so with every passing day for India. A lens that covers the world and time travels into the past, present and future and yet does so in a language that resonates with the everyday reader, distilling academic nuances into simple, summarized facts, is what we desperately need. This book provides that. It is a non-fiction book on such a heavy matter that reads like a can't-put-down commercial fiction. It is a much-needed must-read.

Anupama Dalmia, *multiple Award-winning Blogger; Author; Serial Entrepreneur; Social Influencer; and Karmaveer Chakra Awardee*

Tanushree Ghosh's work is a monumental exercise in reframing the debate around and beyond #MeToo in India as well as America from her vantage point of being familiar with both the cultures. Ghosh gives a masterly account of the movement, its achievements, aspirations and future. It fills a much-needed gap in the scholarship around the subject with women's voices and experiences from the ground.

Kaveree Bamzai, *Author; Senior Journalist,* India Today, The Indian Express *and* The Times of India; *and Former Editor,* India Today

With a much-needed incisive look at the impact of the #MeToo movement in India, *Beyond #MeToo* is an important book that analyses the global movement, the upheaval it created in India and the post-#MeToo world.

Kiran Manral, *Author and Founder, India Helps*

It is brutally honest; I am unable to stop crying.

Sandhya Renukamba, *Senior Editor and*
Community Manager, Women's Web

The author deals with this complicated topic with clinical precision—presenting facts and viewpoints of experts in the field to substantiate her argument. The book is structured well. Each chapter takes up an important point of the issue, as she goes on to explain it. The chapters have been conceptualized in an orderly manner, moving linearly towards denouement. The author keeps on giving hints about what is to follow and rarely digresses from the thread that is being presented to the reader.

There is a nice mix of interviews, articles and references to the Indian culture, delineating the nuances of a woman's status in the Indian society and how the patriarchal system creates hurdles for the victims wanting a 'fair deal'. The author has a firm grip on the moral ethos of India as well as that of the Western world and uses this expertise well to portray how these change the equation for women. There are enough evidences of thorough research that the writer has done to understand this complicated situation, and more or less she maintains objectivity in her argument. It is an academic and analytical work, which has some valuable insights on the issue of sexual vulnerability of women in society in general and at workplace in particular. It throws light on certain areas that need to be dealt with if #MeToo has to have a significant impact after it loses the 'shock and awe' effect.

Geetu Vaid, *Chief Sub-editor,* The Tribune

Beyond
#MeToo

Beyond #MeToo

Ushering Women's Era or Just Noise?

Tanushree Ghosh

Los Angeles | London | New Delhi
Singapore | Washington DC | Melbourne

First published in 2022 by

SAGE Publications India Pvt Ltd
B1/I-1 Mohan Cooperative Industrial Area
Mathura Road, New Delhi 110 044, India
www.sagepub.in

SAGE Publications Inc
2455 Teller Road
Thousand Oaks, California 91320, USA

SAGE Publications Ltd
1 Oliver's Yard, 55 City Road
London EC1Y 1SP, United Kingdom

SAGE Publications Asia-Pacific Pte Ltd
18 Cross Street #10-10/11/12
China Square Central
Singapore 048423

Published by Vivek Mehra for SAGE Publications India Pvt Ltd. Typeset in 11/14 pt Adobe Caslon Pro by Fidus Design Pvt Ltd, Chandigarh.

Library of Congress Control Number: 2021950940

ISBN: 978-93-5479-381-3 (PB)

SAGE Team: Namarita Kathait, Satvinder Kaur and Rajinder Kaur

....

To my daughter, my mother and my sister.
To all daughters, mothers and sisters
alive today. And to all daughters, mothers
and sisters yet to be born. Dedicated in
preparation of the day on which no one will
have to walk with them for their safety.

....

Thank you for choosing a SAGE product!
If you have any comment, observation or feedback,
I would like to personally hear from you.

Please write to me at **contactceo@sagepub.in**

Vivek Mehra, Managing Director and CEO, SAGE India.

Bulk Sales

SAGE India offers special discounts
for purchase of books in bulk.
We also make available special imprints
and excerpts from our books on demand.

For orders and enquiries, write to us at

Marketing Department
SAGE Publications India Pvt Ltd
B1/I-1, Mohan Cooperative Industrial Area
Mathura Road, Post Bag 7
New Delhi 110044, India

E-mail us at **marketing@sagepub.in**

Subscribe to our mailing list
Write to **marketing@sagepub.in**

This book is also available as an e-book.

CONTENTS

FOREWORD

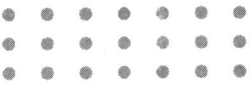

Issues of rape and sexual assault, especially at the workplace, go beyond social justice. It eliminates the routes to economic justice for women and creates a perpetual cycle of oppression, discrimination and further violation. Decades prior to the dust storm of the MeToo movement, Bhanwari Devi's fight in India itself started the fight for a woman's safety while she did her job. And the struggle—the question of a woman's right to safety and for her to have equal rights—continues.

The struggles fought by Bhanwari and her husband have been multifold. At the personal front, she has to confront her husband's issues regarding purity of body after rape where her husband found it difficult to have a physical relationship with her. Fighting this prevailing concept was tough at many levels. As her project director and friend for a lifetime, I cherished the relationship with Bhanwari where she could talk about this issue openly with me in the presence of her husband. I feel that the shift of thought about fighting for justice has a higher sanctity than the physical touch of a male. But I was also broken literally by her and by her husband after counselling them.

The social boycott and notions prevailing around the purity of the body in the society resulted in the use of abusive language by people, including her boys. Bhanwari's sons could not cope and slowly started feeling that their mother didn't do the right thing. They felt that she had made their life miserable. Bhanwari never thought of giving up despite the fact that the rapists continued to live in the same village and interfere in her life. Till date, two sides of her life have continued. On the one side, she is the icon of women's struggle in Rajasthan, India, and the world, for which she received respect and accolades. But the other side is grim and painful.

Bhanwari Devi's struggle broke the silence around the feudal mindset of the state of Rajasthan, role-modelling courage to fight against majority rich political influencers. But all this while, Bhanwari struggled financially. Her fight for justice resulted in the end of their livelihood (making earthen pots and pulling rickshaw in the city by her husband). After the incidence, they stopped making and selling earthen pots. Her main livelihood is saathin's honorarium and award money.

At the backdrop of Bhanwari's fight, I also wished to pen down the fight for women's rights in India which Tanushree has now accomplished to do. I am happy that this book and the author are committed to keeping #MeToo alive for posterity. The change needed is in the mindset because the assault on a woman is never just the assault alone.

Dr Pritam Pal
Vishakha Chairperson; Former Women's Development Programme Project Director for Bhanwari Devi, UNICEF

PREFACE

Over the years that this book has been in progress, many changes have transpired. Such changes are expected to transpire every day. For example, as I am writing this preface, I hear of the Bombay High Court judgment on POCSO Act that groping a minor's breast is not to be considered sexual attack (January 2021). These changes will make many such laws which are analysed in this work differently from what they were at the time of writing. Some will be rendered toothless. New legal provisions will emerge. But what will not change is what I felt as a little girl, groped by a stranger who squeezed my breasts (which happened to me multiple times as a child, and if anything can be said from reading social media posts of my friends today, it happens to all of us again and again). What will not change is what I feel reading the Bombay High Court judgment today as I learn that it was passed by a female judge. This feeling is why I wrote this book. This feeling is why I hope you—man or woman—will read it.

Disclaimer: *Reference to allegations in this work doesn't prove or disprove any accusation. The intent of this work is to explore how such allegations were received, processed and dispositioned in the contexts of MeToo, gender parity and harassment prevention.*

ACKNOWLEDGEMENTS

This book wouldn't have happened if not for an entire tribe coming together. Of this tribe, some I knew well, some I had merely crossed paths with and some I had simply cold called. And yet they had all graciously offered their support. This tribe, which consists of each and every person quoted in this book, is the foundation on which this book stands. There are quite a few pillars on this foundation that I leaned against often. Two of strongest ones are my closest friends R. Prasad and Chakravarthy Akella, whose support makes not just this book but my entire journey in gender activism possible. Over the past few years of crafting this book, they brainstormed with me and provided me with thoughts, materials and concepts. My other pillars are my mother Manu Sengupta, my father Pradeep Ghosh and my sister Madhumanti Ghosh. They stayed with me when I gave up and didn't let me fall.

I owe Suhail Mathur of The Book Bakers for his audacity of pushing me to write on this topic. Suhail saw in me what I didn't see myself and urged me to venture into non-fiction.

My husband Ashish Dhall bore the brunt of the extra hours after work, and my daughter is my reason for all that I do. I do not have enough words to thank them, nor can they be thanked. My noting them here is to thank the universe that I have them in my life.

INTRODUCTION

For almost everything of significance in our lives, it is not hard for most of us to recall where we were at the exact moment of the matter unfolding or of us coming to know of it. The most factual examples of this that I can think of are events of mammoth proportions and tragic. I was walking into our living room chucking my school bag on the sofa, as the television set that was almost always on had started showing images of a tower on fire from a plane crashing into it. I was walking by a salon in Central Kolkata on one of my trips back home when I had heard the news of my closest friend jumping off a building. Even the displays on that salon's glass panes are still vivid in my memory. I was eating dinner with some friends visiting, almost full-term pregnant, when the news of a gang rape on a bus started running on NDTV, from the city that I was in just a month back. A lot of these memories visit me often as flashbacks, outlining the exact vistas which were etched the first time, placing them firmer into my conscience.

But the breaking of #MeToo (by which I mean the start of the hashtag on Twitter in October 2017 and its almost immediate viral spread) is different. For the life of me, I can't remember the point in time when I came across the phenomena unfolding for the first time. It may be so because I had been travelling through Japan, Singapore and India—out on a multi-nation business trip. Or, more possibly, it may be because although #MeToo is a movement whose strength lies in its formalization, MeToo was always with me. And I am sure that I am not the only woman who can claim this.

On reading the words of Tarana Burke[1] (an activist from The Bronx, New York, who had started using the phrase 'MeToo'

---

1 https://www.nytimes.com/2017/10/20/us/me-too-movement-tarana-burke.html

in 2006 to outline and emphasize how prevalent sexual violence is, especially among young black women), I felt this realization reinforcing.

'The "MeToo" Movement started in the deepest, darkest place in my soul,' Burke writes in the 'Inception' segment on her website. She continues to outline how, on hearing a heartbreaking tale of assault from a vulnerable victim, she had identified yet shunned both the victim and her own experience out of her sphere of acknowledgement.[2]

This is where and how MeToo had really started for me too.

This is where MeToo starts and ends for a lot of us.

This is why the 2017 hashtag went viral.

And this is why it is impossible to identify the exact moment when MeToo unfolded for me. Because even though #MeToo, thanks to Harvey Weinstein, is now spoken of mostly in the context of 'workplace sexual harassment', Burke's MeToo, and that of most of us, is about acknowledging that we all have experienced violation at some point in our lives and have yet stayed silent. We all know someone who is being assaulted or has been assaulted, or of institutions and individuals who perpetuate abuse. And we all have been silent—for ourselves and others.

MeToo had unfolded for me when I had first shared with my mother the mal-intent I could feel in the physical touch of a close relative. MeToo had unfolded for my mother when she shut me up saying how it must be a misunderstanding, as she had probably died inside, praying that I indeed am mistaken while knowing very well that I wasn't.

MeToo had unfolded for me when I heard the same narrative in my late 20s from a friend who co-authored a Huffington Post piece on abuse with me.[3] Listening to her explain how, in spite

---

2 https://metoomvmt.org/the-inception/
3 https://www.huffpost.com/entry/for-all-the-women-in-indi_b_9833702

of her deep love and respect for her mother (who she described being her inspiration for everything she has pursued in life), she couldn't forget and forgive her mother's silence. MeToo unfolded for me when I realized, as I listened to her, that of all the grudges I had for my mother, this incident hadn't even found a real place! That is how commonplace and compliant I had become to sexual abuse. That is how understanding I was willing to be of anyone who couldn't raise their voice, for I couldn't raise mine either.

MeToo had unfolded for me when sitting in a brightly lit room in gorgeous upstate New York with sounds of gorges and intellectual chatter reverberating all around me, I had realized that almost all the men in the room were expressing some amount of surprise on hearing the women in the room who were talking about how they had been touched inappropriately, even molested, in crowded public transportations. While every woman in the room was saying that they had experienced this at some point in their life, I had wondered how this could be possible.

Abuse. So commonplace. So not acknowledged.

MeToo had unfolded for me in my IIT days where tales of misdemeanours of certain professors were known up and down the halls, yet were impossible (and even deemed unnecessary) to be raised for complaints. That is why MeToo rekindled in me when Raya Sarkar published her list.[4] Just like the arguments ('boys will be boys' and 'locker room talk has its place') acceptable as counterarguments to the current US president's hot mic mishap, certain things were deemed acceptable of 'brilliant' men. As it has transpired since Raya published her list, formal accusations are seldom made and mere 'concerns' needn't be investigated, creating a perfect catch-22, therefore. Why formal complaints won't be found, as we all know, has to do with how impossible it's to successfully prove, let alone have any action taken, indict or

---

4 https://www.huffingtonpost.in/2018/10/25/metoo-in-india-75-professors-30-institutes-what-happened-to-raya-sarkar-s-list-of-sexual-harassers_a_23571422/

prosecute the accused in most of these cases with the current tools we have in hand for outlining, investigating and proving anything outside of gross sexual misconduct in most of these settings while lack of formally documented records (and informal concerns that needn't be investigated) prevents better tools getting put in place. Instead, there are often (or used to be at least) indirect attempts of protecting the women which are even more tragic. For example, it was well-known that a certain faculty didn't accept female students in his lab, for he didn't want any distraction for his male students or have 'incidents' happening to the women.

This we will talk about in detail later in this book, for this is a vital risk in the post-MeToo era with real potential to harm. To quote Gloria Feldt, former CEO and president of Planned Parenthood,[5] author and activist, 'The danger of falling right out of sexual harassment into sexual discrimination is real.'[6] I interviewed Gloria on three aspects of MeToo which I summarize below and will bring forward in appropriate later segments for further review.

1. **Using MeToo post MeToo:** Not just men but also women, especially in workplace scenarios, have expressed views on how MeToo will hinder career aspirations of young women by causing men to be 'cautious' about mentoring or 'promoting' women. It has also been expressed (famously by Catherine Deneuve in her open letter and less famously by numerous others we meet every day) that women mostly use such advances for their convenience until it's not convenient anymore, and that this factor is not getting acknowledged anywhere. A social worker friend of mine working with city law enforcement office in the greater Phoenix area, Arizona, USA, tells me that even in the law enforcement (where they have to process anywhere around 20–40 cases per week on

5 'Planned Parenthood Federation of America, Inc., or Planned Parenthood is a nonprofit organization that provides reproductive health care in the United States and globally' (https://en.wikipedia.org/wiki/Planned_Parenthood).
6 https://time.com/5120607/companies-leadership-metoo-era/

sexual harassment), MeToo is in kind of an 'awkward funny satiric sarcasm' space for her male colleagues, with most of them joking or commenting on how they don't want to be 'MeToo'd' for something harmless. This is not very far from jokes I have been privy to in parties where men express a need for 'He Too' when someone bumps into them and 'I would buy you a drink, but I don't want to be MeToo'd.' The USA has workplace sexual harassment criteria and guidelines which are quite strong in some cases (just like the Vishakha Guidelines[7] and now POSH in India which will be discussed in detail later). However, it's obvious that something is still not working. The regulations and guidelines seem to be lacking effectivity even in the USA. Sexual harassment at work or in most settings is hard to prove or prevent, neither do the current processes and definitions successfully address concerns around subjectivity. So, what can and should be made better and how to ensure that the post-MeToo momentum is used in countering sexual harassment—not in creating confusion, digression and discrimination?

2. **MeToo and the age of 'women':** Just like the late 1960s, 1980s and 1990s, and possibly quite a few times yet to come, MeToo has been celebrated for ushering in an era of women with increased sensitivity towards and prioritization of questions of equality and justice for women beyond sexual harassment. Yet what we see happening with abortion laws popping up in multiple states in the USA (2018–2019), for example, the abortion debate has been a constant consternation in the USA in spite of Roe v. Wade,[8] seems to be completely countering

---

7 A. Kulkarni, 'Background and Legal Framework of Sexual Harassment of Women at Workplace in India', *Social Sciences International Research Journal 2*, no. 1 (2016): 443; https://www.livelaw.in/sexual-harassment-at-workplace-the-journey-of-the-law/
8 D. V. Bolton, 'Abortion: Roe v. Wade', *Journal of Criminal Law & Criminology* 64 (1973): 393.

this (latest laws propose to outlaw abortion even in case of rape or incest after eight weeks—a nearly impossible timeline to be able to keep up with for most women in terms of even knowing of an unwanted pregnancy). In the today's USA, legislations like Equal Rights Amendment[9] (ERA), if brought to the floors, will not pass, while restrictive legislations seem to be on the rise. Although this is not uncommon and is often agnostic to the issue, especially in the USA political system (e.g., increased mass shootings have coincided with relaxing of the weapon possession laws instead of tightening),[10] this is worth pondering on. Starting with a global lens and then zooming in on India, it is important to examine whether or not movements like MeToo truly usher in 'women's era' or they merely create noise.

3. **Counter MeToo post MeToo:** A backlash against feminism, or any social movement for that matter, is given. Does MeToo face an additional risk of the same for being 'anarchic' and 'non-definitive' (in other words, a social media-generated movement)?[11] Should we be extra cautious and be prepared for a stronger backlash? What are some other risks (in addition to gender discrimination becoming rampant in practice—point 1) that a strong backlash can drive?

All of these are important for understanding the 'after MeToo'. Will MeToo live? If yes, how? Or is it on its death leg already,

---

9 'The proposed Equal Rights Amendment (ERA) to the United States Constitution is a political and cultural inkblot, onto which many people project their greatest hopes or deepest fears about the changing status of women. Since it was first introduced in Congress in 1923, the ERA has been an issue with both rabid support and fervid opposition. Interpretations of its intent and potential impact have been varied and sometimes contradictory' (https://www.equalrightsamendment.org/faq#:~:text=The%20proposed%20Equal%20Rights%20Amendment,the%20changing%20status%20of%20women).

10 William J. Vizzard, 'The Current and Future State of Gun Policy in the United States', *Journal of Criminal Law & Criminology* 104, no. 4/5 (2015): 879. https://scholarlycommons.law.northwestern.edu/jclc/vol104/iss4/5

11 https://www.livemint.com/Leisure/LhMn4nQG1Rmic88lB1ZDaJ/MeToo-is-anarchic-and-thats-a-good-thing.html

and will leave behind a legacy of just a few hopeful years? Ironically, the #MeToo, with its Harvey Weinstein saga origin, both widened and narrowed the concept MeToo, which pre- and post-dates the hashtag. But it did create the needed focused momentum. The sister movement in India, also breathed into life through focus with the Tanushree Dutta allegations, did the same. But a closer look, beyond the tabloid headlines, is needed to ensure that we don't box MeToo out of the bigger question on gender, for such a segregation will not only be unfortunate but also erroneous.

Let's start with the fact that we didn't think of India having its MeToo when scores of women posted on social media in solidarity of the hashtag. India's MeToo movement specifically and largely refers to the breakout of accusations against stalwarts in the entertainment and media in late 2018, not the joining in of thousands of Indian women sharing their stories with #MeToo right alongside their global counterparts in the October of 2017. How common sexual harassment is, for Indian women, was alas no surprise to most of us. Barring a few responses (possibly from the likes of my Cornell mates) to the posts where men expressed shock and some hint of sadness, the chatter was limited to 'it's a known sad state of affairs', for even though we are tabooed to talk about it in most settings and find solace in segregating what happens and to whom, we know that in India, women's harassment is commonplace. I will discuss shortly (and in further detail later) where 'India' is especially special in this vs where factors applicable to any nation comes into play. But the point can't be denied that we have a widespread problem here, which we tackle often with condescending protections or segregation (from anti-Romeo squads and family escorts to ladies' compartments in trains and ladies' queues in Puja pandals—latest examples include rideshare bans in some tech cities).

Besides these measures, we mostly bear, until when particularly dastardly incidents take the nation to its boiling point (the early 1980s' custodial rape in Bombay, causing nationwide campaign against rape and rise of Forum Against Rape (FAR); the late

1990s' uprising and outcry, following the case of Bhanwari Devi and Vishakha Guidelines; the 2012 Delhi gang rape and mass protests; and the 2013 Criminal Law (Amendment) Act[12]). However, because as a nation we seldom have time to focus on gender and the widespread effects of patriarchy on the same, we default back to the status quo. 'Movements get triggered by incidents, but gender consistently remains second and secondary for both India and Indians to class, caste and survival'.

The interesting (and possibly quite unapparent to most) fact might be that we needn't feel excessively pre-historic for where we were, and possibly still are. India is quite notorious for its patriarchy—both soft and hard—and it goes beyond sexual harassment. From female infanticide to dowry and discrimination, there is no dearth of discussions on issues India has and how unfairly it treats its fairer sex. But what is seldom discussed is that India wasn't always the nation of rampant objectification and discrimination, and neither were other societies too far ahead too long ago.

For example, rampant and unchallenged sexism in America, just like racism, is not a thing of a very distant past. Post war (and until the late 1960s), a woman's place was quite solidified in the US society with a downgrade from their wartime and pre-wartime participation in breadwinning roles.[13] Especially for the middle and upper classes, the 'woman's place' was quite reinforced in both practice and preaching. Career for a woman was mostly looked down upon, and many American women lived under laws which gave the husband control of their earnings and property (They couldn't go into business without their husbands' permission or get credit without male co-signers[14]). Not hiring women for most

---

12 G. Gangoli, *Indian Feminisms: Law, Patriarchies and Violence in India* (Farnham: Ashgate Publishing, 2007); http://pldindia.org/wp-content/uploads/2013/04/The-Crimnal-Law-Amendment-Act-20131.pdf
13 G. Collins, *When Everything Changed: The Amazing Journey of American Women from 1960 to the Present* (New York, NY: Little, Brown, and Company, 2009).
14 Ibid.

positions, across industries and academia, and objectification of the ones hired, was the norm. Most importantly, none of this was frowned upon—even by most women.

Quoting a friend whom I had invited to a panel on sexual harassment in December 2018 post MeToo (Gerri Burke, my friend, now in her 90s, had spent her prime years working in Manhattan offices as an administrative assistant in advertisement): 'Pleasuring men in whatever way he chose to be pleasured was necessary.' It is easy to see why Gerri, although sympathetic, has trouble demarking the lines of abuse, consent and consensual. Because the lines indeed were (and to a lot of folks still are) blurred.

But while 'everything changed' for women in America quite suddenly[15] along with a radical revision of convictions, it didn't for India. Post 19th-century reforms, women's rights in India stayed either constant or spiralled down (with a myriad of devastating mutations of socio-economic norms sprouting in face of change—all worsening the state of women). For social reformation, as one of my friends put it: 'It's a question of stagnation vs acceleration.' The starting point in time is immaterial; a higher velocity towards change is material. Although there is widespread belief currently that we are on an upward trend, our one-step forwards few steps back cycles have caused us to be on a significantly low of a slope for a long time, mitigating our overall position on the graph. In this, India is unlike the USA therefore, where the civil rights movement in the 1960s and the heightened consideration for equality and human rights driven by it and other simultaneous and subsequent movements (the Vietnam War and the anti-war movement following) caused a high-velocity ramp towards gender equality.

So India needed a MeToo, badly, arguably more than any other reformative renaissance—from cleanliness to corruption—as

---

15 Ibid.

gender equality defines the moral fabric of the civil society. Women's rights are human rights, and women's empowerment, which is stalled by abuse, is a documented solution to issues across the spectrum, affecting socio-economic progress (demography, conflict, food and resource security, and sustainability).[16]

But now what? As referred to earlier, speaking out against workplace sexual harassment pre-dates MeToo significantly in India, but social movements (primarily driven out of the activism segments) didn't quite result in a mindset change and, therefore, change in on-ground realities, despite the landmark Vishakha Guidelines. In fact, it has been argued that legislations and guidelines have often been counterproductive for the feminist movements and women's causes in India.[17]

Quite possibly, with global mindset shift and the 2012 Delhi gang rape that shocked the nation's conscience, the ground in India was built up for MeToo. But can the impact of MeToo and its efficiency of aggregation be credited for the ground yielding at last?

Yielding what, many will ask. What solutions have been put in place? How many prosecutions have happened, leading to how many convictions? Are women safer today? What changes are on the way apart from the whole lot—a howl and cry? Fair questions. We will explore this both factually and informally. But as Supriya Nair so eloquently wrote: 'It (MeToo) shifted the whole conversation from the realm of legality to that of cultural responsibility.' And I will argue throughout this book that the latter is far more important, particularly for India.

Caste is preserved through the bodies of upper-caste women.
—R. Prasad, Activist, Arizona

---

16 World Economic Forum, 2013.
17 Gangoli, *Indian Feminisms.*

What also begs consideration, when talking of Me Too for India, is whether or not the movement cuts across and unifies segments or if it amplifies the intersectional distinctions gender is further subjected to in India. Just like with race in the USA (which plays into the marginalization and harassment of black women, causing their experience and reality to be quite distinct in the overall gender equality dialogue), the lens of caste and religion needs to be applied while capturing women's plights in India. Therefore, a movement like MeToo, when explored for its potential, needs to be measured on its universality. It has been consistently placed (and with significant merit) that the use of sexual violence as means of subjugation and placement of authority (primarily on the minority segments) in times of turbulence plays deeply into the outlook towards gender.[18] Behaviours percolate and persist, and an ethos is created. We will not only explore how India is not necessarily unique in this matter but also attempt to understand where we are and how that plays into where we stand today. 'It is said that the strength of MeToo lies in its universal appeal. Cutting across divides, it creates a problem statement all women, irrespective of national identity, race, caste, creed, strata or ideology, can relate to. But does it? Or does this argument fall apart in India—India vs Bharat style?'

Summing up the thoughts here, MeToo, for the sake of bringing into light how commonplace sexual harassment is, was no bang for India. MeToo, for triggering a mindset revamp, can be.

Alisha Chinai's allegations two decades back, as well as Tanushree Dutta's initial reporting to Cine & TV Artistes' Association (CINTAA),[19] were in a different India, and that can be seen in the archives of comments and discussion in any publication from the time. The inclination to believe and the baseline sympathy

---

18 K. Kannabiran and V. Kannabiran, 'Caste and Gender Understanding Dynamics of Power and Violence', *Economic & Political Weekly* 26, no. 37 (1991): 2130.
19 https://indianexpress.com/article/entertainment/bollywood/tanushree-dutta-cintaa-supports-case-nana-patekar-5382822/

seemed to be lying with the accused—at least equally, if not predominantly. The 'could be true' opinions weren't also equipped with 'it would be so wrong if true' but with 'this is what is expected in certain professions, of course' followed with 'it's better not to get into such matters'. But in 2019 India, there was outrage against the year's release: Kabir Singh. Severely demented and detrimental movies were rampant in the earlier decades too, but thank god, we are changing!

Or are we? And if yes,

1. Did MeToo cause the change?

    Or

2. Are these parallel phenomena with no causal relations?

    Or

3. Did the change cause MeToo (referring to 2018) in India?

4. Is the change to stay, and does it cut across the many Indias that lie within India?

5. And why does any of this matter?

It does, for in this exploration lie some answers on how much MeToo can help the gender question in India. For India, the key potential of MeToo, in my opinion, lies in paving the way for a 'culture of belief'.

Globally, the aftermath of MeToo has been prolific. Beyond sexual harassment, it has led to wider discussions—from equal pay for women to transgender and LGBT rights—showing potential to usher in a social nirvana of equal citizenships.

But grander the promise, larger is the risk of missing or misusing its aptitude. As I write this, the sentiment that all this might have been in vain is quite predominantly emerging as some of the high-profile accused getting acquitted one after another.[20]

---

20 https://www.tribuneindia.com/news/spectrum/from-metoo-to-hetoo-not-guilty/807666.html

This sentiment is apparent in the conversations I present on this matter in the following chapters. For now, I will place the point that if anything, acquittals and 'disappointments' highlight the need for a closer look into the aspects of prevention and prosecution. It's not a dismissal of the movement itself.

But what would be worse than not realizing any benefit from the movement is a backlash and/or exhaustion-driven anti-MeToo wave. The possibility of that is quite real, especially in India, because even if we set the additional odds propped against a movement primarily birthed through and proliferated via social media aside, an overdose of best and brightest of ideas is a repercussion waiting to happen. It is important, therefore, to be guarded against incorrect associations and indiscriminate overstepping.

Let's take feminism for example, which literally is the most basic of concepts required for a functioning human society. (In the most basic sense, feminism is exactly what the dictionary says it is: the movement for social, political and economic equality of men and women.)[21]

Feminism is the radical notion that women are human beings.[22]

Yet in both its normative and descriptive forms, feminism has fought incredible backlash throughout its history and is still fighting the same. Because the association is whole another beast. The portrayal of feminists has been far from flattering, perpetuated over the years by commercially motivated media and personally motivated public figures. For example, 'Feminists leave their husbands, kill their children, practice witchcraft, destroy capitalism, and become lesbians.'[23] Thanks to such associations

---

21 Jennifer Baumgardner, *Manifesta: Young Women, Feminism, and the Future* (New York, NY: Farrar, Straus and Giroux, 2000).
22 Cheris Kramerae, *A Feminist Dictionary* (Champaign, IL: University of Illinois Press, 1996).
23 Pat Robertson, 'Christian Evangelist', *The Washington Post*, 1992.

over decades, when surveyed (2007), most women, let alone men, didn't want to be associated with what they believed feminism represented.[24]

We will leave alone for now the eerie similarity of such abrasive and abusive stigmatization to terms like 'presstitutes' coined recently in India to address women journalists (but will revisit later, for roots of sexual abuse lie not too far from what causes immediate association of a woman's viewpoint to her moral character) and continue with MeToo. Akin to feminism, MeToo has been associated already, as mentioned earlier, with women going too far and a hindrance to normal, healthy inter-gender interactions (again, #MeToo denouncement by Catherine Deneuve and other French women as a witch-hunt and threat to sexual freedom being the widely known, but not the only, example).

As the saying goes, those who don't understand history are condemned to relive it. Understanding MeToo, therefore, is not just a 'ride the wave' interest. It is a vital responsibility.

'Almost five years after, the ultimate story of MeToo is yet to be told, for it needs to be scripted in the context of where we go from here. As the nation basks in the glory of a new (and long overdue) sensitization towards sexual harassment, the dust of emotion is maybe yet to settle. But once it does, will India, a nation grappling with patriarchy at every stratum of its being, be ready for the new reality?'

---

24 Christina Fisanick, *Feminism: Opposing Viewpoints Series* (New York, NY: Greenhaven Press, 2008).

CHAPTER 1

TOWARDS THE CULTURE
OF BELIEF

What do you think will happen with the Tanushree Dutta accusations? The question started making rounds in dinner parties almost a full year after #MeToo had broken ground in the USA. The Harvey Weinstein saga had been followed by multiple other, including that of Steve Wynn (the Las Vegas casino mogul and Wynn Group CEO, whose resignation was cited by several sources as a milestone quite powerful, given his political and business clout). By that time, *The New York Times* was reporting 200+ powerful men to have been 'brought down' by #MeToo[1] and Bloomberg was reporting 400+ accused in the USA itself (calling it a conservative estimate).[2] This excludes the earlier accusations against stalwarts and role models like Tarun Tejpal, the case against whom, incidentally, was dismissed this year in a low court.[3]

I didn't pay much attention to the question for quite some time. Somewhere within, I didn't connect the 'Tanushree Dutta' and 'MeToo' dots seriously. To me, at that time, MeToo had already happened. New revelations could and would appear, but what

1 https://www.nytimes.com/interactive/2018/10/23/us/metoo-replacements.html
2 https://www.bloomberg.com/graphics/2018-me-too-anniversary/
3 https://qz.com/india/2014367/tarun-tejpal-judgment-by-kshama-joshi-is-the-antithesis-of-metoo/

could be a 'significant start' or a 'milestone moment' after a year plus of the unfolding of a movement?

MeToo had had CEOs ousted, empires toppled, candidates defeated, institutions sued and a Supreme Court nominee in the USA testifying to answer decades-old accusations. In addition to the above and the international community joining in on social media, one-year milestones of #MeToo included 'Time's Up' and French and Arab world adaptations of the hashtag. Mainstream conversations in the USA were shifting to broader gender equality discourses (e.g., pay and discrimination), leaving harassment behind.

I too (in the USA at that time) was busy organizing and participating in talks on 'after MeToo'. How to make sure that workplace policies get toughened? How to ensure that men (and women), willingly or unwillingly, don't make prevention of sexual harassment (POSH) a premise for sexual discrimination? India's MeToo also had already happened for me. It was with the scores of Indian women joining in on social media sharing their stories, reinforcing how widespread the problem of non-consensual sexual advancement is in daily life in India. I didn't expect any new revelation (whether in India or globally) to have the power of channelling a further formalized and standardized movement. And that is where I had misunderstood MeToo.

I had thought of MeToo as an opening, a permission almost, a glamorization if you will, of a matter that needed to be acknowledged. In one person's raised hand, years of silence had made place for raised fists in the mainstream (outside of the activist circle) discourse of top issues. Replacement of discomfort with pride when it comes to sexual harassment. All the words I use here, it's quite important to stress, are in a positive connotation, for I truly believe that this is how it should be. Glory and pride of courage in face of abuse should be celebrated. MeToo did that for me and many others, more so in the context of India, where the commonplace nature of the problem might not have been a surprise, but the permission to be proud instead of ashamed, previously lacking, was validated through the social media declarations. I couldn't ask for much more.

But I had missed that MeToo could also be continuous. Just like chain reaction initiators, it could perpetuate and form a multitude of cluster movements. By catalysing structured and focused explorations of the issue of sexual harassment in targeted problematic domains (in this case, Bollywood, then print media and then academia in India), MeToo could create successfully not just a broad ecosystem but also microcosms. Both are tremendously important, but if a rating is needed, I will vote for the former, for the former creates what makes the latter possible— a culture of belief in place of the culture of silence, denial or dismissal that will open doors for meaningful and specific dialogues on gender equality.

To make this case, it is important for me to admit right here that the dots didn't connect between Tanushree Dutta and MeToo within me not just because of the time lag, the shift in focus or my engagements but also because of the archenemy of action against sexual violence: perception.

From somewhere within my subconscious, I had dismissed Tanushree Dutta for reasons that are hard to express or elaborate and dangerous to confess to (especially with the label of liberal or progressive) yet are so real in making this fight so difficult.

I had watched *Aashiq Banaya Aapne* and *Chocolate*. My subconscious association of the woman I share my name with and knew only of through these movies was not with the voices of dissent protesting sexual harassment. I had assumed her to be a woman who would never have to face such advances or someone who could take these into her stride or, worst of all, someone who'd be OK in spite.

Shame on me for this. But no matter how terrified I feel to admit this here, I must. It is because of these assumptions that we make, even as 'liberal', educated elites, about both the perpetrators and the victims, that a culture of silence and tolerance can perpetuate. Who has the right to be a valid victim? Who should be believed? We think we know—whether we admit it or not. With social conditioning, our definition of morality and even preferences come from an ambiguous, often 'can be altered per convenience' place. Instead of acknowledging this, we turn these into tools against the victims. This is soft patriarchy—residing within both genders— and a tenacious challenge. This is also why gender issues can fall secondary to other pertinent matters—from caste and religion to survival. Again, it's a perfect catch-22. This strengthens the culture of silence, which in turn strengthens this. Therefore, the strength of MeToo lies first mostly in creating an ecosystem where populations are forced to challenge their perceptions through witnessing of mass behaviour on the same.

Let's take the subset of workplace sexual harassment and India for example. It is important to remember that a quarter of a century before #MeToo, the 1992 gang rape of Bhanwari Devi had provided India the opportunity to acknowledge, outline and prevent workplace sexual harassment. However, although with the Vishakha Guidelines, India did outline and acknowledge, it never succeeded in preventing and prosecuting the problem. Effective prosecution leading to conviction is rare (Bhanwari Devi herself still awaits justice, 27 years and counting,[4] and the in-house complaint committees (CCs), again and again, have proved to be not only ineffective and gross violation of the guidelines but also to be more of mouthpieces for the perpetrators than the victims). According to a World Economic Forum (WEF) report,[5] 59 countries, pre-MeToo, had no laws against sexual harassment

4 https://scroll.in/article/899044/dalit-womans-rape-in-92-led-to-indias-first-sexual-harassment-law-but-justice-still-eludes-her
5 https://www.weforum.org/agenda/2015/09/why-discriminating-against-women-keeps-countries-poorer/

at work and only 18 countries out of the hundreds have no laws, which disadvantages women.[6]

In legal and cultural environments most like the United States (e.g., Canada, the United Kingdom, Australia, South Africa, and Israel), the American model (as codified by the EEOC i.e. Equal Employment Opportunity Commission and legitimized by the U.S. Congress and the courts) has been adopted almost whole cloth and with similar results. But across Europe, Africa, and Asia, the American approach is culturally and legally incongruent.[7]

International policies against sexual harassment and violence against women include the following.

- **The United Nations Convention on the Elimination of All Forms of Discrimination against Women (CEDAW):** Adopted in 1979, it is mostly a recommendation which recognizes that sexual harassment at workplace impairs equality in employment and states that 'all parties should take all legal and other measures that are necessary to provide effective protection of women against gender-based violence, sexual assault and sexual harassment in the workplace.'[8]

- **United Nations Fourth World Conference on Women:** Held in 1995, it's an adaptation of a platform for action, including provisions on sexual harassment in the workplace which calls on 'governments, trade unions, employers, community and youth organizations, and NGOs to eliminate sexual harassment'.[9]

6 Ibid.
7 http://oaji.net/articles/2016/1115-1460723528.pdf
8 Ibid.
9 Ibid.

Mostly, as noted above, sexual harassment is covered under discrimination prevention laws.

....

In many countries, provisions on sexual harassment have been included in their equality and sex discrimination laws, including in: Australia (Sex Discrimination Act); Austria (Equality of Treatment Act); Denmark (Gender Equality [Consolidation] Act); Finland (Act on Equality between Women and Men, 1995); Germany (Act to Establish Equality for Men and Women); Guyana (Prevention of Discrimination Act, 1997); Honduras (Law on Equal Opportunities for Women); Iceland (Act on the Equal Status and Equal Rights of Women and Men); Ireland (Employment Equality Act, 1998); Japan (Equal Employment Opportunity Act); Republic of Korea (Equal Employment Act); Lithuania (Law on Equal Opportunities); Malta (Equality for Men and Women Act); Mauritius (Sex Discrimination Act); Netherlands (Equal Treatment Act); Norway (Gender Equality Act); Romania (Law on equal opportunities); South Africa (Employment Equity Act); Sweden (Equal Opportunities Act, 1991); Switzerland (Law on Equality); and Venezuela (Organic Law on the Rights of Women to Fairness and Equality)[27]. The argument made is that, since sexual harassment is directed primarily at women, they are disproportionately subjected to detrimental treatment in the labor force and it is therefore a form of sex discrimination. The sex discrimination approach is particularly prevalent in countries in which equality or anti-discrimination legislation is the only route available to victims of sexual harassment.[10]

Labour laws and criminal provisions (in some countries) are also used for sexual harassment. Countries with criminal provisions against sexual harassment include Venezuela, Sri Lanka, Spain and Bangladesh.

....

10 Ibid.

Although sexual assault (and rape) is criminal in most nations, it is important to note that what constitutes so is defined variedly. For example, only 8 out of 31 countries in the European Union recognize sex without consent to be rape.

A legal definition of rape based on the absence of consent is not new or ground-breaking. It is a recognized international human rights standard. The Council of Europe's Convention on preventing and combating violence against women and domestic violence (The Istanbul Convention), widely hailed as the most comprehensive legal framework to date to tackle violence against women and girls (VAWG), obliges signatories to criminalize all non-consensual acts of sexual nature. Although the Istanbul Convention has been ratified by more than 20 European states, the majority of them have yet to amend their legal definitions of rape.[11]

On other gender-based violence (GBV), 144 countries are reported to have laws against domestic violence (vs 154 for sexual harassment). Specific crimes such as acid attack and female genital mutilation are criminalized in most countries; nations with high prevalence have called out separate segments and increased punishments for such offenses.

In summary, legalities in the matter of sexual harassment are complex and contingent, from statute and age of consent to definitions of assaults. Sexual harassment, however, contrary to expectations, has been called out under both civil and criminal provisions (countries with criminal provisions against sexual harassment are relatively few). India has comparatively rigorous and comprehensive criminal provisions in place, especially owing to the 2013 modification of the penal code. Women, however, in

---

11 https://www.amnesty.org/en/latest/campaigns/2018/04/eu-sex-without-consent-is-rape/

most nations, should be able to bring about complaints against GBV, as they are also covered under international policies and recommendations. Now, seeking justice vs achieving are two different matters. As we have seen, again and again, laws and policies can only take us so far and, although are necessary tools, can often be rendered useless as judgments delivered by courts can be highly contingent.

Sexual harassment is rooted in cultural practices and exacerbated by power relations at the workplace.[12]

Most CCs (in-house CCs which needed to be formed as redressal forum for women facing sexual violence) have failed to adhere to guidelines of formation and action and have instead been used by management to intimidate and further victimize victims. From accusation of students against their supervisors (Chandra, PhD student, MS University, 1999) to employees coming forward against supervisors (NALCO molestation case),[13] either dismissal of complaint or revictimization of the victim through blaming, motivated interrogations and even termination followed in place of victim advocacy, due process and prevention, and was carried out by or with the CCs.[14]

Below are a few quotes directly from an article on the issue of sexual harassment by Radhika V.[15] for the post-Vishakha, pre-MeToo picture on workplace sexual harassment across the spectrum.

....

'Every day is as traumatic as the other,' said Kala Devi, who works in a factory in Ghaziabad. 'The supervisor loses no

....

12 Tejani Sheba, 'Sexual Harassment at the Workplace: Emerging Problems and Debates', *Economic & Political Weekly* 39, no. 41 (2004): 4491.
13 *The Indian Express*, 2004; Sahara Manoranjan Case, *The Telegraph*, 2004.
14 Sheba, 'Sexual Harassment at the Workplace', 4491.
15 Radhika V., *The Week Magazine*, 1999.

opportunity to use foul language, make obscene gestures and brush against us.' With two kids and an alcoholic husband, she can't quit the job.

....

Liar, inefficient, psychologically disturbed, the labels flew thick and fast at 34-year-old Mridula Karhadkar right from the moment she complained to the National Commission for Women (NCW) of sexual harassment by G.K. Malik, the honorary director of Chowgule Sishu Vidya Mandir in Delhi. She was an accounts clerk in the school and almost two years and three inquiries later, her battle is far from over.

....

'Initially when he patted my shoulder or put an arm around me I thought it was an appreciative gesture by a 63-year-old man,' said Jayashree who joined DPS in 1995. 'But I realized soon that his physical conduct was not decent, and he openly started demanding sexual favors.' It was the same with the other two and when the women complained they were allegedly victimized. Jayashree said her seniority was brought down, while Shayista's child was denied admission.

And so, the saga has continued in all workplaces, for everyone, just like sexual abuse and harassment within other environments. But why? 'Why despite the intention and institutions formalized, inaction—and even worse counteraction—commenced?' Is it because India is somehow worse standing as a nation? Or is it because cultures change last and require avalanches, not guidelines?

Let's take the Larry Nassar example from the USA for a closer look. On 22 November 2018, Nassar (a former USA Gymnastics national team doctor and an osteopathic physician at the Michigan State University [MSU]) pleaded guilty to 10 counts of sexual assault (charged with 22 counts of first-degree sexual misconduct on minors). All the 10 victims (a fraction of the total number of girls he is believed to have victimized) associated with this case were under the age of 16, and 3 were younger than 13, at the time of the abuse. By the time of his sentencing, Nassar was already sentenced on possession of child pornography.[16] To be technically correct, the start of Nassar's downfall pre-dates the #MeToo breakout, but it is the coinciding in time with the MeToo movement of his trial and sentencing and it's both gaining from and providing impetus to MeToo that is of tremendous significance. Not to discredit in anyway the immensity of the saga itself—from the sheer number of victims to for how long it had continued (first of the accusations against Larry Nassar is now known to have surfaced in 1994)—but even after it had started becoming clear that Nassar was done for (2014–2015), there wasn't much noise made by his strongest prior sponsors. Because that is how it could be with even the grimmest of sexual assault narratives pre MeToo (or in more general terms, pre mass-anti-harassment sentiment), just like it was with daily reports of rapes in the newspapers in India in the inside pages pre 2012.

USA Gymnastics quietly cut ties with Nassar in 2015, following a 2014 investigation. The MSU, instead of leading an outrage in the redemption of their repeated failure to protect the victims, reassigned him to teaching duties in place of clinical ones. It is now known that by this time, MSU had received multiple instances of complaints of sexual assault and had yet cleared him of wrongdoing. It was only in 2016, after *The Indianapolis Star*'s publications of the saga, that MSU fully fired Nassar. As one of the reports had outlined, USA Gymnastics had a long history of sweeping sexual assault complaints under the rug—a culture of tolerance spanning decades.

As some analyses of the Nassar case depict, as a doctor of osteopathic medicine positioned with USA Gymnastics, who was tasked to perform osteopathic manipulations including pelvic

---

16 https://www.nytimes.com/2018/01/25/sports/larry-nassar-gymnastics-abuse.html

floor treatments on his patients (young, often underage athletes and gymnasts), Larry Nassar was preordained to be believed over his victims. Perception! Of who can't be a perpetrator! And he was believed, again and again. Even law officials in Ingham County questioning Nassar over the allegations of sexual assault believed him when he used technical terms and descriptions to convince them of his innocence. This was in 2004. Nassar successfully got himself cleared of allegations of sexual assault by explaining that his violation of a young girl was a required treatment that had been misunderstood by his victim because of her unfamiliarity with such medical procedure.

What he had done, had been doing and continued to do for another decade to multiple others was abuse which would not have been hard to prove. In court testimony, victims stated Nassar being visibly aroused as he penetrated them vaginally and anally, without gloves, and massaged their breasts. Yet Rachael Denhollander[17] (one of Nassar's victims who had been abused by him in 2000 at the age of 15 years and had filed a criminal complaint against him in 2016) had to come armed with years' worth of research on pelvic floor treatments, testimonials from other medical professionals and other documentation before she could approach the authorities. She was fully prepared to be not believed.

It was a decade after the first criminal complaint of abuse was filed against Nassar that accusations against him were taken seriously. Larry Nassar's victim count by this time is now known to have risen to over 300 underage and young girls.

NPR USA did a segment comparing the first round of police interrogations of Larry Nassar to the second in search of answers. They outlined the most important difference between the two times (the second time led to Larry Nassar confessing and

---

17 https://www.detroitnews.com/story/news/local/michigan/2018/01/24/nassar-denhollander/109787862/

getting indicted vs the first time, which is discussed above) to be the fact that in the second instance, the investigating officer came in believing the accusers. The investigating officers in the first instance, having come in with the perception of what Nassar had seemed to be, had believed Nassar—Nassar: a tremendously respected, veteran medical professional and expert in the field. His accuser(s): young, immature girls.

Did the MeToo movement (or, in a broader sense, change of attitude towards sexual harassment) play a role in defining how the Nassar story ended? Absolutely. Because just like the culture of silence that allowed Nassar to have over 300 victims, there is a culture of belief. Societal mental spaces, whether in the USA or India, need to be shifted. Movements do that. Otherwise, isolated cases, no matter how landmark, perish.

Yes, a properly put together case against Nassar would have brought him to an investigation, maybe even prosecution, whether or not the MeToo movement had preceded his fall so close in time. But properly put together cases don't get put together against men like Nassar so often and so easily. And even when they do, they end in guidelines rendered ineffective by erroneous implementation practices.

....

Nassar, as *At the Heart of Gold* documents, was uniquely positioned to get away with what he did. He was a trusted, even beloved figure in his Michigan community, volunteering at his church and local high schools, and offering free therapeutic sessions to girls who were cheerleaders, rowers, dancers. He had almost unchecked access to young athletes in his role as a sports doctor for USA Gymnastics and Michigan State University. And, crucially, he was operating within a sport in which girls are primed from the beginning to silently endure what happens to their body, one with a philosophy of 'athletic Darwinism' where only the strongest and most stoic will go all the way. 'It's almost like being a wounded animal,' the former

Olympic gymnast Kathy Johnson tells Carr. 'You don't show your weakness. You don't show that you're hurt.'[18]

My daughter trains as a gymnast, and my mother was a gymnast too (a gene trait that completely skipped the middle generation somehow). My mother's ambitions as a gymnast had to be halted, owing to my grandfather's objections to the body-hugging costumes which are required for the sport but were raising eyebrows in his circles, and late into evening hours that were needed to be put in with mostly males in the club gym. My daughter doesn't have to worry about such matters. But the Nassar case proves that she still has to worry. And it doesn't have much to do with gymnastics. I do see in the little girls I see training day in and out the culture of endurance getting drilled in, just as *The Atlantic* has described. I see their little bodies getting it from kindergarten years, slowly learning to persist. But all that said, the rest of the 'uniqueness' of Larry Nassar, unfortunately, is not very unique. Neither are the gymnasts 'uniquely' vulnerable victims who are not going to be able to come forward although, having their physician as the abuser does increase their risks of getting abused enormously.

When we look into our homes and our lives, how unique is it for many of such abusers to be 'uniquely positioned' to be able to perpetuate and get away with abuse, from family members in a high position of trust and influence to trusted community members (teachers, gurus, godmen)?

Not very.

Everyone can be an opportune abuser, especially in countries with high-value attachment to shame, honour and purity. Opportunities are farther hardened through hardening of the culture of silence.

---

18 Sophie Gilbert, 'A New Film Reveals How Larry Nassar Benefited from a Culture of Silence', *The Atlantic*, 2019. https://www.theatlantic.com/entertainment/archive/2019/05/new-film-exposes-how-larry-nassar-was-able-abuse/588571/

Re-victimization of the victim is the worse form of abuse
there is and that's what we do to everyone here in
India where you have to prove and re-prove your
innocence again and again. Who is she? What was
she doing? Even for eleven-year-olds.
—Maitabi Banerjee, Blogger and Activist, India

Looking at women and their history in India, scholars agree that it is difficult to measure and quantify their status. Indian Constitution, through Fundamental Rights, grants equality under the law for men and women (Article 14), equal opportunity in matters of employment (public) and equal pay for equal work (Articles 16 and 39), and equal access to public spaces (Article 15). In addition, statutory provisions (Equal Remuneration Act; Maternity Benefit Act; Dowry Prohibition Act; Section 498A; Hindu Succession (Amendment) Act, 2005; Sexual Harassment of Women at Workplace (Prevention, Prohibition and Redressal) Act, 2013; and Criminal Law (Amendment) Act, 2013—Sections 326A, 326B, 354A, 354B, 354C and 354D) have existed and have continuously been put in place—often triggered by movements which were in turn triggered by serious incidents. Comparing to the USA, for example, where ERA is yet to and would possibly never pass and bills floated are often repressive towards women, a mere glance at India's legislative ammunition given its reputation for women's right inspires pride. However, as it's known, legislation can't address outlook and approach.

Other socio-economic pointers, such as women's access to education and employment, age at marriage, social and personal tolerance of domestic violence, women's mobility to pick a few, tell a different and wide-ranged story.[19] GBV statistics—from sexual harassment, assault, domestic violence, acid attacks and trafficking into prostitution to specifically and primarily Indian

---

19 Gangoli, *Indian Feminisms*; Kishore and Gupta, 2004.

dowry-related violence and female infanticide—paint quite grim a picture of India.

Obviously, just like for any nation, the cards dealt out to India through the nation's history play an integral role in this, as does how and by whom women's rights were championed for in India.

In the early 19th century, women's rights were championed primarily by elite upper-caste Hindu men. Then, in the late 19th-century, social reforms and intentions on improving and equalizing women's status weakened—a causality of rising national sentiment against colonial rule and colonial intervention. Holding on to the roots took the form of defense of regressive practices in the name of preservation of Indian and Hindu identity (e.g., the age of consent of marriage controversy). As a result of indigenous opposition, the liberal arm of the colonial state was disabled and upper-caste patriarchal norms were entrenched into legal structures.[20]

The floundering of women's rights in the name of prevention of intervention by governing authorities and states into personal business and beliefs is not uniquely Indian and neither is it outdated (from abortion rights in the USA to the not-too-old triple talaq debate right here again in India). But what is possibly additionally detrimental for us women and our fight in India is how easy it is to make gender secondary here to other identities we associate with. We will visit this in the next chapters.

India's initiation of MeToo pre-dates the 2017 breakout of the hashtag. It happened in 2012, with the brutal rape and murder of Jyoti Pandey in Delhi. The horror of 2012 shook a country long-festering with the problem of not only sexual assault being rampant but also a terribly patriarchic mindset towards it to its core and started building of the counterculture. But Indian feminism and movements for women's rights in India have had a long history.

---

20 Gangoli, *Indian Feminisms*; Sen, 2000.

'Upheavals have happened, as have legislations and reforms, but as history shows, "patriarchy" was never challenged as a thought process in India—which has a lot to do with not just how men but even women think, thanks to years of habituation.'

Looking at the USA and the entire history of women's rights in the West for comparison; in spite of where the US attitude towards women was in the 1960s, what happened within a few decades can seem almost 'overnight'. I summarized this earlier and am elaborating on here. As Gail Collins puts it in her book on the matter:[21]

Then, suddenly, everything changed. The cherished convictions about women and what they could do were smashed in the lifetime of many women living today. It happened so fast that the revolution seemed to be over before either side could really find its way to the barricades. And although the transformation was imperfect and incomplete, it was still astonishing. A generation that was born into a world where women were decreed to have too many household chores to permit them to serve on juries, and where a spokesman for NASA would say that 'any talk of an American spacewoman makes me sick to my stomach' would come of age in a society where female astronauts and judges were routine. Parents who hoped for a child to carry on the family business, or for another doctor in the family, or for a kid to play ball within the backyard at night, no longer drooped with disappointment when the new baby turned out to be a girl. It was the liberation that countless generations of American women had been waiting for, whether they knew it or not. And it happened in our time.

However, even if the change itself, like change often is, was rapid, building up to it was required for the initiation. A mindset overhaul

---

21 Collins, *When Everything Changed.*

for a population—from one of segregation, hierarchy, domination and social positioning to equality—was initiated with the civil rights movement in the USA. Increased sensitivity to justice and fairness sets the tone for the broader dialogue on the stature of other oppressed or unequally treated segments, including women. Experiencing the civil rights movement is associated with women becoming cognizant of their treatment and stature in the society. This is the known magic of revolutions. They serve as inciting instances.

But India's path to revolution, for women, has been back and forth in spite of mass movements, toiling grit and landmark wins. This point can't be emphasized enough, for it is critical we draft the roadmap for gender parity in India keeping this in mind. Below is a breakdown of this key trait proved with a walk down the history lane.

In the 1970s, dissatisfaction and disillusionment with political structures following the emergency increased educational and employment opportunities for women, and the rise of feminism in the west contributed to the emergence of feminist movements in India, focusing on demands for equal opportunities and curtailing violence against women. Strong links and parallels, keeping in line with the international theme, formed between the women's movements and other people's movements and political upheavals (the Naxalite movement). However, Indian feminist movements formed stronger dependencies and partnerships with other left agendas (e.g., in the 1980s, with the trade union, anti-price rise and such), arguably compromising the gender focus for the sake of economy, caste, corruption and other inequality fights (socialist instead of gender conceptualization of rape). Also, the anti-rape campaigns of the 1980s and 1990s had a focus on the fighting of state power and oppression of women by the state. This again begs a question of whether gender equality as a question was fostered through these or if it was lost behind the question oppression and systemized structural violence. Besides, the use of the 'Westernization' argument by associating it with loss of

'Indian' identity has been consistent and successful against women's rights movements in India, silencing activists and keeping India from benefiting from the international developments towards women's freedom (international decade of women—1975–1985).

In the 1990s, with globalization, economy and opportunities increased. But it's debated till date whether globalization served women of India well or was it a detriment to their progress.[22] Deregulation of the economy, foreign capital, global influence and adaptation of global standards are challenged with questions of exploitation of disadvantaged women in free trade zones, losing of 'Indianness' because of objectification and commodification of women's bodies.

Interestingly, India and even Indian feminists seldom see a woman capable of making a choice of exposing or commodifying her body, and Indian legislative actions on matters like surrogacy follow this line of thought. It is for the nation to decide who should not lose 'Indianness', and it's mostly women. Indian women fail to see the loss of the war with the winning of this battle when they succumb to this thought process. This has a critical role to play in the gender struggle in India, and we will discuss this through stories in a later chapter.

In sum, for now, these are the points to recap: Indian women's rights movements, often triggered by inciting incidents, largely failed to create systemized realization of the concept of equality and acceptance of gender equality as a value. This saga is consistent from the first major campaign of the women's movement in free India rising out of the gang rape of a tribal girl in Mathura by policemen to Nirbhaya protests of 2012–2013. In addition, high value placed on Hindu and Indian identities (often through careful, motivated intention) and de-prioritization of gender[23] to the three Cs (caste, class and corruption) have been instrumental

---

22 Gangoli, *Indian Feminisms*; Ghosh, 1996.
23 M. Subramaniam, *The Power of Women's Organizing: Gender, Caste, and Class in India* (Lanham, MD: Lexington Books, 2006).

in making women and champions of women's right feel lesser and shamed, digressing their focus and preventing national focus on gender rights. The high and almost exclusive focus on legal reforms is also a characteristic prominent through the history of women's rights in India. These, instead of focusing on Indian patriarchy and its nuances (e.g., the role of women in marginalizing women and upbringing of Indian men as honour bearers playing into their treatment of women) for targeted action, have cost India dearly and will continue to cost if not remedied.

No country in the world has successfully eliminated discrimination against women or has achieved full equality.[24]

For the sake of understanding what societal tolerance does to women, and therefore, inevitably to the society itself, let me digress a bit. I had met Dr Saltanat Childress and Professor Jill Messing in a panel while searching for research groups working on applications for women's safety. Professor Messing's associates are developers and researchers behind the app myPlan, which assists women facing violence find safety.[25]

Dr Childress is working specifically on translating this application for women in Kyrgyzstan, her native land. Just after I spoke to her, she was to be leaving on a summer-long assignment to Kyrgyzstan to study violence in various forms against the women there. In one of her papers on intimate partner violence (IPV), she specifically explores the effect of culture and tolerance on whether IPV is normalized or brought to prosecution. Just like sexual harassment, especially by close contacts, known perpetrator, and perpetrators in position of influence, IPV (more commonly known as domestic violence) thrives on soft patriarchy, defining the victim's position in terms of shame and consequence (i.e., no point in speaking

24 United Nations, 2018.
25 http://www.fox10phoenix.com/news/arizona-news/asu-professor-creates-app-to-help-women-deal-with-domestic-violence

up—the culprits can't be brought to justice anyways, and you will instead be prosecuted in the court of opinion). In her works, Dr Childress explores the attitude of women towards IPV in Kazakhstan, Kyrgyzstan and Tajikistan[26]—three countries sharing historical ties. Her work offers a cross-country perspective from the region. The nations have their differences (e.g., Kazakhstan is middle income, while Kyrgyzstan and Tajikistan are low income) and similarities (they all have experienced significant conflicts—a known contributor to worsening of women's status—including a violent civil war after independence in Tajikistan in which women were subjected to horrendous atrocities). The summarized conclusions are not hard to guess and are eerily representative of what the reality is with sexual harassment and women in India.

Lubna Tabassum, an activist from Bangladesh now based in Phoenix (a long-time worker for South Asians for safe families and now working with the Arizona Department of Justice), and Christie (last name withheld), a single mom who is now in the USA but has spent years in Columbia before leaving her husband and moving back to the USA, shared similar thoughts when asked about MeToo and its impact on their respective communities. Sharing experiences ranging from how her mother-in-law getting hit on the bum and women getting abused by partners are considered within the sphere of acceptance (and hence not abuse) in some Latin American communities and how marital sexual harassment, even severe, is apparent in many of the cases she works on but not to the victims, they both stressed on 'culture', not as ethnicity but as ethos. A culture of speaking out (or questioning at least of things that don't feel right or are hurtful) can't be practised without awareness and a supportive ecosystem. A dialogue on prioritization also ensued because in many societies which have

---

26 M. Joshi and S. Childress, 'A National Survey of Attitudes toward Intimate Partner Violence among Married Women in Kazakhstan, Kyrgyzstan, and Tajikistan: Implications for Health Prevention and Intervention', *Social Work in Health Care* 56, no. 4 (2017): 294.

prevalent gross violence against women, the bandwidth is often consumed in tactically addressing such incidents and offering rehabilitation. Strategic tackling of the underlying themes and redressal of anything that's not 'major' take a back seat. A saying quite familiar, by Heinrich Heine, comes to mind as I ponder on these consistent themes that span nations and cultures: 'Where they burn books, they will also ultimately burn people.' I think of it this way: 'Where butts are pinched, or a woman is slapped for no reason, they will ultimately rape and maim.'

For protesting against abuse—it has to register first that it is abuse indeed and not something that's normal and acceptable. For that to happen, there needs to be counter-conditioning of the society.
—Christie, Activist and Restaurant Worker,
Columbia and the USA

So the importance of a movement or even a structured sustained effort that brings voices together, which in turn leads to targeted, strategic action, can't be denied. As Maitabi Banerjee, a blogger and an activist from Bengaluru, put it when I interviewed her as one of the MeToo voices:

The suffocation that yes it has happened but I can't speak out, for the cost of doing so might be higher to me than the incident itself, is what caused the mass resonance with MeToo. It couldn't have happened if no one else spoke up, or even if everyone did but no one was going to believe.

In a November 2018 article, U.S. News & World Report[27] quotes Ruchi Narain, an Indian filmmaker visiting LA just a few months prior. She expresses that it'd be at least 10 years before Bollywood could have a Harvey Weinstein like phenomena if accusations

---

27 https://www.usnews.com/news/best-countries/articles/2018-11-12/metoo-reshapes-attitudes-in-india-about-sexual-harassment-in-the-workplace

came forward. Narain assessed the Indian society to not be ready and the system to be too loaded against women. I would have thought the same. But what I love most about my motherland is its power to awe. We have it in us, more than any other people I know, to surprise ourselves—again and again.

The 2012 Nirbhaya incident started India's shift towards the culture of belief, as did the 2017 breakout of the hashtag. And I believe that why Tanushree Dutta was believed the second time around vs the first has to do with the winds changing already towards a culture of believing women, acknowledging sexual harassment, and intolerance of the same. The similarities of Tanushree Dutta's experience with CINTAA and the Larry Nassar case described above are not coincidental.

Therefore, arguably, we are at least in the middle of a shift. But does it cut across? And is it sustainable? What difference does it make in the lives of women in India that MeToo happened? If MeToo disappointed, but history shows that only persistent social revolution can urge in a meaningful change, how do we bring one about without having to go through another Nirbhaya? Incidents like the firing of 56 housekeeping employees of NIFT Hyderabad in place of the accused (we are talking Hyderabad aka urban India here, that too a leading tech hub) begs for these questions to be asked. I will ask these in the following chapters.

CHAPTER 2

THE FIGHT BEFORE

During the time of writing this chapter, I was participating in a journalism cohort in the USA as an instructor. The year was 2020 and the month was right after George Floyd's[1] death was on the forefront. Race had emerged in the USA as a stronger conversation than the ongoing COVID pandemic[2] or gender. The cohort, which we had expected would be overwhelmingly applauded (the goal was to train these women for leadership, which, in turn, we hoped, was going to drive gender parity on all fronts—from prevention of gender violence to equal pay), wasn't appreciated at all. We were hitting road bump after road bump. It was not that gender wasn't important anymore. It was just that the fervent anger against years of prejudice experienced by women of colour was overtaking gender solidarity. In some cases, it was getting directed against other women who had had more privileged (read better) experiences. Now this, as examined in several chapters of this manuscript, has been a forever bane for women's rights. Particularly in India, this has caused gender to become either a sub-identity under other identities (religion, caste, and class) or an apparatus for furthering the exploitation of segments. A US example we have discussed in this matter is the political identification by women (Democrat vs

---

1 https://www.nytimes.com/2020/05/31/us/george-floyd-investigation.html
2 https://en.wikipedia.org/wiki/COVID-19_pandemic

Republican) coming in their way of activism for gender rights,[3] from Bill Clinton to Donald Trump and Brett Kavanaugh. But as I listened on to the women in the cohort, vehemently placing arguments on how race needed to be a more immediate conversation coming just off the heels of MeToo, I felt an extra pang of sadness. An amplified concern. I wondered if sexual harassment, gender discrimination and women's status in the society are already yesteryear issues? Or was it that the issue of race in the USA—like that of 'intolerance' against minorities in India—is really a matter of subjugation which ultimately is the real thing to talk about when talking about gender? After all, whether it's through violence or discrimination, the result for women, ultimately, is subjugation. As 'gender diversity' and 'women' corporate statements got revised through 2019–2020 to 'diversity and inclusion' and 'women and inclusion', I sat in front of my computer pondering on highlighting gender—specifically the female gender—as a unified problem statement. And as I did so, it occurred to me that I needed to write this chapter, in which I had originally intended a mere factual analysis of the ground realities regarding sexual harassment, gender discrimination and gender rights during the late 1980s–early 2010s (post affirmative action, civil rights and globalization but pre MeToo, ERA and the 2013 criminal rights amendment)—very differently. I needed to apply a human lens on the systems and vice versa. I realized that if I did so, the gender question might become apparent. Because the question of before and after (not just before and after MeToo but also the status of gender in the 2020s vs that in the earlier decades) is further nuanced than it appears to be.

The promise of #MeToo was—or rather is (as we still might be in the middle of it)—manifold: awareness, unification, inspiration and change. On the surface, gender rights awareness (globally and in India) through the 1990s and well into the 2010s has propelled miles forward with the Internet, social media and MeToo stacking

<hr>

3 L. Hirshman, *Reckoning: The Epic Battle against Sexual Abuse and Harassment* (Boston, MA: Houghton Mifflin Harcourt, 2019).

one over another. We have talked so far in this manuscript quite some on awareness, unification and inspiration, and I was intending to start the process of demarking change by marking a before and an after. But as I held a human lens on the earlier decades, looking for nuggets of all that #MeToo promises, not just awareness of the pervasiveness of sexual violence against women, I felt a strong need to first understand if there indeed was a before and if there will be an after. The conclusion on this will be a matter for the later chapters, but we will start the journey here.

Now, one quick but important point is that inspiration might be considered an addendum to awareness by some. But I would like to consider it separately. Although inspiration is hard to occur without awareness, awareness doesn't necessarily cause inspiration. Instead, it can deter and suppress (e.g., a multitude of incidents of violence against women, some of which we will review here and in the following chapters, are perpetrated and publicized with the intent of inducing horror).

Earlier, we reviewed how, despite Vishakha Guidelines, real-life experience with sexual harassment at the workplace didn't evolve that much for women in the decades, leading up to MeToo and POSH. In fact, in many cases, the very committees that were tasked with prevention, investigation and redressal failed the victims. Instead, they contributed to revictimization and retaliation.[4] However, that doesn't in any way reduce the importance of Vishakha (and similar landmark legislations which offer frameworks for marking a matter as a problem). In Chapter 7, with Professor Reicha Tanwar,[5] we will compare Vishakha and POSH[6] as redressal and prevention mechanisms for workplace

---

4 http://www.doccentre.net/docsweb/sexual-harassment/sexual-harassment-cases.htm; Sheba, 'Sexual Harassment at the Workplace', 4491.
5 Professor Reicha Tanwar is a celebrated women's rights activist and the director of the Centre for Women's Studies and Development at Kurukshetra University.
6 https://en.wikipedia.org/wiki/Sexual_Harassment_of_Women_at_Work place_(Prevention,_Prohibition_and_Redressal)_Act,_2013

harassment and evaluate their pros and cons. In this chapter, I present the accounts 'before #MeToo'.

THE ACCOUNT OF BHANWARI DEVI (1992–2020, CONTD)

For recounting Bhanwari Devi's case, the appropriate start is probably what she was quoted asking in a relatively recent, post-MeToo interview. 'What can I possibly tell you that people don't know already?'[7]

The revival of interest around Bhanwari Devi in the MeToo era is understandable. She was internationally recognized and through her fight, guidelines for workplace sexual harassment including the definition of 'workplace' beyond the office (vital for fieldworkers) were instated[8] which, in essentiality, recognized the right of Indian women to be able to work safely. Her case is remembered not only as a success story for women's activism but also as a notable success of the public interest litigation (PIL)[9] mechanism. As Kavita Srivastava[10] was noted to have said on the matter, Bhanwari Devi's case was not just a case of achieving justice against a gang rape, but it was also an indispensable one to ensure that 'saathins' (village-level social workers for the women's development project by the Government of Rajasthan) could be convinced to do their work, which in turn was critical to ensure that grassroots fieldwork for socio-economic development could have female volunteers and workers. But despite the well-deliberated facts, a plethora of articles and interviews of Bhanwari Devi herself, references in

7 https://www.news18.com/news/india/the-story-of-bhanwari-devi-indias-metoo-woman-1682995.html

8 https://onefuturecollective.org/the-history-behind-sexual-harassment-at-the-workplace-law/

9 https://bnblegal.com/article/pil-cases-of-india-which-changed-the-legal-system/

10 https://wikipeacewomen.org/wpworg/en/?page_id=2589

books[11] and a movie,[12] there indeed is a lot that people need to know, especially for the context we are after.

The premise of the matter is Bhanwari Devi's gang rape by five men in September 1992 after she opposed child marriage (of a nine-month-old baby) following her employer's (Government of Rajasthan's) dictate issued on the same. She did try to have conversations to persuade the families to do otherwise (including with the family head—Ram Karan Gujjar). However, economic (long-established methodology of marrying daughters off as children and all at once to prevent separate ceremonial and future dowry expenses) and social (pulling out of such commitments at the urging of the government or a lower-in-caste woman worker is a social black eye) motivations caused the men to remain adamant. Bhanwari reported this, as she would have to as a saathin which caused the law enforcement agency to show up during the wedding. They didn't enforce anything, however. They offered customary advice, enjoyed the hospitality of the family and left believing in the ruse that it was not a child marriage ceremony but a mere family celebration of Teej. The wedding of the infant had to be delayed but was completed the next morning. Ram Karan Gujjar and family viewed this as an unforgivable blow to their prestige and blamed Bhanwari for their public shaming (i.e., the showing up of the law enforcement agency at their event). Bhanwari's reporting of the incident was seen as a betrayal by the family (and the village).[13]

---

11 W. Dalrymple, *The Age of Kali: Indian Travels and Encounters* (London: Penguin Books, 2004), 97–110.
12 https://en.wikipedia.org/wiki/Bawandar
13 Gujjar was panchayat head and highly influential. According to reports, Badri Gujjar held (and continues to hold) unlimited authority on marriage, employment, social interactions of the Gujjar's in Bhateri and the Gujjar community in broader Rajasthan. The Gujjar influence, given the unshakeable caste hierarchy that the elected panchayats back, controls the fates of the other castes too.

Several references note a broader context around this matter of reporting, holding the Government of Rajasthan responsible for a 'knee-jerk reaction' to statistics published in Delhi. The Government of Rajasthan is noted to have acted imprudently and erratically by issuing the dictate and forcing saathins to report child marriage without a mechanism in place to implement such prevention in the fields, understanding the risk this would pose to its community workers and acknowledging the nexus between police, government officials and the village panchayat. Some reports therefore criticized that the government is thereby accused of 'jeopardizing years of patient work by the saathins' and destabilizing its own communities.

The rape, of course, had transpired to teach Bhanwari a lesson for her defiance, to put her in her place (lower than that of the upper-caste men who raped her). A PIL filed by Vishakha and four other women's groups (in 1992) led to the Vishakha Guidelines (August 1997). However, the criminal act of rape and assault is yet to be punished. In the interim, the five years to Vishakha judgment also had the following happening:

- Bhanwari Devi and her husband were boycotted socially and economically, which had started before she was raped and continued after. An open threat was issued against her and the villagers largely sided with the Gujjar family.

- After her rape, Bhanwari Devi was mistrusted, ridiculed and mistreated by the police. The first incident report was not registered, and she was made to wait. She was also harassed non-stop with the support of political and social bodies.

- Gross negligence occurred in processing and preservation of evidence, including her being sent from one centre to another and delaying critical steps (like vaginal swab) beyond the needed within 48 hours.[14]

14 T. Abraham, *The Politics of Patriarchy and Saathin Bhanwari's Rape: Women and the Politics of Violence* (New Delhi: Har Anand Publications, 2002), 277–279.

o She was made to leave the police station sans her skirt (which was confiscated as evidence), covering herself with her husband's blood-stained turban.

o The evidence (including her skirt) was undoubtedly tampered with, which remains a major roadblock in the path of criminal convictions of the accused.

- The social workers fighting her case were demonized.

- She and her family were ostracized and stripped of means of earning a living in the village before and after the incident of gang rape.

- Reporters have quoted villagers calling her slut and Ram Kumar Gujjar a good man. Years later, finding a wedding match for her son was problematic.

- Bhanwari Devi, however, received international (and national) recognition for her courage after her fight came under the limelight.[15]

In the years that followed, although the civil suite (PIL) materialized into judgment, the accused were acquitted by a trial court. Twenty-eight years later, at the time of this writing, those still alive remain free men. The case is now awaiting a trial date at Delhi High Court.

- Five judges were changed in the case.

- The reasoning(s) for trial court acquittal was preposterous at the least and deeply problematic for future India if considered with care.[16] The verdict cited the impossibility of Bhanwari Devi's husband witnessing such a matter passively because he had taken a vow to protect his wife in front of a fire (her husband was beaten and physically restrained by two men), the improbability that family members would commit such

---

15 https://www.thebetterindia.com/7199/the-irony-of-iconhood-the-life-and-times-of-bhanwari-devi/

16 http://ssr-net.com/issues/Vol_4_No_1_June_2018/3.pdf

acts in front of other family members (the accused had an uncle–nephew pair) and the impossibility of upper-caste men desecrating their bloodline by having intercourse with a lower-caste woman.

In summary, despite statements of previous judges who noted their conviction that the incident of gang rape had happened and was an act of revenge, the accused were acquitted with garbage put forward as reasoning.[17]

What is significant, out of every iniquitous detail of this case, 'is the fact that the sense of justice, or rightfulness—as in which side is correct in this matter—still remains a question in her village and therefore, puts a question mark on a woman's right to be not sexually abused against a community's right to be able to maintain its hierarchy and traditions'.

To understand this, let's review Rajasthan. Rajasthan is celebrated and commemorated as a land of incredible colour and beauty (and as India's face on international tourism brochures), masking the state's lack of socio-economic progress under preservation of heritage. This wouldn't be terribly relevant, if not for the fact that most valour stories that resonate with and about Rajasthan have to do with 'honour'. Guarding of religious and sociocultural purity from invaders extrapolated into guarding of family honour—men dying, and women killing themselves, in the name of honour (read sexual purity)—from tales of Padmini to practices such as *jauhar* (self-immolation) and sati (burning a widow on the pyre of her husband). A state with incredible heritage in art, architecture and music has consistently guarded the wrong pride and has reglorified regressive practices in the name of heritage.[18] The fairly recent right-wing fight involving Karni Sena,[19]

---

17 https://www.bbc.com/news/world-asia-india-39265653
18 https://feminisminindia.com/2020/08/07/roop-kanwar-last-known-case-sati-india-relevance-today/
19 https://indianexpress.com/article/explained/rajasthans-karni-sena-a-political-profile-padmaavat-protests-rajput-5039550/

who had its women's arm ready to commit *jauhar* to ban a movie, is an example. The Karni Sena women believed that their honour was being defiled by a movie showing fictional queen dancing. The gender issue (of men guarding women in the name of guarding honour) was used for nationalist Hindu gains, no doubt[20]; but the problem pertinent to gender this brings to light is significant, nevertheless. Of the many Indias that reside within India, the one in Rajasthan has repeatedly proved itself to be particularly backward when comes to gender and caste.[21]

- In 2017, a survey found 98 per cent of women in Rajasthan between ages 18 and 25 years to wear a veil.[22]

- In 2017–2018, masses protested the release of *Padmaavat* before knowing what the movie showed, believing that it would show a Hindu queen to be dishonoured. Saying that they protested, however, is an understatement. Death threats were issued against the movie's lead actress, including threats of cutting off her nose (a common method of chastising and labelling women, especially as a mark of her character). Buses were burnt and, most importantly, women were ready to commit mass suicide by self-immolation.[23]

- In 2019–2020, campaigns urging women to uncover their faces during casting ballots were deemed controversial.[24]

20 https://indianexpress.com/article/beyond-the-news/how-is-karni-sena-the-group-behind-padmavati-protests-so-powerful-4948391/
21 Dalrymple, *The Age of Kali*, 97–110.
22 https://www.theguardian.com/global-development/2020/jan/23/rajasthans-women-encouraged-to-remove-veil-in-state-campaign
23 https://www.huffingtonpost.in/rituparna-chatterjee/karni-sena-now-says-padmaavat-glorifies-rajputs-heres-a-reminder-of-what-their-u-turn-has-cost-india_a_23351795/
24 https://www.ndtv.com/jaipur-news/women-cant-progress-till-ghoonghat-exists-says-rajasthan-chief-minister-ashok-gehlot-2127811

Below is a paragraph from a 2018 report on women in Rajasthan:

In Rajasthan, the child sex ratio is 888 girls per 1000 boys and Jaisalmer specifically has a ratio of 874 girls to 1000 boys. The census also revealed that of total deaths in Rajasthan, over 20% of them were infant deaths. Overall, the female child population (age 0–6) between 2001 and 2011 dropped by 3 million. One journalist referred to this as 'the silent genocide'. Female infants are sometimes tragically killed by opium poisoning, starvation, or even being crushed with stones. The reality of this 'silent genocide' is revealed in the village of Devda, where a low sex ratio meant that there were only 18 girls in a population of 25,000 men. Even past infancy, things do not get easier. Rajasthan is the third largest state in India and ranks as the worst for female literacy. The latest census revealed that only 52.12% of women are literate in Rajasthan, compared to the already low national average of 65.46%. Many families pull their daughters out of school as they often see it as an unnecessary cost. With only 72.1 % of girls between 15–17 years attending school, Rajasthan also has the lowest female school attendance in the country.[25]

In the 1990s, Rajasthan lagged disastrously in almost every gender metric—from female infanticide and child marriage to female literacy and the average age of first-time mothers (which is noted to have increased to 16.5 years in 2007,[26] thanks to work by saathins like Bhanwari Devi).

Before her stance on the planned marriage of the nine-month-old daughter of Ram Karan Gujjar (in adherence to the government's child marriage prevention campaign), Bhanwari Devi had worked on several issues, including attempted rape, and had good support from her villagers. Meaning, she wasn't someone who wasn't

25 https://citta.org/wp-content/uploads/2018/11/Jaisalmer-Report-2018FT.pdf
26 https://web.archive.org/web/20120527074809/http://www.tehelka.com/story_main34.asp?filename=hub131007A_MIGHTY.asp

socially respected. In fact, although caste and class hierarchy placements are well established in a village, so was hers as someone wise and aware of social matters. However, after her efforts of persuading the Gujjars and the police visit on the day of Akha Teej,[27] she and her husband faced tremendous boycott. This is as significant to note as the fact that the child marriage did happen the next dawn—a nine-month-old infant was married off, despite visits from the deputy superintendent of police the evening before.

The rape and what followed on the surface seem to show that the Gujjar men were beyond enraged by her defiance. But the act itself and the broader behaviour of the community speak to the stronghold of the concept of 'honour' in the Rajasthani society. I believe that it is significant to note this concept here and in chapters throughout this book, not in academic terminology but as a concept—the obsession with honour and what keeps it going.

Human beings have a social need for ideologies and pride. For poorer demographics, loyalty (e.g., to rulers and owners) and honour (stemming from behaviours they imbibe) serve to fill the vacuum that lack of resources and power creates. This often develops over generations as the only thing that is within a family's (or a community's) control. This is milked and fuelled, of course, for political, national and even societal gains. But this anthropological shortcoming is a disaster in the path of progress. This manifests in several different forms across religions and nations and has been classified as a wide range of things—from fear and resistance to change, to loss of control (American Civil War).[28]

In Rajasthan, the reason saathin work (or, in a broader sense, permeation into communities via community members) has been one of the very few effective routes for social change is that this mode placates the fear of loss of control and takes an appeasement

27 https://www.hindustantimes.com/bollywood/karni-sena-to-oppose-padmavati-screening-if-facts-are-distorted/story-i3p3EAb50HfxVR5FdWiSeK.html
28 https://en.wikipedia.org/wiki/American_Civil_War

route instead. The same was expressed by non-profits working with Afghan women—slow, patient infiltration of the communities without challenging their beliefs proves to be the only effective route.

Is awareness different from permeation and appeasement? Absolutely. Learning the downsides of child marriage or female infanticide won't do much for the cause in communities where it can be ignored as an absurdity—thanks to centuries of conditioning. Bhanwari Devi's case is textbook study material for several different concepts: from societal behaviour to individual traits. Mass adherence to beliefs that encourage disproportionate and seemingly illogical actions to prevent loss of control is a key one out of that list.

The next matter is that of the power equation in sexual harassment, especially workplace sexual harassment. I had watched *Bawandar*[29] in a showing that Nandita Das[30] herself had presided (at the Cornell University). More memorable than having done so with the immensely talented actress was a quote I read in an interview of the film's director, Jagmohan Mundhra, published at the time.[31] Mundhra was being discredited (in an attempt to discredit the movie itself) as an erotic second-grade thriller director who commercialized sexuality and his response to whether or not he was doing the same with *Bawandar* was that 'rape is about subjugation, not sexuality.' Bhanwari Devi's case is a textbook one supporting this argument. Although I can't discard the sexual desire and deprivation factors that are co-modulator in some cases, in matters of workplace sexual harassment, more often than not, the ones with positional authority or influence abuse their subjugates. Power dynamics played a key role in Bhanwari Devi's rape, although she was not abused by her superiors or colleagues but for doing her job. She was also raped in the village—which was

29 https://en.wikipedia.org/wiki/Bawandar
30 https://en.wikipedia.org/wiki/Nandita_Das
31 https://en.wikipedia.org/wiki/Jag_Mundhra

her workplace. As we will discuss in Chapter 7, the definition of workplace is key for workplace sexual harassment regulations like Vishakha and POSH. However, the lack of existing protections at that time for fieldworkers like her caused her fate in the police station (a government agency) while filing an FIR to be no different than any commoner. Now, given the caste and class imbalance in a land ruled by the same,[32] could it have been the case regardless? Yes. And that is where movements come in over laws, but we will come to that later. For now, let's just recognize that the saathin work and similar tireless efforts by bands of activists over decades in Rajasthan didn't become stronger movements rallying around inciting incidents that came into the limclight. It is the tireless rallying that pushed these incidents into the limelight and created movements around them.

The case of Roop Kanwar[33] is another example. It is much lesser known that the trial for the glorification of her death on her husband's pyre (a crime in India) reached a verdict over 30 years after the incident. Roop Kanwar and the act of her dying on her husband's pyre is still largely worshipped in Rajasthan, with memorials and mementos.[34] Whether or not she did so voluntarily is disputed (from reports of her getting dragged, appearing drugged and beaten before getting pushed into the pyre under heavy logs to testimonials of her jumping into her husband's pyre herself existing side by side).[35]

Expectedly, the women in social service in Rajasthan who have been part of the landmark struggles is the primary group I consulted with for this chapter. Renuka Pamecha has been in

---

32 https://swarajyamag.com/politics/battle-of-rajasthan-caste-calculus-will-play-a-key-role-in-determining-the-winner
33 https://www.nytimes.com/1987/09/20/world/india-seizes-four-after-immolation.html
34 https://timesofindia.indiatimes.com/city/jaipur/in-sati-village-roop-kanwar-still-burns-bright/articleshow/70984735.cms
35 https://www.hinduismtoday.com/modules/smartsection/item.php?itemid=472; https://www.nytimes.com/1987/09/20/world/india-seizes-four-after-immolation.html

this field for 45 years, currently heading Mahila Suraksha Evam Salah Kendra (which is located in the very premises of a women police station), helping women in distress. In the past, Renuka has acted as the head of rehabilitation centres for women, Vividha,[36] and has co-founded Rajasthan University Women's Association (RUWA). And, of course, she has been part of the landmark movements out of Rajasthan which gave India Vishakha and the Sati (Prevention) Act (discussed below). In short, Pamecha has been closely associated with both the accounts (Bhanwari Devi and Roop Kanwar), and the women's rights movement in Rajasthan has been her daily cause for decades. I asked her what she thought of the fact that most people believe that Roop's act of burning on her husband's pyre was voluntary. And what, if anything, a state could do if so. She said,

Marji koi shabd nahin hoti (Free will is not even a word). Even if I want to commit suicide, shouldn't my family stop me? Or should they celebrate all around me? *Trance ho jati hain—mahol create hota hain ke mandir banega* (The woman gets into a trance—atmosphere is created that a temple will be made). It's widow murder. *Iccha ya aniccha koi maine nahin rakhti* (Wish or no wish doesn't matter here).

Several matters in the Roop Kanwar case parallel the Bhanwari Devi account. For example, Roop's in-laws were long acquitted, absolved of any responsibility in her death, and reports mention that even though police were informed of the incident beforehand, they were unable to reach on time to prevent the ceremony which happened in presence of a large crowd. Also, like in the case of Bhanwari Devi, the activism following her death led to the Sati (Prevention) Act[37] by the Government of Rajasthan and its adaptation by the Parliament of India. Although Roop's case is

---

36 https://janchetna.org/profile/strategy/networking/
37 https://www.indiacode.nic.in/handle/123456789/1814?view_type=browse &sam_handle=123456789/1362

not a case study we are focusing on, for understanding the broader gender rights vs the sociopolitical liaison picture, let's summarize the sociocultural similarities between the two cases.

- **Blind, misguided, harmful faith persisted and morphed from aggressive defiance to ambivalent justification.** As recently as 2019, the youth of Roop Kanwar's village have been quoted saying that they light incense sticks for her.[38] There is nothing glorious or honourable in getting a nine-month-old married or a woman immolating on her husband's pyre, no matter how many years of tradition supports it. It is worthwhile to note here that the statements you will read on the matter of Roop Kanwar's sati are not too different from what you might hear close friends or even family members say on dowry. 'We are dead against it, but if it's someone's will and a supreme act of love, how can we disrespect such an action?'

- **The accused were mostly acquitted despite a high amount of activism, and law enforcement agency largely failed to prevent or punish the involved.** The deep religiopolitical infrastructure that exists as a guarding net around patriarchal practices makes it impossible for any other outcome to happen.

Chunari Mahotsav bhi humne stop kiya—court order ke saath, just like sati (We stopped Chunari Mahotsav too with court order, just like sati). *Police ka pehra raha, par court roke to bhi nahin rukti—kaise rukegi? Samajh parivartan ka kaam humne kam kiya, bas political changes hi laye* (Police presence was there, but even if the courts stop it, nothing can stop if the society doesn't change. We haven't done much with changing the society, only political changes have happened).
                                        —Renuka Pamecha, Activist, Rajasthan

---

38 https://timesofindia.indiatimes.com/city/jaipur/in-sati-village-roop-kanwar-still-burns-bright/articleshow/70984735.cms

- **Activism around the incidents leads to indirect gains in the form of guidelines and laws.** These do serve an important role by allowing the problematic incident to be recognized as illegal and, therefore, need to be highlighted again and again.

- **To the communities in Rajasthan (and greater India—we will come to that), women's rights are less important than honour.** 'Community' includes the women—men are not solely to blame. Bhanwari Devi was called a liar by Bharatiya Janata Party's women's wing and just like in Karni Sena matter with actress Deepika Padukone, many women were quoted shaming her for bringing disgrace to Rajasthan's honour. In Chapter 6, we will provide some causal analysis of this matter.

Coming back to the case study, as stated earlier, Bhanwari Devi was asked to remove her lehenga (skirt) as evidence in the police station and had to walk back covering herself in her husband's blood-stained turban. This is quite well-known. It is also well-known that when the case went to the court, she was harassed on the witness stand with narratives commonly used on rape victims: whether they enjoyed the act. These are additional tactics implemented, of course, to embarrass and deter the victim and ensure others are dissuaded from coming forward. But what is incredible and most noteworthy to me in this account is how Bhanwari Devi and her husband persisted and continued to persist in face of mass ostracization, threats from neighbours and relatives, a boycott by extended family, loss of livelihood and awards that offered no real resolution (reports note that the funds from Neerja Bhanot Award remained locked away in charity trusts,[39] while the family struggled to make ends meet).

What is there to fear? They can kill us only once.[40]

---

39 http://www.ambedkar.org/News/News112701.htm
40 Mohan Lal, Bhanwari Devi's husband (https://www.bbc.com/news/world-asia-india-39265653).

Not only did she not fear shame, but she also is defiant—till date refusing to leave her village, confident that she has done no wrong and has nothing to be afraid of (after the next case study, as we recount Drew Dixon's story, it will be clear why this is tremendous). Twenty-eight years later, with 4 out of 5 of the accused dead (and the fifth one enjoying power and prestige) while she awaits justice, Bhanwari Devi's activism continues. In 2020, she participated in a 2-month-long tour of rape survivors through 24 states.[41] Some reports quote her to be understandably bitter, others quote her urging action for other women. Possibly because India can't, in the current ecosystem, award her a court victory, she was awarded a plot and a grant by Rajasthan's then Chief Minister Ashok Gehlot (2002).[42]

The similarities drawn here between incidents spanning decades from the state of Rajasthan are not to present Rajasthan as a problem state in isolation. But rather, it is to offer substantiating evidence of causal factors towards the gender subjugation problem in the context of highly patriarchal and belief-dominated societies. The origins of such beliefs were more often than not motivated, and their popularity was designed (to be discussed in Chapters 4, 5 and 6). But with the history forgotten, these have now manifested into laws of the land, manipulated for political and religious control.

I also interviewed Kamini Shukla (another woman who has spent her entire life for gender rights, was part of the women's development programme and has been with Vishakha, including on the executive board). She is now associated with SMILE alongside Pritam Pal, Bhanwari Devi's original project director and a good friend of Shukla. I asked both Pamecha and Shukla the question of Rajasthan (and similar apparent microcosms which seem to be unique and specifically lagging in development). Their

41 https://www.telegraphindia.com/india/bhanwari-devi-and-a-long-march-to-wipe-out-the-stigma-of-rape/cid/1685303
42 https://www.rediff.com/news/2002/jan/10rajas.htm

views differed on this matter. Renuka is strongly of the opinion that even though there's some amount of historical component that plays a role in Rajasthan being extremely hierarchical—because it was a feudal state after all—women's and social movements of Rajasthan are not weak.

> *Jitni awaaz yahan se uthi hain, utni kahin se bhi nahin uthi* (The amount of voice that has come out of here, there is nowhere else that has had the same amount of voices raised). The media here is very strong also. Print media before the Internet. Any movement is because of media—but then, the media slowly becomes pro-structured government. If you say Rajasthan for the 90s, now you will say Kerala is for domestic violence. Why would that be then? Doesn't Kerala have the highest education? So, it's not any state in particular for any particular reason. It is because of the broader outlook towards women and the mindset of the entire society.

'Just gender?' I probed her, 'Seems like caste issues are worse here too.'

> Gender and caste are not separate. Gender will get divided for caste. Or anything for that matter. *USA mein kya hota hain* (What happens in the USA)? Gender caste—gender race—black and white will divide—*sare* (all) Thakur(s) will be on one side, *sare* (all) Rajput(s) will be on one side. Maybe the Rajasthan, or rather India, factor might be that the political vote bank is based on that.

Kamini Shukla disagreed.

> *Rajasthan mein NGOs at the village level are less* (In Rajasthan, there are fewer NGOs at the village level). *Karna bhi chahte hain to panchayat rok dete hain—log peeche hat jaate hain—niptara panchayat se hi hoti hain and panchayat is too strong here and too backyard* (Even if NGOs want to be there, panchayat will stop them—people will have to retreat—resolutions can happen only through panchayats and panchayats are too strong and too backyard here).

I can't conclude here on Rajasthan, or India or on all the factors that caused (or continue to cause) gender rights violations; the next chapters are for that. But Pamecha's point on gender vs other identities will come to the forefront in the next case study.

DREW DIXON (AND OTHERS) VS RUSSELL SIMMONS (1983–2020)

- In 2017, Russell Simmons[43] (an African-American entrepreneur and music mogul reported to be of net worth upwards of 300 million in 2011) was accused of rape by four women and of sexual harassment and assault by others, who cited incidents persisting over a decade (1983–2014).[44]

- One of the accusers, Drew Dixon (an executive at the record label Mr Simmons had co-founded), had Mr Simmons harassing her on work calls and sometimes in front of co-workers over a period of time—from showing her his erect penis to remarks on how she aroused him—before the actual incident of rape.

- The incident of rape is alleged to have happened when Mr Simmons had asked Ms Dixon to come over to his apartment for work and had made her go into his room to retrieve an artist's demo they were to review together. Dixon has said that she saw a pair of handcuffs, remembered Simmons forcing her to have intercourse and had blacked out. She said that she later regained consciousness in his bathtub, naked.

- Dixon noted that she had spiralled into depression because of the persistent harassment.

- Several folks stated that they were told about the incidents at that time. Reports of inappropriate behaviour including outright assault against Russell Simmons surfaced again and

43 https://en.wikipedia.org/wiki/Russell_Simmons
44 https://www.rollingstone.com/music/music-news/russell-simmons-sexual-assault-allegations-a-timeline-202515/

again through the 1990s, although it isn't clear if legal action or public reporting was pursued before 2017.[45]

- Following the incident of rape, Simmons is said to have expected regular physical intimacy with Dixon, normalizing his aggression towards her through the expectation of regular sexual engagements. It is worthy to note this here as a signature, for in a similar saga at the Fox News, the powerful executive (Roger Ailes)[46] is reported to have told his employee that all could be made better through them initiating and pursuing a sexual relationship.[47] Note that although we are not deliberating the Fox News sexual harassment case here, the case, just before MeToo and often noted as an early MeToo (alongside the accusations against Bill Cosby),[48] is significant because Gretchen Carlson's lawsuit against Ailes, who allegedly fired her for rejecting his sexual advances, led to scores of women to come forward with allegations against Ailes.[49]

- In November 2017, in the wake of #MeToo, *Los Angeles Times* reported former model Keri Claussen Khalighi's accusations.[50] Keri told the paper that Simmons had made aggressive advances and had briefly penetrated her without her consent.

- One week following *Los Angeles Times*'s reporting, screenwriter Jenny Lumet published her column in *The Hollywood Reporter*, accusing Simmons of sexually violating her in 1991.

- Drew Dixon came forward with her story after reading Lumet's column and said that she was inspired by other women coming forward through the #MeToo movement.

45 Ibid.
46 https://en.wikipedia.org/wiki/Roger_Ailes
47 Hirshman, *Reckoning*.
48 https://www.bbc.com/news/world-us-canada-43915033
49 https://www.politico.com/blogs/on-media/2016/07/gretchen-carlson-files-lawsuit-against-roger-ailes-alleging-sexual-harassment-225162
50 https://www.washingtonpost.com/arts-entertainment/2020/05/28/russell-simmons-on-the-record-documentary-hbo-max/

- By the time the 2020 documentary on this, *On the Record*,[51] was released, 20 women had accused Simmons.

- The primary concern Ms Dixon shared in the 2020 documentary (which has a saga of its own that we will discuss in detail, for the controversy surrounding it is equally relevant) was how she would be viewed by her community for coming out against a fellow black man.

- All the women said that they felt empowered to come forward after the Harvey Weinstein accusations became public (aka initiation of MeToo).

- *On the Record* was originally slated for release on Apple TV+ as part of Oprah Winfrey's multiyear deal with the streaming network.[52] Despite MeToo, Oprah Winfrey pulled herself from the film (controversially)[53] and later admitted to having been pressured by Simmons. She, however, maintains that her decision to pull from the film was purely because of creative differences with the filmmakers and stresses on her strong support for the women in the movie.[54]

Note: It will probably read ridiculous and might require a segment worth of explanation, but to me, as I read transcripts of the Rajasthan incidents and media reports of Oprah's statement, Mr Gehlot granting a plot to Bhanwari Devi in support (Rajasthan, India) but her high court dates getting pushed out year after year, and Oprah Winfrey supporting women in the documentary but pulling her channel out of releasing the film (Los Angeles, USA), don't look very different.

51 https://en.wikipedia.org/wiki/On_the_Record_(film)
52 https://www.latimes.com/entertainment-arts/movies/story/2020-01-31/drew-dixon-tina-perry-oprah-russell-simmons
53 https://variety.com/2020/film/news/russell-simmons-documentary-on-the-record-sundance-alexia-norton-jones-1203479964/
54 https://www.theguardian.com/film/2020/jan/25/on-the-record-oprah-winfrey-russell-simmons

- The accusers are noted to have faced 'devastating' personal and professional fallouts because of the abuse.

- Drew Dixon left Def Jam (Simmons's company) and joined Arista. However, her experience with harassment was repeated at Arista when L. A. Reid[55] took over the label. Dixon had accused that Reid made 'frequent, unwanted advances' which she rebuffed, facing increasing professional consequences in retaliation. Dixon left the music industry altogether. In 2017, Reid stepped down following sexual harassment claims by another employee.

We all lose when brilliant women go away.[56]

The cost of sexual harassment, to the economy, is high. Harassment or lack of safety at workplace is a key factor in women leaving the workforce. However, how replaceable are the women who leave? The answers can be very different. As noted in the previous case study, the Bhanwari Devi incident could have done irreparable damage to the saathin programme with women refusing to do similar work, given the risks associated. In the hip-hop industry, as in some other entertainment fields, that is not the case.

DIFFERENT? OR NOT?

New York, USA, and Rajasthan, India, don't bring forward relatable images to our mind, definitely not in the context of sexual harassment. But with a deeper look, underlying similarities which should be reflected upon, and differences, which should be explored, can be found.

The music industry in the USA, especially the hip-hop scene, had (pre-MeToo) an ecosystem normalizing objectification and harassment. Although shaped through completely different

55 https://en.wikipedia.org/wiki/L.A._Reid
56 Amy Ziering and Kirby Dick, *On the Record* (HBO Max, 2020).

histories, it's no different than what we have noted for Rajasthan where female lives remain less valuable to date.

A 2017 *The New York Times* article states that the reason the music industry seemed to have been relatively unaffected as MeToo rocked Hollywood is that sex and debauchery are built into the music industry.

Where the boundaries between work and play blur in late nights at clubs and studios, and many women have scant power or incentive to complain about being mistreated. These women still face powerful industry gatekeepers like Mr. Simmons, whose pedigree and ability to make or break careers allowed his abusive behavior to go unchallenged for decades, his accusers contend.[57]

Celebrated singer–songwriter and record producer R. Kelly,[58] just like Bollywood's Salman Khan, had remained untouchable (and as some reports accuse, protected) despite decades of accusations of abuse of teenage and underage girls, including indictments on charges of child pornography.[59] R. Kelly is noted to be the most successful rhythm and blues (R&B) artist of the 1990s and one of the world's bestselling artists. However, repeated charges of sexual harassment of minors (including marriage to an underage woman) getting overlooked are something else altogether. In 2019, Kelly was facing 18 counts of federal charges, and MeToo had had a lot to do with that (victims broke non-disclosure agreements to come forward in 2017 post MeToo).[60] Before MeToo, as several reports have alleged, R. Kelly's continued invincibility and

57 https://www.nytimes.com/2020/05/27/movies/on-the-record-russell-simmons-review.html
58 https://en.wikipedia.org/wiki/R._Kelly
59 https://www.bbc.com/news/entertainment-arts-40635526
60 https://www.buzzfeednews.com/article/jimderogatis/r-kelly-underage-woman-speaks-out#.gyzJNR3DWA

repeated acquittals created wrong and dangerous precedence. 'The awareness of what "didn't happen" to him didn't inspire confidence.'

Second is the matter of gender rights vs loyalty to a community (like in the cases out of Rajasthan). The USA has a tough history to tackle on this front. Black men have been falsely accused and lynched as sexual predators, causing the community to rally together. The fight against this prejudice, in the USA, has been 'do or die' for the black community. Bringing accusations forward against black men—especially by black women—therefore, could be perceived as an act of betrayal. 'Whatever it is, no matter how evil, we don't air our dirty laundry to the world' is a sentiment that is not too foreign for close-knit communities, especially for the ones priding themselves on being unique or fighting prejudice for the same.

Drew Dixon talks about this several times, from not wanting to 'let the culture down' (talking of the hip-hop culture) to a fear of being viewed as someone who is opposing her own community, doing further damage to blacks in America. Dixon also talks about the experiences of Anita Hill[61] and Desiree Washington, other black women, reputed and powerful, who were disbelieved and discredited when they came forward with accusations of sexual harassment and violence.

....

Black women are subjected to both racism and sexism—a double bind that puts black women at higher risk for sexual violence and contributes to a 'culture of silence' that prevents them from telling their stories.[62]

....

61 https://web.archive.org/web/20111107034024/http://www.gpoaccess.gov/congress/senate/judiciary/sh102-1084pt4/41-124.pdf
62 https://www.washingtonpost.com/arts-entertainment/2020/05/28/russell-simmons-on-the-record-documentary-hbo-max/

This matter of differentiated and worse experience of women of colour is no different from the experience of lower-caste women in India. In Chapter 4, we will showcase this in detail. In Chapter 8, Anugraha Kumar Sharma speaks about this when speaking of Dalit women. But for now, let's just reflect on the fact that despite the tremendous responsibility towards women and girls that Oprah Winfrey is celebrated for, she quite possibly chose race over gender when it came to *On the Record*, not too different from villagers who chose tradition and the women who'd self-immolate. Whether it's for race or honour/caste/family, when it comes to gender, making a strong argument for gender rights is difficult for women.

Now, let us consider the protagonists in these stories. Drew Dixon is the daughter of a former mayor of Washington. She lives in the USA, that too in New York City, and is an executive herself. She was raped in an apartment. She was not in financial distress. She disclosed to friends what had happened to her but couldn't come forward publicly until 2017. She spiralled into depression and appears visibly affected in several of her interviews, a decade plus later.

Bhanwari Devi is a child bride herself, of a lower caste, and had meagre means when the incident happened to her. She was gang-raped by five men in an open field and had to bear public humiliation and ostracization. She went to the police and was sent back without her skirt. She has faced years of threat and acute poverty but remains defiant.

This comparison isn't in any way to shed unfavourable light on Ms Dixon. This comparison, on the contrary, is an attempt to understand abuse and it's varying effect. I brought up my observations to some friends despite the risk of being called a victim-blamer. One of them said that just like immunity, exposure to pain and suffering overtime creates resilience. Another noted that when there is nothing left to lose, fighting becomes easier.

I called Renuka Pamecha and Kamini Shukla back, and then Pritam Pal (Bhanwari's project director who has been with her since the starting days and is, to date, a close confidante of hers).

I learned from Shukla that just a few days ago (October first week of 2020), Mohan Lal ji, Bhanwari Devi's husband, passed. Mohan Lal ji was noted to be a key source of Bhanwari Devi's strength in multiple articles that studied the couple, including by Nandita Das while shooting for *Bawandar*. 'What keeps her so strong? What gave her the strength?' I asked, sharing accounts of other women I was studying who were having tremendous struggles with depression resulting from abuse.

Shukla credited the support structure, the programme and her project director—Pritam Pal.

> *Pritam project director ki post pe thi—thoda power to hoti hain—par it's her personality too, and Pritam's* (Pritam was in the post of project director and some power came from that, but it was her personality too. And Pritam's). Also, the whole WDP (the Women's Development Program)—all saathins—all prachetas—were together. I was in Dungapur at that time, the southern part of Rajasthan—but we all gathered, from everywhere, for one cause.

Renuka Pamecha echoed what Shukla had said. '*Bhanwari Devi ka support structure bahut strong hain* (Bhanwari Devi's support structure is very strong).' I noted as she spoke that she speaks in the present tense—28 years later—knowing that criminal conviction is going to be impossible (which we will talk about in later chapters)—it's still an ongoing fight for her.

> *Pritam, Roshan ji—kisi ne bhi use akela nahin choda* (No one left her alone). We closed the secretariat gates. The gates were closed until they let the appeal happen. And Bhanwari's convictions were unshakeable from the beginning. She has done nothing wrong—so she had her conviction taking her through.

I don't want to go down the line of validating or repudiating personal strength arguments here. But I do want to make a note of the importance of community and support structure. Just like a community association beyond gender can rip the gender problem statements apart, gender coming together as a community— even when no other anthropological connection exists—creates strength. Before, after and during MeToo—as women fall apart or feel ashamed of being feminists—if they rally closely instead, a feudal society where lives can be at risk for raising voices (Pamecha has needed police protection a few times, as have many of the others, and, of course, Bhanwari Devi has been under constant threat—she is just too visible to be harmed again) and where time seems to be at still can come very close to a movement driven out of the richest nation of the world, via the Internet, decades ahead in time.

The other thing I want to note through this capture of the contrast in the two protagonists is that abuse can have very different effects on different individuals. Investigation of accusations should be based on facts, not expectations of human behaviours. We will come to that in the statute of limitation discussion.

The last matter here is that of plausibility. In the Bhanwari Devi case, accusers were acquitted with the court giving them the 'benefit of the doubt', as some reports quote. An incident that would appear to be the only rational thing that could have happened to anyone with even bare minimum know-how of the 1990s Rajasthan is thrown away as improbable. Bhanwari's story can't be true because her husband would have intervened (her husband was restrained). Bhanwari's story was marked as a matter that can't be true because upper-caste men wouldn't rape lower-caste women and family members won't engage in gang rape together (multiple documented cases exist showing the contrary).

Drew Dixon's account, depending on the report I was reading, had several discrepancies (which could very well be incorrect reporting and not incorrect recollection on Dixon's part). For example, some of the reports I have cited quote Dixon to have passed out on seeing handcuffs, some have her quoting she remembers being kissed forcefully when she blacked out, others have her saying that she remembers being forced into intercourse. She has consistently said that she wasn't under influence of drugs or alcohol. I believe that because she came forward in 2017, on the heels of the breakout of MeToo, she didn't have to face disbelief and questioning of her accounts which she'd otherwise have had to. Other women corroborating similar experience with Simmons of course helps. If she had come out before MeToo, there's a good chance that her account would be torn apart and suppressed. After MeToo, there is a good chance too that the story gets ripped in court or is settled out of court. My point here is not that Ms Dixon is being untruthful. My point is twofold. One, when without the right climate and with a motivation to disprove, anyone can be discredited. Two, it is absolutely possible for a victim to blackout and have hazy recollections. The building of a case against the accused, therefore, relies on evidence and parallel accounts. Bhanwari Devi was dismissed not because of improbabilities, but because of the state mechanism and caste politics that stand behind the Gujjars. Drew Dixon would be most possibly discredited too (especially if there were no other allegations) in a climate where the opposition of sexual harassment came secondary to other matters, especially in a jury trial.[63] But the fact that multiple accusers and similarity in their narrative have put Simmons out of commission highlights what inspiration can do.

It is probably clear now why we discussed Drew Dixon alongside Bhanwari Devi—two women and accounts so different prima facie. But it's probably not clear yet why I have an after-MeToo incident placed in this chapter. Why have I placed a story from the so-called era of awareness following accounts that possibly resulted from a lack of awareness? Well, Dixon was raped in 1995, three years after Bhanwari Devi's rape and long before #MeToo (which is true for several MeToo accounts, including the Harvey Weinstein saga credited as the #MeToo starter). So, as I said,

63 https://www.americanbar.org/groups/criminal_justice/publications/criminal_justice_section_archive/crimjust_standards_jurytrial_blk/

before and after, like awareness and inspiration, is quite nuanced and fluid. There are a few additional reasons for my selection of these particular accounts, and I will get to them as I wrap up this chapter— after the third, and final, case study.

RUPAN DEOL BAJAJ VS K. P. S. GILL (1988–2017)

In 1988 (29 July), Ms Bajaj, then an officer of the Indian Administrative Service in the Punjab cadre, lodged a police complaint against Mr K. P. S. Gill, then Director General of Punjab Police, alleging for offenses ranging across multiple Indian Penal Code (IPC) sections (341, 342, 352, 354 and 509).[64] The incident that prompted her complaint had taken place at a dinner party (18 July), where Mr Gill had repeatedly pursued Ms Bajaj and had, ultimately, slapped her butt, in the full view and presence of other guests. The sequence of events has been noted quite diligently in the references, given the high profile of the case and the background of the plaintiff. Below is how one source lists the same.[65]

- Around 10 PM on the said night, Dr. Chutani and Mr. Gill walked across the garden and sat in the ladies' circle.

- Bajaj, who was talking to Mrs. Bijlani and Mrs. Bhandari at the time, was requested by Mr. Gill to take a seat next to him as he wanted to talk to her about something.

- Responding to his such request when Mrs. Bajaj went to sit in a chair next to him Mr. Gill suddenly pulled that chair close to his chair.

---

64 Section 341: punishment for wrongful restraint; Section 342: punishment for wrongful confinement; Section 352: punishment for assault or criminal force; Section 354: assault or criminal force to woman with intent to outrage her modesty; Section 509: word, gesture or act intended to insult the modesty of a woman.
65 https://www.latestlaws.com/case-analysis/sc-case-analysis-rupan-deol-bajaj-anr-v-kanwar-pal-singh-gill-anr-by-vatsala-walia/

- Bajaj was a bit taken aback when she put that chair at its original place and was about to sit down and Mr. Gill again pulled his chair closer.

- Realizing something was wrong she immediately left the place and went back to sit with the ladies.

- After about 10 minutes Shri Gill came and stood in front of her so close that his legs were about 4" from her knees.

- He then, by an action with the crook of his finger asked her to 'get up immediately' and come along with him.

- When she strongly objected to his behavior and asked him to go away from there, he repeated his earlier command which shocked the ladies present there.

- Being apprehensive and frightened she tried to leave the place but could not as he had blocked her way.

- Finding no other alternative when she drew her chair back and turned backward, he slapped her on the posterior in the full presence of the ladies and guests.

When I had interviewed a journalist in Chandigarh (she requested anonymity) who knew the matter, she had characterized both the incident and the punishment meted to K. P. S. Gill as 'small crime, small punishment'. As we will argue in many parts of this manuscript, sexual harassment can't be classified as 'small' (or 'trivial', as some counter-views classify certain instances) based on just the act itself. We will also compare how POSH is much more comprehensive in this matter than the US workplace sexual harassment laws. However, in this context, it's easy to see where she was coming from. The 1980s and 1990s saw gang rapes, women getting cut and killed in the most horrendous of ways (from Anita Dewan[66] and Girija Tickoo[67] to cases we have already discussed) and

---

66 https://en.wikipedia.org/wiki/1990_Bantala_rape_case
67 References that outline what happened to Girija Tickoo can be found easily through an Internet search if the reader is interested. However, I am not linking

dowry deaths-dominated newspaper headlines. Therefore, done by a superior or not—to a woman in a high place or not—butt slapping would seem like something that should be forgotten and forgiven.

The courts seemed to hold a similar view (delay and detouring hearings and investigations and openly saying so in judgments), as did the mainstream opinion. I reached out to Kalpana Kannabiran[68] (renowned sociologist and lawyer whose papers I will be quoting in several chapters of this manuscript) specifically on the K. P. S. Gill account and MeToo, for she has written extensively on both. She directed me to one of her works,[69] which lists multiple examples of how Gill's conduct was viewed as an unfortunate matter that had happened to him—not an incorrect action he took. Below are the direct excerpts from Ms Kannabiran's paper.

....

The sentence of three months' rigorous imprisonment. Although well within his discretion and powers under the relevant section of the Indian Penal Code looks somewhat harsh considering that Gill had an outstanding record as a Supercop. If today Punjab is rid of militancy which had taken a heavy toll of human lives in the state a great deal of the credit goes to Gill.[70]

....

It somehow makes the law of the land look grotesquely odd and incongruous that a man who has done signal service to

....

them here. Post the Article 370 matter in Kashmir, 2019/2020 Internet is flooded with references that are blatantly propagandistic and inflammatory. The references on Girija Tickoo that I was able to find (outside of scholarly papers in which the actual matter is buried quite deep within) were of the said nature. Although I was able to gather the case details from those articles, I would like to not include propagandistic sites in this manuscript to the extent possible (Note: in some cases, the discussion topic in hand would require including references and details of such sites). This stance of mine for this work is agnostic to any religion or political ideology.

68 https://en.wikipedia.org/wiki/Kalpana_Kannabiran
69 http://www.csdhyd.org/gritwp18kk.pdf
70 Editorial, *The Hindu*, 9 August 1996.

the country by ridding a state of the dread and oppression of terrorism should have to spend five months in jail for a minute's exuberance provoked by the charms of an attractive working woman.[71]

....

KPS Gill's conviction by a Chandigarh court prompts a moral dilemma. India's most celebrated policeman, the man who contributed most in crushing terrorism in Punjab, and one of the country's most authentic living heroes, has been held guilty of using 'criminal force' and 'intruding upon the privacy of a woman.' There was no political dimension in Rupan Deol Bajaj's charge.... It was a plain and simple charge of sexual harassment.... Under the circumstances, should Gill's enormous national contribution be allowed to gloss over a personal misdemeanour? Conversely, should Gill's record in Punjab be allowed to be subsumed by a flood of righteous indignation.... No Indian who is aware of his role in defeating secessionism in Punjab 3 Suchita Srivastava v. Chandigarh Admn. 2009 9 SCC 1 5 can be happy at Gill's misfortune.... Unfortunately it is not his humiliation alone; the country too feels a little small today.[72]

'The country feels a little small today.' It is worth noting and remembering that this was said in the context of delayed justice at last being meted for sexual harassment. In the months following the FIR, Mr B. R. Bajaj, Rupan Deol's husband, filed an additional complaint (citing the same offenses and concern on Punjab Police's investigation and action on the matter) in the Court of the Chief Judicial Magistrate. However, in 1989, against the appeal filed by Mr K. P. S. Gill (under IPC Section 482, both the complaint and the FIR were thrown out by the high court. Of the reasons[73] cited for doing so, the following are noteworthy:

....

71 Editorial, *Deccan Chronicle*, 8 August 1996.
72 Editorial, *The Indian Express*, 7 August 1996.
73 https://indiankanoon.org/doc/579822/

- 'The allegations made therein do not disclose any cognizable offence.'
- 'The allegations are unnatural and improbable.'
- 'There was unreasonable and unexplained delay of 11 days in lodging the F.I.R.'

'Improbability or implausibility', or in other words, doesn't seem like something like this could have happened, as noted in the cases discussed earlier in this chapter, is a subjective but potent armament in dismissal of complaints. Specifically, for judgments out of India, it seems to be a 'when all else fails, throw out the case' reasoning used often, especially at levels below the Supreme Court. Technically, going by the legal texts, implausibility is a valid defence for all cases in which circumstantial evidence only exists. However, as discussed for the Bhanwari Devi case, material evidence can be tampered with, and witnesses can turn, not appear (happened in the Gill case) or shown to be unreliable. If the judge is looking to dismiss, he will do so anyway by marking a very probable incident improbable, like in the case in discussion—Rupan Deol Bajaj vs K. P. S. Gill. Allowing subjective reasoning to be a valid dismissal in a compromised judiciary system allows for the dismissal of all cases—evidence or no evidence.

In a trial by the jury (as followed in the USA), the subjectivity of singular opinion is expected to be dispersed by having a group instead (expected to be comprised of diverse and blind selected individuals).[74] However, it is far from fail-proof, and selecting or influencing juror bias is a technique followed effectively by both prosecution and defence.

It's noteworthy that there is a widespread perception that India did away with jury trial following the case of K. M. Nanavati vs

74 https://www.uscourts.gov/services-forms/jury-service/types-juries#:~
:text=A%20trial%20jury%2C%20also%20known,but%20jury%20deliberations
%20are%20private

the State of Maharashtra,[75] because of the subjective and biased opinion of the jury affecting justice. The judiciary system was severely shocked and displeased with the acquittal of Nanavati in the first trial and the case was re-tried.

I say that it is noteworthy here for two reasons. Since we will talk again and again of criminal convictions in the context of sexual offenses (from due recourse and fair processing requirements to determination of actual happening of incidences—a lot, as we will see, is going to be relying on conviction rates), it's necessary that we point out again and again that what determines conviction, often, is not what should. In Chapter 8, we will discuss this in the broader context of law, not just conviction under the law. We will review how the law is not what it seems to be: an absolute fulcrum based on marked standards of right vs wrong that determines social behaviour, but rather is a matter that is itself quite influenced by social sentiments and popular opinion.

The second reason for noting is to note the point that murder and acquittal for murder are largely unacceptable to the judicial conscience. But sexual assault (including grievous) is not.

Coming back to Rupan Deol Bajaj vs K. P. S. Gill and 'the matter of "no big deal"': The high court noted the act to be not a cognizable offense and brought about IPC Section 95 (an act causing slight harm), which amounts to the fact that if the wrong precedence got set with the judgment passed in this case, women would have a hard time bringing criminal charges against slap on the butt, stroke on the back, touching of the breasts (all of which can be argued to be accidental or without malicious intent) and so on.

'A slap on the wrist for a slap on the butt.' That's what my source in Chandigarh had said.

---

75 http://archive.sarai.net/files/original/d50d1f5e2a0a59a67e9c8787901c66f8. pdf

Doesn't seem fair but legally, at the time in discussion, that is what would most possibly happen for defendants who weren't Ms Bajaj.

—A Senior IAS Officer

Lastly, on 'the matter of delay': 11 days' delay on the filing of the FIR. Now, it is quite easy for even a commoner to guess why, being in the same profession and social circle, it would take a husband and wife days of consideration and discussion on what to do on such a matter, especially since the case needed to be filed is against the Director of Punjab Police and according to the court's own words, 'not a matter that causes too much harm to the defendant'. However, the courts need to use, and often use, the delay in filing argument against victims in cases of sexual abuse. This became a key point in the MeToo debate with public opinion deliberating 'why it took so long if it's true?' Hopefully, MeToo (including cases like the ones we have discussed here where strong women with means suffered for decades before coming forward) has created some awareness on the 'time' factor.

However, there are legal barriers that haven't been eliminated, not just societal ones. Statute of limitation had a reason to be put in place (prevention of convictions based on unreliable witness testimony/memories of events that have weakened over time). But without an understanding of the emotional, societal and physiological dynamics of sexual assault, its existence has done a great disservice to justice and prevention in this space and is continuing to do so. In the USA, whether a criminal statute of limitation exists on reporting of a sexual crime is dependent on which state we are talking[76] (most states continue to have them, though quite a few have exceptions granted, e.g., for DNA evidence). Also, in the USA, just like in India in Ms. Bajaj's case, felony vs misdemeanour is a matter, as is whether or not there was an intent and repetitive pattern.

---

76 https://www.rainn.org/state-state-guide-statutes-limitations

In recent years, evidence that does not erode over time is often available, such as DNA, audio or video recordings, emails, texts, and other digital communication. These newer forms of evidence play an important role in investigating and prosecuting crimes of sexual violence. The society also has come to understand more about the physical, emotional, and psychological effects of sexual violence and the reasons why a victim may not immediately report the crime. As the understanding of these crimes and their effect have evolved, so have states' laws.[77]

The statute of limitations in India is defined by the 1963 Limitation Act, governed by Section 468 of the Code of Criminal Procedures and extremely contingent, to say the least.[78] There are lists of exceptions listed, against rigorous time limits based on the maximum punishment for the crime. For example, for an offense punishable by fine only, it's six months. If the offense is punishable with imprisonment, the statute is mostly proportional to the maximum number of years of imprisonment allowed for the offense.

This fogginess remains in the case of child sexual abuse too, and the recent laws (e.g., the Protection of Children from Sexual Offences Act, 2012) do not specify a period for a survivor to report the crime. It is also unclear whether or not a survivor can report the crime after turning 18. Section 19, which details the procedure for reporting abuse, assumes the complainant to be a child, defined as 'any person below the age of 18 years'. So the Limitation Act and the Code of Criminal Procedure remain applicable. Section 468 states that any offense, including child sexual abuse, punishable with a minimum of three years in prison must be reported within three years, with the limitation period starting on the day the offense occurs. Section 473, on the other hand, mentions that the

77 https://www.rainn.org/articles/statutes-limitations-sex-crimes
78 https://timesofindia.indiatimes.com/home/education/news/Law-of-Limitation/articleshow/1012807.cms

limitation period can be extended where 'delay has been properly explained', and it is in the 'interest of justice'.[79]

> Govindarajulu, 53, says she was abused by a male relative from the age of six to 13, in the southern Indian city of Chennai where she grew up. She moved to Canada when she was 21. It wasn't until years later, while watching a television show on child abuse, that repressed memories surfaced, and she realized she had been abused. She gathered her nerves and told her family 20 years ago. No one doubted her accounts, and another cousin also spoke of being abused by the same man, who is now in his 70s, she said. But she was told she had no legal options to report him.[80]

Coming back to Bajaj vs Gill, it is hopefully apparent now that the 11 days' delay is not a legal violation (it doesn't violate even the most rigorous of statutes), but rather an excuse for discrediting and dismissing. What it means is that in a commonplace situation for most of us commonplace folks, if your supervisor squeezes your rear and you take a few days to remain in shock, there might be an issue of your being able to seek criminal justice against him. A civil suit is going to be your only option.

> *MeToo ke bare mein yeh hi bolungi ke immediate accusations hi nahin sunte hain, to das saal baad kya sunenge—par mahilayon mein himmat aayegi—Akbar jaise log hat jayenge* (What I will say about MeToo is that they don't want to listen to immediate accusations, so how will years' old ones stand a chance—but yes, it will give women strength—and people like Akbar[81] will get removed).
>
> —Renuka Pamecha, Activist, Rajasthan

79 https://scroll.in/article/897644/grey-area-activists-are-sceptical-about-removing-time-limits-on-reporting-child-sexual-abuse
80 https://www.reuters.com/article/us-india-children-crime/decades-on-a-survivor-campaigns-to-change-india-law-on-reporting-abuse-idUSKCN1GB0A5
81 https://en.wikipedia.org/wiki/M._J._Akbar

Bajaj vs Gill was appealed at the Supreme Court following high court dismissal where it was duly deliberated. Of the IPC sections alleged, deliberation was mostly on Sections 354 and 509 (on outraging the modesty of a woman). Case analysis files have recorded the deliberation on 'modesty' itself, since it wasn't defined. From the consideration of dictionary definitions (Oxford and Webster) to understanding if a slap on the butt is suggestive of sex or not, what constitutes outraging the modesty of a woman became the primary matter. The court decided that with or without sexual intention, slapping a woman on her butt is disrespectful to a lady and hence counts as an act of outraging her modesty. The defence argued intention and the proof of it. The court considered the sequence of events throughout the evening and ruled that Gill's behaviour through the evening indeed allows for an inference of culpable intention.

Let's pause and note one more point here: Proving that an event has happened and proving that an event has happened as an event that's punishable by the law are two different things. We will deliberate more on this in Chapter 7, but for now let's just note that if Mr Gill wouldn't have gone through the shenanigans of chair pulling and such, and had just sneaked up behind Ms Bajaj, slapped her butt in full view and walked away, the Bajaj vs Gill judgment would have looked very different.

For the sake of completion, here is how the different sections under consideration were dispositioned. Sections 341, 342 and 352 were ruled to be not applicable, as wrongful restraint was found to be not a matter in this case. Section 95, which was brought about by the judiciary, not the complainant, was found to have no applicability based on precedence set by Veeda Menezes vs Yusuf Khan.[82]

82 https://www.latestlaws.com/case-analysis/sc-case-analysis-rupan-deol-bajaj-anr-v-kanwar-pal-singh-gill-anr-by-vatsala-walia/

The Supreme Court held that the High Court had committed a gross error of law in quashing the FIR and the complaint. Accordingly, it set aside the impugned judgment and dismissed the petition filed by Mr. Gill in the High Court under Section 482 Cr.P.C.[83]

However, before coming to the judgment, let's take a look at the defendant, Mr K. P. S. Gill, and understand who he was so that we can deliberate 'entitlement to impunity', as Kalpana Kannabiran calls it in her work, and whether or not such entitlement is reserved for certain individuals or is available to any man, thanks to our outlook on gender.

Gill, an Indian Police Service officer who started his career in the Northeast and served as the Inspector General of Police in Assam and twice as Director General of Police for the state of Punjab, is widely referred to as the 'man who single-handedly ended Khalistani terrorism in Punjab' and the 'terminator of Khalistani terror'. He is exactly the kind of alpha male India likes to celebrate in its tales of celebrating valour (from Rajputs to Sikhs to Shivaji). For example, during his tenure in the Northeast, he was tried for kicking a demonstrator to death.[84]

In the 1990s, when India was reeling under separationist and insurgent movements, Gill was hailed as exactly what was needed for India. He was appointed to curb terrorism in the state of Punjab, and so he did, with reports noting his iron resolve and equally ruthless techniques creating a culture of terror in Punjab.[85] Serious human rights violation accusations, including Human Rights Watch reports and the killing of human rights activist

83 Ibid.
84 https://www.financialexpress.com/india-news/former-punjab-dgp-kps-gill-dead-at-82-10-things-to-know-about-the-supercop-who-uprooted-militancy/687609/
85 https://www.nytimes.com/1993/10/26/world/though-sikh-rebellion-is-quelled-india-s-punjab-state-still-seethes.html?pagewanted=1

Jaswant Singh Khalra, for the most part, were overlooked. Now, the body count he and his force left behind didn't matter much, and looking at the history of insurgency and the impunity granted to forces to counter (Chapter 4), this is not surprising. Gill has several other accomplishments—including Operation Black Thunder,[86] founding of the Institute for Conflict Management in India and being the president of the Indian Hockey Federation. In the 2000s, Gill was appointed by the state of Chhattisgarh as an adviser to help with the Naxalite movement, and international publications reported on his Punjab mechanisms, highlighting the applicability of his techniques to other nations (e.g., for defeating the Taliban in Afghanistan); such was his legacy and reputation.

In the matter of Bajaj vs Gill, Gill was convicted (for outraging the modesty of a woman) and was sentenced with three months of rigorous imprisonment, followed by two months of ordinary imprisonment and then probation. His sentence included a monetary fine (of ₹200,000) to be paid to the complainant (which Ms Bajaj refused to accept and hence was later donated to women's organizations—the irony will hopefully not be lost on the readers). The imprisonment statement was later changed to probation on appeal, and therefore, Gill didn't serve time for his offense.

We have already seen how the nation reacted. From calling it harsh and unjust to feeling 'small' as a nation for what was happening to a man of Gill's stature, the excerpts included earlier show how enamoured India was with Gill, or rather is. There is a reason why I marked the timeline of Bajaj vs Gill as 1988–2017, not 1988–1996. The discomfort India felt with 'outraging of the modesty of a women' becoming significant enough to have caused the inconvenience of a legal judgment against a man like K. P. S. Gill came alive again in 2017—the MeToo year—with death. Multiple articles celebrated Gill's life, marking how unfortunate it

---

86 https://en.wikipedia.org/wiki/Operation_Black_Thunder#Operation_Black_Thunder_II

was that the incident had to happen to a man like him.[87] 'Several publications discussed Gill's courage, praising what it must have taken. It is sad (for the lack of any other term that I can think of) that the courage of Ms Bajaj—what it must have taken for her to up against a man like Gill in India—is not celebrated till date.'

It is worth considering if the sympathy and the willingness to forget and forgive are reserved for men like Gill in India (or for Kelly and Simmons in the music community) for who they were? Well, Kannabiran points out, comparing K. P. S. Gill's account to Bhanwari Devi's, that it's not necessarily so (and I should dare say here that I was delighted to find out in my discussions that my choice of case studies for understanding 'before' MeToo and MeToo aren't very different from that of someone of Ms Kannabiran's eminence). Below is the excerpt she sent on 'entitlement to impunity' and its widespread applicability to men in India, not just the ones hailed as national heroes.

....

Indian culture has not fallen to such low depths that someone who is brought up in it, an innocent, rustic man, will turn into a man of evil conduct who disregards caste and age differences—and becomes animal enough to assault a woman. How can persons of 40 and 60 years of age commit rape while someone who is seventy years old watches by; particularly in the light of Bhanwari Devi's acceptance that one of the rapists is a respected man in the village.[88]

So sympathy lies with the Gills, Gujjars and Simmons. If the matter is 'trivial', it is because it is so. If the matter is grievous, it is because of who they are. And then there is the 'it can't be.'

....

87 https://feminisminindia.com/2017/05/31/kps-gill-sexual-harasser/
88 Excerpt from trial court judgment as quoted in Kalpana Kannabiran, 'In the Footprints of Bhanwari Devi' (Working Paper, November 2018), http://www.csdhyd.org/gritwp18kk.pdf

Yes, Donald Trump did say grab them by the pussy.
But who doesn't say stuff like that? Surely, he didn't mean it.
A man like him wouldn't say a thing like that seriously.
—Dawn Schroder, Retired Factory Technician, Arizona, 2016

It seems like we can skin the cat whichever way, the relationship between sexual harassment and tolerability remains strong for one reason or another. While gender as an identity suffers when it comes to women's rights, a strong male identity can weather caste, race, religion and other such alliances. Several references quote villagers belonging to the same caste as Bhanwari Devi saying that Badri Gujjar is a good man, so such a matter couldn't have happened. And when there is a strong female gender statement, it forms a community of its own. We will discuss these points quite a few times in the next chapters, but for now, let us look into some other aspects we have covered.

I selected to showcase these particular cases for quite a few reasons, some of which, like the need for exploration of the nuances (in the behaviours, concerns, considerations, similarities between widely different societies, differences between individuals, timelines and MeToo factors—aka inspiration, awareness and unification), I have explained already. In addition to that, I also wanted to select accounts that present as many variants of workplace sexual harassment as possible. For example,

1. Harassment at the workplace or outside for the nature of the work done or for doing a job (apart from the Bhanwari Devi account, another widely known account of such is the Aruna Shanbaug case)[89]

2. Harassment at the workplace by outsiders (personnel not employed by the place of work)

---

89 https://www.reuters.com/article/india-nurse-death/aruna-shanbaug-dies-four-decades-after-being-sodomised-and-left-in-a-coma-idUSKBN0O310O320150518

3. Harassment at the workplace or outside by co-workers or supervisors

4. Harassment at the workplace or work events by persons of authority outside of the direct chain of command, including personnel of authority in the same field employed at different institutions or companies and such (note: assaults by people of power in the same profession, whether at workplace or work event or not, understandably will have a very different implication and, therefore, are considered as workplace harassment, as it can affect the victim's employability and livelihood. For example, when we discuss LOSHA and MeToo in academia, we will discuss how the careers of victims can get affected when their assailants are in the same field)

No social change can come about if laws and society both don't change. Mahila vikas was started in 1984. *1992 tak jab saathin successful ho gayi, to programme hi khatam kar di. Inka koi forum hi nahin hain* (The women's development programme was started in 1984. By 1992 when the saathins started seeing success, they closed the program down—there is no forum even these days). So, the problem is that initiation is there but monitoring isn't there—*Women and Child Department khud hi bimar hain* (The Women and Child Department itself is not healthy). The only way is intervention through gaon (village) structure. Sarpanch and panchayat are elected—we have to bring change into them. We need that, and we need a monitoring plan.

Political, administrative and civil society—all three have to join hands. Otherwise, movements on the forefront will leave the cause untouched.

Can you bring the Constitution into your home? That's my only sentence. Then you can have movements.
                              —Renuka Pamecha, Activist, Rajasthan

Covering a multifaceted matter with a limited number of case studies is challenging, and the takeaways are numerous. But if there is one that I want to end this chapter with, it's the realization

I came to as I spent nights reading through the reports and articles. Sexual harassment, workplace or not, is not an isolated matter, neither in its happening nor in its pursuit of justice. Awareness, inspiration, identities that unite and differences that divide are not one-dimensional. So for establishing a before and an after, for any movement at a point in time, considerations beyond the movement need to be made. The most pertinent of such considerations, to be able to demarcate matters, is what constitutes a movement? Scope and reach? Mechanism? Impact? Legacy?

As we have discussed and will continue to discuss, women's rights and feminism—globally and India—have had no shortage of movements. Maybe that is why academics like Kannabiran classify feminism in waves, not in terms of movements (MeToo is often noted to be the fourth wave). We will continue this charter of understanding in the next chapter.

CHAPTER 3

THE COST

The cost of violence against women (GBV) is estimated to be around 2 per cent of the global GDP ($1.5 trillion). The projection for the COVID pandemic (which is considered a deep recession) is a 4.4–5.2 per cent GDP shrinkage.[1] So, in other words, eliminating GBV saves the world half a severe recession. Since the top 20 economies (which include the USA and the UK, key European nations, China, India, Japan, South Korea, Australia and Mexico) contribute almost 80 per cent to the global GDP,[2] eliminating GBV in nations such as the USA, India, China and Australia is expected to have a significant impact. Below are some additional numbers.

- Annual costs of intimate partner (and domestic) violence range from $1.16 billion (Canada) to $32.9 billion (England and Wales), including $5.8 billion for the USA and $11.38 billion in Australia.[3]

Domestic and intimate partner violence causes
more deaths and entail much higher economic costs
than homicides or civil wars.[4]

1 https://www.cnbc.com/2020/10/13/imf-world-economic-outlook-2020-amid-coronavirus-crisis
2 https://www.investopedia.com/insights/worlds-top-economies/
3 https://www.unwomen.org/en/news/stories/2016/9/speech-by-lakshmi-puri-on-economic-costs-of-violence-against-women
4 Ibid.

- The costs of sexual harassment to businesses include legal and liability costs, increased insurance premiums, loss of talent, productivity loss, and loss of business and reputation. It is estimated to be upwards of $6 million per Fortune 500 company per year.[5]

- A meta-analysis of some 41 studies of workplace sex-based harassment estimated that, on average, organizations lose about $22,500 in productivity per harassed individual. Individual costs include the impact on health, loss, and lack of opportunity and earning.[6]

- The cost of sexual harassment to the economy was estimated to be $3.5 billion for 2018 for Australia.[7] This includes health-care and justice system costs in addition to cost to businesses. Similar estimates for the USA or Indian economy are lacking; however, alongside the cost to corporations, a 1994 study found the annual cost to the US federal government to be $327 million (including job turnover [workforce loss], sick leaves [absenteeism] and loss of productivity).[8]

It's impossible to draw up a balance sheet for all the accusations of sexual violence that have come out in recent times because so many of the cases are settled privately and sexual harassment is still under-reported. What we do know is that sexual harassment and assault exacts a heavy toll not only on the individuals who have gone through it, and on our society as a whole, but also on a company's bottom line.[9]

5 https://fee.org/articles/the-economic-costs-of-sexual-harassment/
6 https://iwpr.org/iwpr-publications/briefing-paper/sexual-harassment-and-assault-at-work-understanding-the-costs/
7 https://www2.deloitte.com/content/dam/Deloitte/au/Documents/Economics/deloitte-au-economic-costs-sexual-harassment-workplace-240320.pdf
8 https://www.ineteconomics.org/research/research-papers/metoo-the-economic-cost-of-sexual-harassment/
9 https://www.saiglobal.com/hub/blog/the-incalculable-cost-of-sexual-harassment-in-the-workplace

- For American and global corporations, company payouts and settlements for sexual harassment range in hundreds of millions (e.g., $300 million settlement[10] by Google, 2020; $45 million paid by 21st Century Fox, 2017; and $20 million paid by Fox News, 2016). Sexual harassment payouts are reported to have hit an all-time high in 2019, with companies paying out $68.2 million to those alleging sexual harassment violations through the US Equal Employment Opportunity Commission (EEOC).[11] In 2017, it was $46.3 million.

- For individual settlement (the maximum an individual can receive in monetary compensation by suing an employer under Title VII[12] in the USA), the federal government currently caps victim of sexual harassment compensation at $300,000. Critiques argue that the number (in place since 1991) needs to be updated to match the statistical value of sexual harassment (which the Vanderbilt University estimates to be at $7.3 million or higher).[13]

- For India, although a dollar number is not noted (to date) for the cost of sexual harassment (or other gender violence) to the economy, several studies show sexual violence to be holding the Indian economy back. Since 2004, 20 million women are noted to have 'vanished' from the Indian workforce.

THE COST OF GENDER DISCRIMINATION

Globally, gender parity stands at 68.6% and
the bottom 10 countries have closed just 40% of the gender gap.[14]

10 https://www.cnbc.com/2020/09/29/googles-310-million-sexual-misconduct-settlement-details.html
11 https://www.eeoc.gov/statistics/charges-alleging-sex-based-harassment-charges-filed-eeoc-fy-2010-fy-2019
12 https://www.eeoc.gov/statutes/title-vii-civil-rights-act-1964
13 https://www.forbes.com/sites/kimelsesser/2019/03/26/is-7-6m-the-value-of-sexual-harassment/#7d2f17da312a
14 https://www.weforum.org/reports/gender-gap-2020-report-100-years-pay-equality

There are, of course, several metrics that are used for measuring gender equality. The Global Gender Gap Index used in the WEF data below examines the gap between men and women in 4 fundamental categories and 14 different indicators that compose them. The four categories are economic participation and opportunity, educational attainment, health and survival, and political empowerment. Since this metric is a comparison index, the highest possible score is one suggesting complete parity between men and women across all the categories (marked as 'equality' in the WEF report, and the lowest possible score of zero is marked as 'inequality'. India scores 0.67 for 2018 and the USA scores 0.72 against a world median of ~0.7 (over 153 countries).

The cost of gender inequality globally (141 countries were included in the analysis) due to loss of human capital wealth is estimated at $160.2 trillion if we simply assume that women would earn as much as men (twice the value of GDP globally). Said differently, human capital wealth could increase by 21.7 per cent globally, and total wealth by 14.0 per cent, with gender equality in earnings.

- Per capita (methodology includes children) gender inequality is estimated to cause a loss in wealth of $23,620 per person globally.

- Globally, women account for only 38 per cent of human capital wealth vs 62 per cent for men. In low- and lower-middle-income countries, women account for a third or less of human capital wealth. Fifty-five per cent of women (aged 15–64 years) are engaged in the labour market as opposed to 78 per cent of men.[15]

- Of losses incurred from gender inequality, South Asia ranks higher in percentage loss than even sub-Saharan Africa (2014).[16]

---

15 Ibid.
16 https://openknowledge.worldbank.org/bitstream/handle/10986/29865/126579-Public-on-5-30-18-WorldBank-GenderInequality-Brief-v13.pdf?sequence=1&isAllowed=y

- According to a McKinsey study, India could increase its GDP by $770 billion by 2025 by getting more women to work and increasing gender equality. As of 2012, only 27 per cent of Indian women are in the formal workforce compared to 79 per cent of men. This is noted to be lowest among the major emerging nations and G-20 countries, and better only than Saudi Arabia.[17]

- According to the McKinsey study, the Asia-Pacific (APAC) region could add $4.5 trillion to its collective GDP annually by achieving gender parity.[18] India's economy has the second-largest chunk in this growth potential out of the entire APAC region. In other words, as India debates ways of beating China and becoming Singapore (economically and infrastructure- and development-wise), the biggest knob to turn is achieving gender parity and eliminating gender discrimination.

  Note: loss of women from the workforce in India is largely attributed to women's safety (or lack thereof; therefore, the costs of gender violence and discrimination are heavily interrelated for India).

- On the question of adding to the economy, women in India earn only 65 per cent of what their male colleagues earn. The gender pay gap, in addition to lack of safety, is a key modulator for loss of Indian GDP through the loss of human earning potential[19] (women).

---

17 https://economictimes.indiatimes.com/magazines/panache/sexual-violence-holding-back-indias-economy-more-women-at-work-can-boost-gdp-by-770-bn/
18 https://www.mckinsey.com/featured-insights/gender-equality/the-power-of-parity-advancing-womens-equality-in-asia-pacific#
19 https://www.business-standard.com/article/current-affairs/gender-pay-inequality-decreases-by-only-a-per-cent-in-2018-monster-india-119030700681_1.html

- In the USA (as of 2020), the gender pay gap across races amounts to 82 cents to a dollar, i.e. women earn 82 per cent of what men earn for equal jobs.[20]

In summary, apart from social motivation, there is a strong economic motivation for gender equality and prevention of gender violence. Simply put:

1. Gender equality boosts economic growth.

2. Gender issues have a high cost.

The cost saved from the prevention of gender violence can be invested in development and infrastructure and achieving gender parity. Just the addition of women to workforce and subsequent increase in human earning will impact further economic growth by bounds, especially for India.

20 https://www.americanprogress.org/issues/women/reports/2020/03/24/482141/quick-facts-gender-wage-gap/

CHAPTER 4

INDIA VS BHARAT

Such crimes hardly take place in Bharat, but they
occur frequently in India. Go to villages, no gang
rapes or sex crimes there, they are prevalent in urban areas.
—Mohan Bhagwat, RSS Chief, 2013

In the summer of 2019, a message movie *Article 15*, starring
Ayushmann Khurrana, was released to critical acclaim and hype,
the anticipation heightened given Khurrana's recent string of social
hits. The film illustrates the primary guiding principle of social
segregation in India (aka the caste system) against the backdrop of
gang rape and murder of two underage girls in Uttar Pradesh. The
plot primarily tackles how much of a holy grail the caste outline is
for life in India and how much in denial the 'Delhis' of India are of
the same. Khurrana drives justice for the girls, delivers a message
through his personal awakening (he learns how injected caste is in
India's nervous system) on the Constitution's Article 15, and shows
how, through just a little bit of effort, caste can be left behind
(the movie closes to a scene of men of all caste enjoying a simple
meal together from a presumably lower-caste woman). Khurrana
also rescues the surviving victim trailing through mud, grime
and sloth, literally. However, in the incident of Badaun gang rape
and hanging of 2014[1] (which the movie is presumed to be structured

---

1 https://www.bbc.com/news/world-asia-india-27615590

around), the Central Bureau of Investigation ruled the deaths of the minors to be suicide, despite clear evidence of the contrary.[2] Badaun doesn't need to be singled out or made exemplary, except for the fact that it raised significant international outcry because it came in close succession to the 2012 Delhi gang rape. The 'gender' aspect of the real incident outshining the 'otherwise could be neglected' caste issue is a matter of both fortune and misfortune for modern India.

In January 2018, eight-year-old Asifa Banu was held, gang-raped and eventually murdered in a Hindu temple in Kathua, Jammu. Asifa, belonging to the nomadic Bakerwal Muslim community, is believed to have been targeted deliberately to drive the Bakerwal nomads out of the area. The plot was masterminded by the village head and temple caretaker, had police officers participating, and was backed by members of the currently ruling, proudly nationalist and openly Hindu Bharatiya Janata Party. While nationwide protests[3] erupted following the incident calling for justice, protests also erupted in Jammu (where 'Jai Sriram' and 'Bharat Mata Ki Jai' were shouted) against the booking of the Hindu assailants by the police.[4]

In December 2019, an Unnao Uttar Pradesh rape victim died of cardiac arrest after being stabbed and set on fire by her accused assailants with over 90 per cent burns. Her assailant, an upper-caste Hindu against whom the authorities had avoided filing charge sheets for as long as possible, was released on bail a few days prior. The victim, belonging to the 'lower' Viswakarma caste, was set on fire in a public venue, on her way to meet her lawyers.

2 https://www.dailymail.co.uk/indiahome/indianews/article-2870524/CBI-rules-gang-rape-murder-death-Badaun-girls-concludes-cousins-committed-suicide.html

3 https://www.firstpost.com/india/not-in-my-name-protests-launched-after-kathua-unnao-cases-hundreds-march-over-atrocities-against-minorities-4432897.html

4 https://www.news18.com/news/india/fighting-politics-pressure-protests-how-cops-peeled-off-hidden-layers-in-kathua-rape-case-2182599.html

Another Unnao victim in a separate incident is in the hospital after surviving critical injuries following a deadly car crash. Her father is widely believed to have been framed and murdered in judicial custody, following her rape in 2017. No charge sheets were filed against her accused assailants, including an MLA of the ruling Bharatiya Janata Party, until she had attempted to immolate herself at the residence of Uttar Pradesh chief minister. She had also written to the then Chief Justice, Ranjan Gogoi, who was not too long after accused in the #MeToo allegations and essentially acquitted himself of the allegations, declaring his own innocence. In the same month, Priyanka Reddy, an upper-caste Hindu urban working woman in the IT hub Hyderabad, was gang-raped and murdered. Protest marches clogged the veins of India's metros and primetime channels joined social media in the wave of outrage. Within days, police killed her assailants in what was believed to be a planned encounter.

Caste, class, ethnic cleansing, political rivalry, religion—sexual assault on women has always been a powerful tool in conflict, from the Bangladesh Liberation War to the recent Rohingya genocide in Myanmar and, closest to home, the violence against women during the partition of India. Rape in conflict has three primary groupings: violation of women stemming from the need to violate the enemy's territory/property post victory (history is filled with instances of this war zone practice since pre-medieval times, including mythological references), rape as a deliberate tool (for genocide or colonization),[5] and rape to inflict insult and/or fear for subjugation. In the latter contexts, rape is an intentional tactic, not just a by-product of conflict.[6] The term 'genocidal rape' (which recognizes the use of rape in conflict to implement the genocide itself) was officially accepted for the first time by the International Criminal Tribunal (United Nation) for the Rwanda

---

5 A. Ranjan, 'A Gender Critique of AFSPA', *Social Change* 45, no. 3 (2015): 440.
6 L. Sharlach, 'Rape as Genocide: Bangladesh, the Former Yugoslavia, and Rwanda', *New Political Science* 1, no. 22 (2000): 89.

genocide in 1994 (where half a million women and children were sexually mutilated, raped and murdered). The intention of the use of sexual violence was noted to be the destruction of an entire ethnic group (Tutsis) by the dominant Hutus.[7] The examples cited in the beginning (partition, Rohingya conflict and the Bangladesh Liberation War), including communal riots in India and the violence against Sikhs in 1984, are all examples of deliberate use of rape for ethnic cleansing or suppression. However, what is most important for the matter in hand in this chapter (India and its complicated, layered relationship with its fairer sex) is that even in times of peace, sexual control and subjugation of women have been and are key mechanisms for establishment and maintenance of societal orders. This is more important because what a society intentionally designs into its operational model at times of peace worsens at times of war. Rape as a tool in conflict originates from the patriarchal design of women's bodies as properties of men, violating which amounts as equal to the looting of the conquered territory. We talked about honour in Chapter 2. Designed association of women's sanctity with the honour of men provides the additional motivation of inflicting wounds on the valour of the enemy through assault on the women. India can't be singled out for acts in times of conflict, nor is it unique in having control and subjugation of women as a societal safeguarding methodology (for as early as in the early Mesopotamian society, Gerda Lerner[8] pioneered a work exposing the connections between the establishment of societal structures and subjugation of women of all rank and order through the control of their sexuality).

However, as we will explore here, India is mired deeper into the grime its women have to encounter today because of the deliberate designing of systemic gendered principles for all of its hierarchy-framing needs. Gender has been the common denominator in

---

7 https://www.internews.org/sites/default/files/resources/TheMedia&The RwandaGenocide.pdf
8 G. Lerner, *The Creation of Patriarchy* (Oxford: Oxford University Press, 1986).

the establishment of principles of superiority (and inferiority) in all matters from caste to nationality, religion and even language.[9] The intermingling principles and events specific to India and the Indian subcontinent—from the rise of Hindu empires and Brahmanical patriarchy, influx of invaders and religious conflicts, to colonialism and late colonial rise of nationalism—can be grouped into two interdependent tenets: definition and differentiation (of roles and boundaries for gender within caste, religion and class) for control and subjugation, and normalization of subjugation (through practice and use of reinforcement: symbols, value teachings, portrayal and legalization). The layers substantiating these tenets and how they came into being, and their fate when converged with the effects of globalization in today's India, are significant and unique. In this chapter, we travel both India and Bharat in search of the origin(s) to find the loose ends to pull at. We need those for detangling the weave.

THE CASTE QUESTION

The first, and arguably the most important, of modulators of gendered architecting of the Indian society is the Hindu caste system. As many academic works have cited and common sense can infer, the basic mechanism of maintaining the purity of caste (or any bloodline-controlled demarcation) has to be through control of reproduction—aka the sexual partners the women of a said caste have. Therefore, it is not surprising that the general subordination of women (marked as a global phenomenon dominated by shift of economic drivers from hunting and gathering economy to agricultural and industrial) 'took a particularly severe form in India'[10] with the rise of Brahmanical patriarchy. From the

---

9 C. Gupta, 'The Icon of Mother in Late Colonial North India', *Economic & Political Weekly* 36, no. 45 (2001): 4291.
10 U. Chakravarti, 'Conceptualising Brahmanical Patriarchy in Early India: Gender, Caste, Class and State', *Economic & Political Weekly* 28, no. 14 (1993): 579.

recommendation of pre-puberty marriages to state sanctioning of ritual practices outlining the purity of women, Brahmanical social order (and the safeguarding of the entire caste system) was achieved through the control of women. As Uma Chakravarti puts in her work on Brahmanical patriarchy:

> Safeguarding of the caste structure is achieved through the highly restricted movement of women and even female seclusion. Women are regarded as gateways—literally points of entrance into the caste system. The lower caste male, whose sexuality is a threat to upper caste purity has to be institutionally prevented from having sexual access to women of higher castes so women must be carefully guarded.[11]

From as early as Satapatha Brahmana, through Manu, the control of women and lowering of their status within the caste are brought about via defiling definitions (including in Buddhist literature of the time).[12] Women are repeatedly characterized to be of weaker resolve and character (untruthful, adulterous, sinful and lying) and, therefore, in requirement of higher moral persecution. As it is well known, this is most explicit in Manu. But it's no different in most post-Vedic literature. Notation of women's uncontrollable lust, tales of adulterous wives and punishment imbibed upon them, and of poor fate incurred by kings and sages failing to control their women, are abundant. As Chakravarti states:

> After ruling that women must be closely guarded day and night, regardless of their age, Manu tells us why it is that women must be guarded.... The projection of the fear of women's uncontrolled sexuality was the backdrop to the obsession with

11 K. Ganesh, 'Women's Seclusion and the Structure of Caste', paper presented at the Asian Regional Conference on Women and Household, New Delhi, 27–31 January 1985.
12 Apastamba Dharmasutra, 1975; George Buhler, *The Sacred Laws of the Aryas*, vol. 1 (Delhi: Motilal Banarsidass, 1879).

creating an effective system of control and the need to guard them constantly.[13]

In modern India, Hindu scriptures which have transcended down are quoted to date as absolute guiding principles of life. Quite a few of India's problems stem from the association of identity to pride and pride to 'believed' heritage. It is not uncommon to hear on the streets of leading metros quotes about 'shastras' and 'dharmas' and the role of women depicted in them (which is discussed further in the next chapter in the context of consent). And Mohan Bhagwat, unfortunately, can't be singled out. It is important therefore to trace the path further back, to before the evolution of agricultural society and development of caste and class order.

Just like in other pre-historic cultures, in hunting and gathering economies, the role of women was highly valued (and argued in many articles to be superior owing to their reproductive role). In conjunction, women's sexuality was viewed as an aspect of female existence, and the society was believed to be matristic (one in which women were not subjected to the authority of men, or of other women).[14] Unlike in a rigid patrilineal preservation-required society where the purity of blood has to be preserved, there was, therefore, no need for sexual control of women by men in such societies.[15] The caste hierarchy, therefore, can be duly blamed for gender hierarchy and its disastrous consequences in India.

Tracing the course and methodology of the establishment of this rigour, post its conceptualization, exposes further unfortunate kernels. For effective control of women, like in most matters, coercion and cooperation were both needed. While some of the means of securing the cooperation of upper-caste women for their own subjugation are pedestrian (honour, status, privileges, material

---

13 Ibid.
14 E. Neumayer, *Prehistoric Rock Paintings in Central India,* (New Delhi: Oxford University Press, 1983).
15 Chakravarti, 'Conceptualising Brahmanical Patriarchy in Early India', 579.

possessions and control over lower-caste women (and men)), what Chakravarti defines as a 'masterstroke' is the development and celebration of the concept of virtue in loyalty to husband (*stridharma* or *pativratadharma*). Post channelling of reproductive power away from a woman's sexuality and into motherhood, the notion of an ideal Hindu woman was carefully crafted around her devotion to her husband. Women accepted the dharma of a wife as an ideology and 'chastity and wifely fidelity as the highest expression of selfhood'.

> *It may be argued that the success of any system*
> *lies in the subtle working of its ideology and it that sense,*
> *the pativrata concept was the masterstroke …*
> *one in which women controlled their own sexuality.*[16]

The modern-day manifestation of this carefully crafted mechanism of control doesn't need to be spelled out. From sati, to Chhath and Karwa Chauth, Hindu women continue to cultivate not only fidelity but also self-immolating devotion to husbands as a path to salvation. Some argue that where is the harm in devotion and belief? (2018 examples of scathing responses by Hindu women to Twinkle Khanna's op-ed on Karwa Chauth[17] come to mind.) However, what unfortunately remains the problem is the failure of women to identify and band together for the cause of gender above and beyond the causes of religion, caste or family, which is the designed effect of gender getting carved into a subspace of caste and religious identities.

One interesting phenomenon worth noting here which might ring the bell easier is the 'Bill Clinton and Democratic (read liberal) women' effect. I have discussed this in other chapters, for this shows both the disadvantage and the benefit of gender being

---

16 Ibid.
17 https://indianexpress.com/article/trending/trending-in-india/twinkle-khannas-sarcastic-take-on-karva-chauth-leaves-twitterati-in-a-split-3092184/

present as a common denominator everywhere. It also shows that the matter of gender identification lagging other associations is quite a universal matter that transcends miles and decades. The US women, as Linda Hirshman put it, 'have been stuck between womanizing Democrats or women-hating Republicans.'[18]

Women are a group that makes up the majority ... integrated by the ineluctable law of biology into every human institution.... Because women are a majority, they are intersected by every social diving line.[19]

Despite this being a universal issue, the subjugated role of women in Indian patriarchy has been noted as a key characteristic defining the gender issues that women face in the nation, which have been discussed in other places in this work. From the participation of mothers-in-law in dowry burnings and acid attacks to the denouncement of sexually violated women by other women, a key trait emerges in which women do believe that there is both a behavioural expectation (a Laxman Rekha not to be crossed) and a deserved consequence. The Brahmanical mechanism of imbibing pursuit of sexual fidelity, repression and bounded role as virtue plays heavily into this devaluation of women by other women, who seek both redemption and redressal by being the custodians of the model systems.

This is a bit different from the Bill Clinton effect quoted above, where the association to liberalism and the Democratic Party was valued higher by women. The later phenomenon has also played a part again and again in women's movement in India, possibly more so than in other nations (e.g., as discussed in Chapter 1, the feminist movements arising out of labour movements in the

18 Hirshman, *Reckoning.*
19 Ibid.

1980s in Mumbai rallying for class rights of the mill workers at the expense of women's rights).[20]

Coming back to the implementation of gender hierarchy, the second mode was of law and customs, scripted for situations where ideological control would fail. The woman's male relatives (first in her birth family and then in her husband's) were granted the responsibility of controlling her 'total existence, especially her impulses', again, most explicitly stated by Manu but reinforced in all major Brahmanical texts. And lastly, when the male relatives are unsuccessful, the state is empowered to interfere and enforce, and how!

> *The adulterous woman's nose and ears should be cut off.*
> —*Jataka (I.193)*

An important note to make here is that the caste (or religion) factor is prioritized in such dictates, outshining the crime of adultery because adulterous engagements within or with the upper caste are forgivable.

> *If a woman commits adultery with a lower caste man,*
> *the king shall cause her to be devoured by dogs in a public place.*
> —*Manu (VIII–377)*

In another reference, the king is guided to punish such a woman by shaving off her head, placing her naked on a donkey and parading her along the highway.[21] Honour killing and domestic violence (which rank high in GBV affecting women in the Indian subcontinent)[22] are easy to understand with this context.

India has also had significant influence coming in from the Muslim conquerors. The Islamic codes developing in the Middle

20 Gangoli, *Indian Feminisms.*
21 Chakravarti, 'Conceptualising Brahmanical Patriarchy in Early India', 579.
22 https://www.theguardian.com/world/2010/jun/25/honour-killings-india

East and Africa were no different (although the reasons were) in matters of women. When brought into India, they merged into the existing gender control mechanism. The questions are further complicated for Muslim women in India, because the question of gender justice gets played against religious freedom, minority rights and state vs community rights[23] (a recent example is the triple talaq elimination debate). Personal law is the only law in India that applies to individuals based on religion and divulges from the Constitution-granted equality to all citizens. However, stepping back from modern India and the relatively current power play between state and religious groups on matters of triple talaq and universal civil code, religious minorities (especially women) have often been grouped with lower-caste women and deliberate delineations have been emphasized to ensure distinct behavioural expectations.

COLONIALISM

Although argued (to some merit) to be in the interest of Indian women whose state remained quite subjugated at the time of start of the colonial rule in India (in the years between 1858 and India's independence in 1947: the need for governance and jurisdictive intervention started with the replacing of the East India Company's rule with the British crown's sovereign over India), the colonial reforms are widely considered to have functioned differently than what was anticipated, given India's individuality. The pluralistic and multi-ethnic pre-colonial India did have laws and guidelines, but the segmented adjudication where the rules applicable were dependent on race, religion and caste created an environment of perceived lawlessness and barbarism to Western outsiders.[24] This provided the problem statement the new rulers needed, and the need to focus on the women, whose state was considered to be particularly sorry, was fuelled further for British women by the

23 Gangoli, *Indian Feminisms*.
24 W. H. Rattigan, 'Customary Law in India', *Law Mag. & L.* (1884): 3.

additional motivation of utilizing the liberation of Indian women as a cause against injustice for their own liberation.

> *British feminists claimed that they, rather than English and Indian men, better understood the plight of Indian women. They claimed that by acquiring legal rights at home—particularly the right to vote— they would be able to better protect their native sisters.*[25]

The groups that in pre-colonial times fought to resist a monolithic authority (whether Hindu or Muslim) were expected to demand sovereignty. So the colonial governors judiciously allowed family law matters to stay as is (the law of the dominant religion) while 'negotiating situations that would be governed by the secular (though clearly Christian) colonial law',[26] creating a less than ideal situation for the Indian women who never had a seat at the table. The battle of power remained between the colonial rulers and the native male elites.[27]

....

The tussle over legal and political power between the native elites and the colonialists were fought on the backs of Indian women because it was the alleged degraded position of Indian women and the barbaric actions of the Indian men that justified the colonial mission in the first place.

Therefore, although significant reforms were mandated (from widow remarriage to child marriage and sati abolition), scholars argue that this led to the current state of even secular laws for

25 Jane Haggis, 'White Women and Colonialism: Toward a Non- recuperative History', in *Gender and Imperialism*, ed. C. Midgley (Manchester: Manchester University Press, 1998).
26 V. Chitnis and D. Wright, 'The Legacy of Colonialism: Law and Women's Rights in India', *Washington and Lee Law Review* 64 (2007): 1315.
27 Ibid.

women in post-Independence India being either protectionist and patriarchal or not meaningful.[28] Several works evaluate this by tracing the widely differentiated cause, and therefore effect, of laws brought in around husband's property and widow remarriage, age of consent and contagious diseases, adultery, marriage and other such matter. But what I drew as the most significant for this work's purpose and point is best summarized by Varsha Chitnis:

While the British were busy trying to redefine the pluralist Indian culture into a hegemonic religious one, they were also busy trying to re-define the religious private sphere in secular terms. **This contradiction in the Colonial mission has led to a modern India in which Hindu, Muslim, and Christian women experience profound differences in legal rights and political agency. The British willingness to cede authority in the private realm calls into question their commitment to human rights and women's interests** (emphasis mine).[29]

As a result, gender was further furthered as a subsegment, not a unified experience to fight for. Also, as discussed in the context of restitution of conjugal rights in the next chapter, laws coming in from the British feudal system were eliminated in the UK decades earlier. But these laws continue to fester gender justice expectations in India owing to the nation's proclivity towards patriarchal order and appetite for nostalgia. Interestingly, the validity of British reforms, often furthering British interests in place of that of Indian women, is put forward by feminists and activists as a rationale for resisting global gender reforms, which supplements the touting of heritage and culture as reasons for resisting change—a behaviour that has continued to disservice India through the colonial rule to date.

28 Ibid.
29 Ibid.

THE CONTINUATION OF 'GENDER-ING' FOR PROPAGANDA: FROM BHARAT MATA TO HINDI

Quite ingeniously, the creation of an ideal gender symbol continued well beyond the preservation of societal structures in late colonial India. If defined correctly, the image of a virtuous woman—loving and nurturing—was rightfully speculated to have a wide, emotional appeal which could be put to multitask. From nationalism to language, all concepts are easier to grasp through associations and, therefore, a widely relatable image to create association was cultivated. Scholar Charu Gupta notes this in the context of the Bharat Mata temple in Banaras (foundation laid in 1918, inaugurated by Gandhi in 1936). As Gupta states,

> The temple was an attempt at creating a composite religious and national identity and was seen as a place where all— Hindus and Muslims, high caste and low caste Hindus—could technically come and worship ... yet, there was an overwhelming use of upper-caste Hindu symbols. During its inauguration, there was a 'havan', with offerings and recitations from all the four Vedas by eight orthodox brahmin specialists.[30]

Scholars also note how the depiction of Bharat Mata and, in a more general sense, of Mother Goddess and worshipping of the feminine form changed significantly post injection of Brahmanical norms of virtue from the medieval Bhudevi[31] and feminine power (which is believed to have originated from the life-giving power of women and the presumed power, therefore, of the female over life and death in pre-historic cultures).

From the late 19th century, language became the means of symbol and community creation both among Hindu upper castes and the

30 Gupta, 'The Icon of Mother in Late Colonial North India'.
31 Daud Ali, 'From Bhudevi to Bharatmata: Fragments in the History of Place and Patriarchy' (unpublished paper).

Muslim gentry.[32] In this, Hindi was personified as the mother instilled with virtues of a Hindu wife, while Urdu was personified as 'Begum', equating its romance with erotic, uncontrolled Muslim dancing girls and prostitutes.[33] And again, in the mode of using gender for the definition of boundaries and then using the same boundaries for control of gender, girls' schools had Hindi alone, while Urdu and Hindi were both made available to boys (Arya Samaj).[34] Since women needed to be maintained unadulterated and were not to be seeking employment, they weren't deemed to require having access to Urdu. It was intriguing indeed for me to learn that not only was Urdu classified unsuitable for being erotic, but it was also disregarded for being feminine. This was also used as a methodology to distinguish within Hindi dialects and subs. Braj, for example, was propped as feminine for its preferred use in poetry, especially those considered to be of 'dubious moral nature for depicting the life and loves of Krishna', while 'Khari Boli' was pushed as the 'masculine vehicle for nationalist ideas.'[35]

The gendering of language thus used multiple arguments in different contexts—using the female both to endorse and to condemn, to appropriate and to reject.[36]

The examples of the use of gender symbols to staunchly define and delineate are multiple and continue well into the current decades. But the point that hopefully is already summarized through the above examples is that such definitions, evolving over the medieval, colonial and postcolonial periods in India, were designed to develop certain behaviours—in both men and women. Globalization and the shift of the economy from brawn to

32 Gupta, 'The Icon of Mother in Late Colonial North India', 4291.
33 Ibid.
34 Ibid.
35 Ibid.
36 Ibid.

brain collided head on with this in the 1990s, bringing in the final differentiation: occupation and location.

MODERN INDIA: RAPE AND GEO

Hopefully, it is apparent that the geo question in the title of this chapter—India vs Bharat, aka urban vs rural—was intended to be symbolic. However, although statistics can't conclusively show (ignoring the difference in percentage reporting and other factors such as exposure and opportunity that can confound the results), a clear divergence when it comes to rapes occurring in cities vs in villages and rural communities, India vs Bharat very much exists for gender violence in India. And it is expected to do so for the foreseeable future. Of course, it is not that rapes don't happen in 'Bharat' and only in 'India' or vice versa, but all rapes from all parts of the nation are not equal. Several academic works on the 2012 Delhi gang rape (Jyoti Pandey's gang rape, widely depicted as the Nirbhaya incident) dive into the 'Delhi factor' in the outrage that followed. One such article contrasts the issue against rapes happening in regions under the Armed Forces (Special Powers) Act (AFSPA; which I will dive into in the next section as part of analyses of rape as subjugation) and makes the point as follows:

> What compelled/impelled a large number of people—who usually remain silent or apathetic—to join in the protests in Nirbhaya's case was the space and the time of the incident: the rape and murder were committed on the roads of South Delhi, the center of India's socio-economic and political power.[37]

From my interactions with multiple activists working on the ground with sexual assault victims for this work, I know that rape is often considered acceptable in rural locations (which doesn't mean that the woman raped is accepted—for that depends—rather

---

37 Ranjan, 'A Gender Critique of AFSPA', 440.

that rape is expected to happen), especially by upper-caste members on the lower caste and minorities. Rape is also expected in rural locations as means of raging political conflicts (e.g., in the Trinamool vs CPIM conflicts of the late 1990s in Bengal). The reason that location does emerge as a common denominator here is obvious: rural communities are relatively shielded from both pre- and post-event exposure to wider attention.

In studying caste and racial violence, scholars have observed that even seemingly minor instances can and do instigate disproportionate retaliatory reactions. Especially in transitionary times, increased violence has been noted as a reaction to the weakening of absolute power, which in its most potent form is the lack of articulation or awareness of grievance. Subjugated populations are conditioned to see oppressive wrongdoings as just outcomes. But when awareness increases, this absolute submission is challenged. For obvious reasons, this has an onset rate dependent on geographic and demographic factors, contributing to higher tolerance in certain pockets for sexual violence and injustice. However, it needs to be enforced again that the point here is on tolerance, not the rate of occurrence. Also, the factor of acceptability plays into reporting rates of crimes, adding to the lack of access to infrastructure, and, therefore, further impediments accurate comparison of occurrence rates.

The second factor here is of association. Urban population and the global Indian diaspora relate more to the likes of Priyanka Reddy (whose accused assailants were encountered within days of her death[38] following global outrage) than to the Unnao rape victims. The victim of one Unnao incidence, for example, died around the days of the above-mentioned encounter after being set on fire by her assailants. Yet her plight found lesser place on social media and news reports than the counter-protests to the encounter (which

38 https://gulfnews.com/world/asia/india/priyanka-reddy-case-rage-all-around-as-grisly-details-emerge-people-want-accused-to-be-hanged-1.68188680

were on the police acting as judge, jury and executioner) of the accused in the Priyanka case.

All rapes are not equal in the eyes of justice either. Priyanka Reddy will be remembered longer than the Unnao victim (whose name I couldn't find even after hours of search) because the 'nation' doesn't expect the likes of Priyanka to be raped and sees themselves and their loved ones (living a relatable lifestyle) threatened when such rapes happen. Such attacks therefore drive higher expectations of justice. The 'nation' in this context stands differentiated from the geographical nation of India. The nation here is the mainstream population with access to the national and international reporting channels (social media, television and airwaves), and the criminal justice system operates differently within the boundaries of this nation.

RAPE FOR SUBJUGATION

As stated throughout the previous segments, the design of gender roles has been, from the start, for control. Subjugation, when control mechanisms are challenged, is both a natural continuation and the desired effect. The use of violation of women (including rape) as one of the tools for subjugation has been designed and legalized from the early stages and continues in today's civil society. As described in the caste section, control on lower castes has been institutionalized through sanctioning of punishments that can be meted out to upper-caste women and lower-caste men violating norms of fidelity and lower-caste men and women challenging social hierarchies. Of the many instances that can be chronicled and referenced here, a few are enough to establish the point: parading naked of Dalit women (or of women portrayed or perceived to be of 'lose' morals), often in the presence of and with support of law enforcement agencies[39]; rapes of lower-caste women

---

39 Gangoli, *Indian Feminisms*.

by landlords; the 1990s incidents in Andhra[40]; and the relatively recent incidents of Kathua, Badaun and Unnao, not to mention the gang rape of Bhanwari Devi (which has been discussed in other chapters). Examples are plenty on the use of dishonouring of women, including rape, for the subjugation of the lower castes and minorities. As authors Vasanth and Kalpana Kannabiran note in their work on the matter:

Gender within caste is thus defined and structured in such a manner that the manhood of caste is defined both by the degree of control men exercise over their women and the degree of the passivity of the women of the caste. By the same argument, demonstrating control by humiliating women of another caste is a certain way of reducing the 'manhood' of those castes. This is why, while Muthamma was being paraded naked, the men of her caste who unable to bear the sight, covered their eyes, were derided by aggressors.[41]

Note: The incident referred to here is that of Chilakurti village in Nalgaon, Andhra Pradesh, where 35-year-old Muthamma (a Golla caste agricultural labourer) was beaten up brutally and paraded naked through the streets (with alcohol being forced down her throat) by upper-caste Reddi men for perceived assistance in an inter-caste elopement of an upper-caste girl.

Therefore, on the other side of the caste–gender coin (one side being the control of caste through control of upper-caste women), lower-caste women (seen as either labour or accessible and free of moral expectations) are used for punishing audacities of the subjugated caste. Similarly, gender—concocted to be 'the' object of moral paranoia—is used to influence societal rank keeping and lesson teaching. Perceived or real audacity of lower-caste men

40 Kannabiran and Kannabiran, 'Caste and Gender', 2130.
41 Ibid.

towards upper-caste women are dealt with severe repercussions to men (and women), and upper-caste women are known to support the caste cause, not the gender matter. In the same work by the Kannibarans, the eventual escalation of caste tensions from the matter of a lower-caste man misbehaving with upper-caste women culminating into a full-blown massacre of lower-caste men in the fields in Tsundur is described,[42] after which, upper-caste women marched in support of their men. It is worthwhile to compare this matter to pre-civil rights America, where black men were rampantly lynched, often wrongfully and before accusations were proven, at mere suggestion or suspicion of misdemeanour towards white women. The point, therefore, is that gender association—already a struggling concept—is rendered impossible when placed in an unequal society against the paranoia of dilution of superiority (caste or race).

Caste control through gender and the caste lens obscuring gender common sense goes beyond marches by upper-caste women supporting massacres or acting irrational like in the matter of Karni Sena vs director Sanjay Leela Bhansali and *Padmaavat* that we have talked about in Chapter 2.[43] More subtly and in urban spaces, it plays into matters like MeToo and LOSHA. I interviewed R. Prasad (a caste and gender activist and student at the time, rallying support for LOSHA in university campuses) on this matter, and she had the following to say:

> It seemed like the credibility of the list was being judged based on the fact that she (Raya Sarkar) was a Dalit/Mahajan woman. There was a caste aspect in the criticism—upper-caste Brahmins defending their upper-caste colleagues. This is well known. Round table India, Savari—Dalit organizations, lots of Twitter comments—have all framed it that way. When LOSHA came out, it wasn't the MeToo. But Tanushree Dutta coming out

42 Ibid.
43 https://www.aljazeera.com/news/2017/11/bollywood-film-padmavati-faces-protests-karni-sena-171114114842351.html

was? If we don't confront this, we will keep on mind framing the perfect victim, and women will not come forward. They will judge themselves and see that they don't fit the bill to be believed.

I discussed the matter quite elaborately with Prasad, given her background in women studies and experience of caste in both India (where she spent her early childhood) and the USA (where she finished middle and advanced schooling and now lives). In the USA, she has lived in widely different cities such as Queens, New York (known as the melting pot of immigrants from around the world), and Phoenix, Arizona (a Republican state quite monolithic until recently and infamous for draconic stance on racial profiling). I asked her what got her interested in caste and gender activism.

From a *sidha sadha* (simple) biology student who was destined to probably do pre-med, during sophomore (college) year I got very interested in the activism that came with and after SB1070.[44] People always assumed I am Latino even though I am Indian. But being an immigrant, it was very easy to sympathize with the feeling of racial profiling. So I became very involved and I also started to really explore my caste identity— what it means to be a Dalit?

'How did you come to know you are a Dalit? Did you come to Queens being a Dalit?' I had asked her.

No. Being in a city like Delhi at a young age, you are protected. I got to know what my caste was in my freshman year in high school in world history class. When my professor asked, quite casually, without possibly understanding the impact of his

-----

44 The Support Our Law Enforcement and Safe Neighborhoods Act (introduced as Arizona Senate Bill 1070 and thus often referred to simply as Arizona SB 1070) is a 2010 legislative Act in the US state of Arizona that allowed law-enforcement officers to act on the grounds of 'reasonable suspicion' of an individual being unlawful in the USA. The law is widely criticized for perpetuating racial profiling of Latino immigrants.

question: Does anyone know what their caste is? And I was shocked and surprised to find out that everyone knew, except me. And they stated their caste very proudly. I came home and asked, and it was a delicate situation ... and that's when it was explained to me that I was Dalit, and a Chamar, and slowly I was exposed to the poverty and marginalization my parents had left behind in India.... There were some hints growing up in Queens—my parents would not socialize with the diaspora Indian population. Instead, we stayed in a home owned by a Pakistani family and my mom mostly had a lot of Muslim friends. I didn't understand why. And my dad would constantly talk about, while driving me to college, about Ambedkar....

I asked her, as I listened to the deep pain in her words, why she so strongly felt that sexual harassment had an additional layer of caste in it for Indian women.

Sexual harassment, and the way it fits into the larger picture of gender-based violence in India, is not looked at very often with the lens of caste. *The entire fabric of it is looked at as if the way it exists, it touches all women to the same extent and as if it doesn't have anything to do with the other aspects within a gender. People don't realize that women who are in the highest rank of caste order vs who are in the lowest have a very different experience with sexual violence and harassment,* starting from how its positioned in Manusmriti and other such texts, to how bringing in even the mention of caste causes trolling in social media today. In Manusmriti, there is quite strict guidance on what lower-caste women can do or not do to Brahmin women vs what can or can't happen, by any men, to lower-caste women, especially by upper-caste men.

'But many would say that those are archaic texts with no modern relevance,' I placed the argument I heard from several other upper-caste urban Indian activists in the USA to her as she stared at the ground. 'Also, one reason #MeToo is thought of to be so powerful is because of its aggregative nature: So how will you answer those who say that by bringing caste into this, you are taking power away from the movement?' I further added, trying to prod on her gender vs caste loyalty.

I do agree that sexual harassment can happen to anyone and any argument against that, like if you did this or that, if you wouldn't do this or that, takes away from that. But as we focus on the act itself, it is also important to look at the response, reaction and method of acclimatization to it. It is not the same for us vs say a woman who comes from an upper-caste Brahmin family in Delhi. She can possibly demand consequences for what happened to her. She has power through her caste and class. But a Dalit woman who lives in the outskirts of Delhi in a shack will not have the same level of authority. It is important to understand and acknowledge this, not only from resources, or her access, point of view, but also for who she is. She can't go on Twitter and write a thread on what happened to her and get moral support. Even taking this hypothetical situation out of it, normalization of casual sexual harassment and the history puts her in a different space. The harassers know this too.

In the USA, the intersectionality of race and gender is now a matter of daily dialogue following the Black Live Matters movement. However, caste discussion stays mostly hushed in the diaspora population and the urban India I experience. I was curious to know if Prasad has experienced caste, and how she has experienced gender. So I asked her: 'Is it a fair assumption that growing up in the USA, you experienced gender later than caste?'

Yes, that's true. And it's true even today. It is really with LOSHA when women in India started talking about their experience with sexual violence on Twitter. There is definitely an aspect of working with something that's not formalized yet, but still, the way this played out was that the onus was on the women who provided the names, not on the names on the list. They were (mostly) from upper castes, elites—people who are expected to be allies for this cause, especially in those institutions. A lot of them surprisingly weren't. The upper-caste women expected to be allies to women instead chose their circle. Swa-varna—all four touchable castes. But when journalists came out, suddenly the same due process people were now leading the charge against the perpetrators and were propping this as the actual MeToo for India. There are several factors to this, of course. The factor of prominence, ease of branding is something journalism has vs the invincibility/respect factor India puts on the teaching profession. But there are articles on how when Dalit/Bahujan women do it, it doesn't get the legitimacy and forbearing-ness of a movement. There is a well-documented history of exclusion of Dalit women in the women's movement because *Swa-varna women just don't think caste matters. And they are right because for them it doesn't.*

The next (and arguably the most shameful) matter in the context of rape for subjugation and the differentiated approach to rape in India is the matter of legalization of rape to curb dissent, exemplified by AFSPA.[45]

RAPE AND INSURGENCY

On the topic of rape as a weapon of subjugation, or in a broader frame, the use of gender-differentiated and gendered techniques as a tool, the matter of insurgency and terrorism comes next. Scholars have long analysed the use of broad and abusive regulations to counter insurgency, sedition and terrorism. The now repealed Prevention of Terrorism Act, 2002, and the Unlawful Activities (Prevention) Act, 1967, amended in 2004, 2008 and 2013, have been cited as examples of the state presenting a masculine self by operating on the principles of gender-subjugated governance on all its citizens, not just women.[46] Leaving the academic debate aside, there is an immediate need to raise awareness around the use of rape in independent India to subjugate insurgency by

---

45 https://en.wikipedia.org/wiki/Armed_Forces_(Special_Powers)_Act
46 A. Roy and U. Singh, 'The Masculinist Security State and Anti-terror Law Regimes in India', *Asian Studies Review* 39, no. 2 (2015): 305.

state agencies and on the gender-differentiated effects of anti-insurgency measures.[47]

Rapes in regions of India under AFSPA are not talked about and are carefully avoided in the broader context of women's safety. Just like caste and religion, where identification with the gendered cause at the cost of alienating or opposing the other (and presumed superior) identity is a taboo, national security is marketed as a cause much greater than gender. What remains concealed however is the deliberate design behind that credence.

For reconnoitring and establishing this, the examples—which are aplenty—are recounted in this segment. They demonstrate the scale of a matter so seldom brought to the forefront.

Due to the immunity is given to the personnel acting under this law, in the 54 years of its operation, not a single army, or paramilitary officer or a soldier has been prosecuted for murder, rape or destruction of property.[48]

- Routine leering, extortion, unsolicited physical contact with intent to torture psychologically and violation of women (including minors) during search operations[49]

- Reported rape of seven women in Wavoosa (1997) during a cordon search cited as a routine operation[50]

- The alleged rape of numerous women (number noted to be between 23 and 100, including disabled, pregnant and minor) by 4th Rajputana Rifles unit in Kunan Poshpora (1991)[51]

47 Ibid.
48 Ranjan, 'A Gender Critique of AFSPA'.
49 U. Chakravarti, 'Kashmir Diary: Seven Days in Armed Paradise', in *Speaking Peace*, ed. U. Butalia (New Delhi: Kali for Women, 2002).
50 A. Chatterji, 'Witnessing as a Feminist Intervention in India-administered Kashmir', in *Feminisms in South Asia: Contemporary Interventions*, eds. Ania Loomba and Ritty Lukose (New Delhi: Zubaan, 2012).
51 Ibid.

- Rape perpetrated by security forces in the Kashmir Valley in Chhanpora and Pazipora (1990); Chak Saidpora (1992); Haran (1992); Theno Budapathary Kangan (1994); Bihota (2001); and Handwara (2004)[52]

- Gang rape and murder of Asiya Jan (17) and Nilofar Jan (22) in Sophian (2009) after which the administration first denied and then deflected the issue (despite the rape of a minor) and the police refused to file FIR[53]

- Kunan Poshpora rape (1991), following which the security forces were found to have forced the women into making self-implicating and self-damaging statements[54]

Northeast abuses have been further opaque to attention. These come to the forefront only after alarming and astounding protests by women driven to desperation, for example, Irom Sharmila's hunger strike (since 2000) and women coming out naked in front of the headquarters of Assam Rifles (Manipur, 2004). As Amit Ranjan quotes in his 2015 article, the only case widely known of out of the Northeast is that of Thangjam Manorama,[55] who was taken from her residence in the early hours of a day (2004) by Assam Rifles personnel and found dead later with her body bearing signs of torture and rape. This is the case that triggered the aforementioned protest in which women appeared naked in front of Assam Rifles headquarters, holding signs that decried the Indian Army for raping women in the region over the decade. But several other examples have been studied and cited by activists and scholars which, like in the case of Kashmir, help delineate this matter as a systemic issue rather than a one-off violation. A couple

---

52 Ibid.; Kazi (2009).

53 Chatterji, 'Witnessing as a Feminist Intervention'.

54 R. Manchanda, 'Press Council Report on the Army in Kashmir', *Economic & Political Weekly* 26, no. 3 (1991): 1899.

55 A. Vajpeyi, 'Presenting the Indian State: For a New Political Practice in the North East', in *Beyond Counter-insurgency*, ed. S. Baruah (New Delhi: Oxford University Press, 2009).

of examples are listed below to specifically emphasize the contrast between what happens in mainstream India following the rape of minors vs what happens for cases under the AFSPA jurisdiction. The former state is far from ideal, but the latter is denied even an outcry. This blots India's commitment to gender justice for minors through acceptance of injustice under the pretext of national interest.

- Rape of a 13-year-old and molestation of her mother and grandmother in Karbi Anglong (Assam; 2015)[56]

- Rape of a 15-year-old schoolgirl (confirmed by Manoj Kumar Singh, District Judge of Imphal East) by Army personnel in Imphal (2004) in which the victim committed suicide following the incident[57]

For both regions (Kashmir and Northeast), several reports have been compiled which aggregate the claims of activists. Government and international reports have noted the matter of increase in crimes against women and the impunity factor playing into such an increase. I quote three summarized instances out of one of the articles I have cited on this matter.[58]

....

- A report on incidents that have occurred during 2004–2008 was compiled by a group of serving and retired judges associated with the district courts in Manipur....The report says: 'Crimes against women, more particularly relating to sexual harassment committed by armed forces, are now increasing in some states like ours (Manipur). They (armed forces) think themselves placed at the elevated status of impunity by the legislation and think wrongly that they are given license to do whatever they like (ibid.).'

....

56 http://www.thehindu.com/news/national/other-states/protestsin-guwahati-against-army-after-rape-of-minor/article7096056.ece
57 Ranjan, 'A Gender Critique of AFSPA', 440.
58 Ibid.

- In his testimony presented at the 52nd UN Commission on Human Rights,

Professor William Baker said: 'Rape in Kashmir is not the result of a few undisciplined soldiers but rather an active strategy of Indian forces to humiliate, intimidate and demoralise the Kashmiri people (Parvez, 2014).'

- In 2013, the then Chief Minister of J&K, Omar Abdullah, responding to a question raised in the Legislative Assembly, gave a statement that more than 5,000 cases of rape have been registered since 1989. In 2013 alone, 70 cases of sexual violence were registered against the security forces (ibid.).

However, the tragedy in this matter is the fact that such conclusions remain either highly censured or deliberately masked. For example, in *Dil Se..*, director Mani Ratnam was on the one hand widely criticized for failing to bring forward clearly and strongly the motivation that drove the key protagonist to be so committed towards a self- and mass-destructive goal and, on the other hand, was limited by the Censor Board from depicting elaborately and firmly the matter of abuse by the Armed Forces. As a result, the matter became merely a vague, passing reference in the movie. Bringing Bollywood into this is not trivialization of the matter. It is extremely relevant in the context of mainstream awareness, given the significance of media and film in popularization and creation of culture. Despite its limitations and poor box office performance, *Dil Se..* indeed succeeded in making the matter of 'possibly all is not well' for women under Armed Forces protection a consideration for the rest of India.

In the use of rape, and the terror of rape, for instilling fear, no one group, nation, religion or sect can be blamed. We have talked about universal war time use of rape and rape as tool in conflict through the ages. Use of rape (with intensified violence) for instilling fear or avenging has been used on sectarian groups by all religions and parties. In the exodus of Kashmiri Pandits from Kashmir[59]—an act of ethnic cleansing—rape of Hindu women with aggravated violence was common. The incident of gang rape and murder of Girija Tickoo has been referred to in Chapter 2 and has come under the limelight in the recent years (Girija was gang-raped and cut into halves while alive) as a counter to accusations against Hindus for barbaric rapes of minorities. Girija's account and other similar atrocities have also been more appropriately used to provide context on the Kashmir conflict to the international audience. Understandably, the barbarism in this particular case serves the point well: Inhumanity is not limited to any one religion. The atrocities against Kashmiri Pandits (a minority group in Kashmir) which includes quite few accounts of horrific gang rape and murder should indeed be noted. But if it is used as a justification almost, not just for the matter of fair recording of all incidents, as it is being on multiple propagandistic sites (2019–2020), it's a disservice to the fight against gender violence, for doing so only perpetuates the problem.

Similarly, the left (communist parties in India and in Russia, China and so on) has also used and supported rape for persecution and curbing of dissent. In one of the most high-profile cases out of communist West Bengal of the 1990s, three women health officers were gang-raped and brutalized alongside the driver of their vehicle.[60] The vehicle had had a West Bengal government logo, and the two of the victims including Anita Dewan, who died from the attack and had had inhuman atrocities committed on her (a metal surgical torch was found inserted inside her), were government officers. Despite the same, the government, including the then chief minister of West Bengal, Mr Jyoti Basu, issued statements justifying and trivializing the incident. According

59 R. Pandita, *Our Moon Has Blood Clots: The Exodus of the Kashmiri Pandits* (Gurgaon: Random House, 2013).
60 https://www.epw.in/journal/1991/5/perspectives-perspectives/women-rape-and-left.html

to several reports, the attack and the exaggerated brutality (the driver had had his private parts smashed) were because of a health corruption scandal of the ruling party the officers had had evidence of. Similar atrocities and brutalities committed internationally by communist regimes are not hard to find and, again, prove the point that rape, like brutal murder, is a tool for driving compliance through fear. Unfortunately, as incidents like the Hathras gang rape caused widespread condemnation, the tragic account of Anita Dewan was used to condemn 'liberal' and 'secular' units, potentially by paid propagandists. This is dangerous, not because it's untrue that all parties are guilty of tremendous atrocities against women in India, but because of what I said above: It does disservice to the fight against gender violence and takes the dialogue away from 'gender', again.

INDIA VS THE WORLD: DE-WESTERNIZATION AND INDIANIZATION VS GENDER

The top issues noted by international consortia affecting women of the world are not widely divergent.[61] Reproductive rights, equal pay/opportunity/advancement, sexual and domestic violence (subcategories of the broader GBV) and health are top issues for the USA and key Western countries, while access to education, trafficking, child marriage and GBV (sexual violence, infanticide, female genital mutilation and acid attack) are top ones for Africa, Indian subcontinent and the Middle East. As it can be seen, there's a significant overlap. However, consistently through the history of Indian feminism and women's rights movement in India, the differences and unique challenges of Indian women have been emphasized and celebrated. For example, in the works

---

61 https://apps.who.int/iris/bitstream/handle/10665/85239/97892415646
25_eng.pdf;jsessionid=52F125B56369C99734428DA783B8A048?sequence=1;
https://openknowledge.worldbank.org/bitstream/handle/10986/29865/
126579-Public-on-5-30-18-WorldBank-GenderInequality-Brief-v13.pdf?
sequence=1&isAllowed=y

by Uma Chakravarti, Vibhuti Patel[62] and several others, the issues of temple prostitution, working-class abuse and similar instances have been pointed out, along with the matters discussed in this chapter. The differences and the distinctiveness can't be discounted and, in fact, are extremely critical for understanding and solving the gender issue in India. However, the over celebration of this, in my opinion, has done severe disservice to gender rights in India by further dicing of a problem statement already suffering because of constant de-prioritization. This has allowed for playing right into the hands of groups who continue to design regulations for women that are prejudiced and patriarchal by fronting 'Indian heritage and culture' to foster their motivations. Hostel curfew regulations, anti-Romeo squad measures, forcing corporations to limit working hours for women and regulations against rideshare use by women are not designed for women's safety. They are designed for the control and limitation of women. However, these measures garner widespread support from not just men but also women, for scholars and commoners alike believe in the need for a separate standard of equality for Indian women vs that for the rest of the world because of their unique virtues and goals. Understanding of the deliberate designing that went into creation of these virtues that are merely perfected by practice is not cultivated.

When it comes to gender and human justice, the socio-economic origins and their effects are quite fungible across borders. The Western principles (women's choice to work, choose their outfits and observe or not observe certain lifestyles) are not so Western. Outside of the upper-class experiences, they have existed forever and still exist in India. For example, tribal women and several other subsects have celebrated drinking, working outside of the home and wearing of 'immodest' clothing. The key matter here is that of 'choice' of the Indian women. But attention is diverted from that fact through the use of fear of loss of identity. Preservation of

62 https://newleftreview.org/issues/I153/articles/vibhuti-patel-women-s-liberation-in-india

cultural integrity in a previously colonized country is the sacred deity who can't be touched.

In this chapter, we have reviewed the nodes that have defined modern Indian gender equations: designed differentiation through definition, normalization of behaviours and legalization of subjugation to arrive at the single-most significant cause of gender un-parity in India—the notion of women being citizens whose wishes (a) either don't matter (for they are either unaware or not capable of being in control of their sexuality) or (b) can and should be ignored (for they are (i) secondary to the economy because of their defined roles and (ii) need to be controlled for control of patrilineal purity, land, and sectorial and segmental orders). In the following chapter, we will explore in depth the manifestation of these nodes in modern India.

CHAPTER 5

THE C WORD

Let's admit that consent can be a difficult concept. In my exploration of what consent really means, I found it to be not quite black and white. For example, in the Aziz Ansari account that we will depict later, the woman (overcame from meeting the celebrity comedian) felt obligated and coerced while according to Ansari, he sincerely felt the act to be consensual. Several activists I interviewed for this work held the opinion that whether or not there is consent is a mere matter of having common sense and respect. While the fundamental premise of respect for the partner can't be denied, for it, if fully achieved, is indeed the answer; declining that there are valid misunderstandings that can happen doesn't remedy the issue. Not accepting that there is an issue, in fact, worsens the matter, for example, the matter of feeling coerced yet saying nothing, or trying to stop the act but possibly providing very different signals. I have experienced this myself and have multiple female friends who have. In this chapter, this matter and the dialogue that need to happen around consent will be covered. But India's problem with consent runs deeper and dangerous and is at a much more basic level. Therefore, the modulators of devaluation of consent in India will need to be first established and analysed. ·

WHERE WE COME FROM

In a December 2019 video making rounds on Facebook from ThePrint[1] by journalist Shahbaz Ansar, several Delhi men were once again (for this is not the first neither the last of such street surveys video-graphed) asked about rape and why rapes happen. Anyone on the Internet who has had access to men (and even women) speaking their mind on rape in India can foretell what they will most possibly hear on the video before hitting play:

- If women cover their bodies, they will not arouse men.

- Women need to be in closed quarters/under supervision to prevent rape.

- Women should be respected as goddesses; however, they are the same ones who can (and should) be raped if behaving inappropriately.

- That (above) is what our (the Indian) culture and heritage is all about.

Let's revisit two of the points discussed in the previous chapter regarding the historical context of modern-day gender in India.

1. The push for control on women's sexuality through 'values and scriptures' to serve the purpose of patrilineal purity, and assignment of that control to men: Not only do women and their sexual behaviour need to be controlled by men, but that is also 'the' right thing to do, for that is what salvation and sanctity are derived from. Dharma is literally and deliberately entangled with carnal 'karma' for women and with how they control their women's carnal karma for men.

2. When needed, the use of force is rightful: Indeed, the use of force should be celebrated, for not only are women not in control of their desires and need to be therefore carefully

---

1 https://www.facebook.com/theprintindia/videos/2434872169975136/?v=2434872169975136

guarded, but they can also be not aware of such desires and therefore need to be 'awakened'.

The origin of point 2 can be easily found in point 1.

Below is how this sums up:

- It is an issue if a perpetrator knows of an act to be wrong yet chooses to do so.

- It is a different issue if the perpetrator would usually know right from wrong but was placed in a situation where the matter was just not so clear.

- 'It is a very different and much more significant societal issue if the perpetrator would not know—can't know—what is wrong is any possible way for his act is completely in conjunction with his belief system.'

When it comes to women's safety, we have all three of these happening in today's India. We owe the last one (the only one unique to India) to the late colonial, post-Independence history of gender in India. The need to control women to control the access to them, the 'goddess' symbolism cleverly manipulated away from its origin (the power of giving birth) to representation of virtues that women should imbibe (and, therefore, control their own sexuality with), defined societal roles (that would solidify their positions within homes, not outside) and normalization and sanctioning of sexual assault through religious and legal codes. These panels discussed in the previous chapter form the foundation of India's lack of appreciation for female consent. The next tier on this foundation is formed by the lack of historical context, lack of education and misinformation.

SEX IN MODERN INDIA

Two additional views that were voiced in the Delhi video are that rapes didn't happen before and rape is consensual. The former opinion is often advertised by politicians and lawmakers, and many people in India (including my parents) are firm believers.

However, the fact that the occurrence of sexual assault and rapes is significantly on the rise and is potentially attributable to external factors (Westernization: from clothing to behaviour [e.g., women stepping more out of their homes] and decline of Indian values) is an incorrect one. Globalization in India is largely noted to have happened in the 1990s, following the initiation of the economic liberalization plan by then Finance Minister Dr Manmohan Singh. Following the statistics of crimes against women (which can be compiled out of reported incidents only, of course) through the late 1990s into the present day, a steady increase is indeed seen. However, the delta and jump ratios

1. do not demonstrate clear correlation[2]; bigger jumps (e.g., up to 44% between 2011 and 2015) are noted to be triggered post major incidents and legal modifications;

2. could very possibly, and more accurately, be attributed to increased reporting (which stems from several desirable factors including increased awareness and independence of women as the economy shifted from brawn to brain);

3. have other dependencies. Previous laws were often inadequate for accurate classification and, therefore, noting of GBV (e.g., before 2013 IPC modification with Sections 326A and 326B, an acid attack could only be tracked as violence and, therefore, was impossible to correctly account for).[3]

Therefore, the contribution of globalization (or as many would say it: Westernization) is on reporting, not occurrence rates. Another fact to support this is the coinciding of the Internet and information flow increase with increased number of reported instances. As American social historian Linda Hirshman notes in her book,[4] social movements are almost always brought in by and

2 http://ncrb.gov.in/
3 https://www.huffpost.com/entry/acid-attack-in-india-wher_b_9559790
4 Hirshman, *Reckoning*.

around technology leaps,[5] from printed Bibles driving Protestant Reformation to print media assisting in the abolishment of slavery. Awareness brings change, and technology both brings about and forwards awareness. As discussed previously, the most absolute form of power is the lack of recognition of oppression as such, and exposure indorses recognition of right from wrong. Therefore, this is a welcome change. However, because rapes have now moved from inside-page third columns (where they did find a daily spot all through the 1970s and 1980s in most print publications in India) to 24/7 television and social media discussions, making them much more visible, it is understandable that many presume their rates to have increased dramatically over the last two decades.

The second point—rape is consensual—is natural consequence misinformation and lack of education on intimate relationships. The Quint video-graph from 2018 that went viral on social media (following the notorious 10 rapes in 10 days in Haryana) shows this explicitly.[6] In the video, it is shared by men and women of all ages that consent needn't be verbal and, rather, has to be interpreted, and rape (read intercourse), after a point, has to be consensual or else isn't possible. The Haryana video shows boys and girls describing how a smile, silence or even avoidance of eye contact is interpreted as consent. No visible marks on the body is noted as a telltale sign of consensual intercourse. The gang rape of 16-year-old tribal girl Mathura in the police station that had triggered the anti-rape campaign of the 1980s is worth remembering here. The acquittal, among other assumptions, was based on the 'no visible marks on her body' argument. Although the matters of coercion into consent and submission out of fear not equating to willing intercourse were recognized by an intermediate court, the Supreme Court itself re-acquitted the accused, leading to character assassination

5 Hirshman, *Reckoning*.
6 https://www.hindustantimes.com/india-news/haryana-witnesses-10-rapes-in-past-10-days/story-87vLw3wMHZ3e7yFL00iZcM.html

and re-victimization of the victim.[7] The role of shastras and other motivated doctrines in creating and propagating the notion of women being out-of-control sexual beings has been discussed in the previous chapter. The role of Bollywood in eroticization of assault and delegitimization of dissent is vital as the next and final tier: reinforcement and validation.

S. Anandnathan (name changed on request) is a successful man living in the USA with his lovely wife and daughters. He has a respectable career, a widely successful sister, a mother he would die for (like most Indian men I know) and a multitude of female friends. He is also one of the most libertarian, unconventional and feminist of men I have come across. He believes that during intercourse, it is more important to please the woman (for that part is ignored by most, especially Indian men, owing to lack of awareness). He is an upper-caste Brahmin atheist who is bringing up his children to be non-religious. He also believes that sex outside of marriage should be OK for both men and women, for it is unrealistic and regressive to expect perfect sexual compatibility between every pair of individuals. Particularly for couples in arranged marriages and folks who haven't had a lot of sexual exposure before getting married, it is quite possible that sexual incompatibility is pervasive and irreconcilable. One day over coffee he told me that he grew up believing that women will say no to sex unless they are coerced a bit, for culturally they have been conditioned to think of sex as evil. So they need to be aroused and taken past a certain point to be able to consent.

'Do you still believe this?' I had asked.

'I am not sure,' he had said,

> I grew up believing a lot of things. I did think that forcing a woman or being strong with her is a way to win her and all my school friends believed the same ... and of course I don't believe that now ... but I did believe that only the first part of rape is

---

7 B. Suguna, *Women's Movements* (New Delhi: Discovery Publishing House, 2009).

forced.... Once the woman is brought into it ... she starts enjoying it. I saw it in some movies too, so you know. There was this scene: the woman—the heroine—is in the shower and the man makes a move on her. Initially, he grabs her wrists and her legs are shown to be kicking. But then, their fingers intertwine, and the legs start rubbing. And that's what my friends used to say too in school. It's only a matter of pushing women above a peak....

THE B FACTOR

In India, films are treated like religion.[8]

The 1970s, 1980s and 1990s are teeming with mainstream movies made in India, depicting, on the one hand, persuasive men winning love of fair maiden through criminal acts (decriminalized in the name of love), and on the other, obligatory rape and sexual violence by villains as means of eroticizing the audience. Furthermore, such acts without fail marked the end of the woman's life (virtually and literally), tying the value of a woman's existence entirely to her sexual purity and her preserving of male honour through the same. Let's start with listing out, with examples, the major kinds of criminal acts decriminalized and glorified by Bollywood.

1. **Stalking, persistent harassment:** In Aamir Khan and Madhuri Dixit-starrer *Deewana Mujh Sa Nahin* and similar movies, stalking and persistent harassment are put as the very plot itself. From superhit songs like 'O Lal Dupatte Wali' and 'Yeh Uska Style Hoinga' (in which the lyrics literally say that even though the woman is saying no, she possibly means yes) to subsections and entire movies in which winning love by ignoring the vocalized opinion of the woman are shown as the manly (and loving) thing to do.

2. **College harassment and eve-teasing of women:** From Akshay Kumar-starrer *Khiladi*, Aamir Khan's *Dil* and Ajay

8 Farrukh Dhondy, *The Guardian*, 2010.

Devgan's *Phool Aur Kaante* (all blockbusters) to isolated scenes, the 1990s celebrated unsafe public places (especially in educational institutions). Movies, if involving a college-going protagonist, were required to have at least one song where his love interest would need to be ganged up on and harassed, led by non-other than the protagonist himself.

3. **Full-blown assaults:** There is a brilliant article that I had come across a few years back while researching the movie *Bāhubali* (the highest-grossing film in India and the third-highest-grossing Indian film worldwide at the time of its release) which has a sequence of the hero forcing himself, slowly undressing the heroine who has outrightly rejected his advances and had fought him to be left alone. The article titled 'The Rape of Avantika'[9] summarizes perfectly this category of decriminalized sexual assault in the name of pursuit. Bollywood is filled with such storylines, where the base idea from category 1 (above) has been taken one step further of legitimizing rape and delegitimizing the woman's voiced opinion with one single act of her giving up (and in) eventually.

Prettified though it has been, the lead couple's mating dance in Bahubali is unequivocal in its contention that it is okay to fool around with a woman without her knowing, or to force yourself on her when she resists because that's what courtship is all about.[10]

4. **Marriage to the rapist in place of prosecution:** The Govinda and Juhi Chawla-starrer *Bhagyawan* can serve as a prime example of the possibly most problematic portrayal of rape by Bollywood. In the movie, the rapist is asked to marry the

9 https://www.thehindubusinessline.com/blink/watch/the-rape-of-avanthika/article7433603.ece
10 Anna Vetticad, *The Hindu Business Line.*

woman he has raped. This is noted as not only the only way of re-establishing her (and her family's) honour but also the only way she could continue to live (she kills herself when her assaulter refuses to marry her). Similarly, in another Juhi Chawla (and Anil Kapoor)-starrer Benaam Badsha, the victim (Juhi herself) considers the very act of rape (on her wedding night) as marriage and leaves everything behind to establish a co-habiting, conjugal relationship with her rapist, Anil Kapoor.

Obviously, all the above categories are criminal, and awareness today is significantly higher towards that fact. However, the damage done through decades of glorification has deep effects on the subconscious of a society which can't be easily undone.

A BuzzFeed India YouTube video[11] on this topic accurately traces back the start of all this to the fact that sex is highly saleable, yet, owing to the extremely controlled and skewed outlook of the Indian society in the 1900s towards sex, there was no legitimate way to pass censorship showing sex in the movies. Sex had to be ingeniously designed into scenes through metaphors, suggestive imagery, double-meaning lyrics or shown as a forced act committed by the villain. Before wide availability of porn through the Internet, escapist sequences were weaved into the movies as songs for predominantly male audiences. But the decline of movie-going (owing to the rise of home entertainment and video piracy) is speculated to have caused the film industry to improvise to lure audiences back. This required ability to put in more explicit sexual content, which caused the rise through the 1980s of rape scenes in movies. As the video rightly concludes, 'Given the influence Bollywood has, that's a dangerous precedent to set,' and an almost impossible one to undo, for although rape scenes have declined from movies with the rise of Internet porn (much easier

11 https://www.buzzfeed.com/watch/video/95060

and explicit access to sexual content), the views to the Bollywood rape and assault videos online continue to hold strong.

On a superficial level, Bollywood's dichotomy towards sexual assault might feel contradicting (celebrated as essential when carried out by the hero and considered catastrophic when by the villain), but it is not. The precise message through both, in the context of consent, is the same: The women's opinion is non-existent and/or immaterial before, during and after.

Current Bollywood has moved on to what I would call 'speckling objectification' instead of naming it or putting it in as part of the plot. From slaps on butts in songs to shots of cleavage, and slapstick comedies showing men lusting over women, Bollywood continues to eroticize assault and minimize the importance of consent and also shows assault as a fun and desirable matter.[12]

I had asked Anandnathan on why he believed what he believed for so long.

'But why did you think this? You had a mother and sister,' was what I said.

> Well, there's no source of correct information. Never did I learn about consent in sex nor did I learn that women can want sex by their own will. So where will I learn about rape or sex growing up? Either from the television or from friends, right?

The debate on whether Bollywood merely reflects, or creates, culture has been long raging. However, in this matter, Bollywood's role in the victimization of women is beyond debate. They are not the only ones to blame; nor did they create the beliefs, but they also surely role-modelled assault into every home.

'In a 2011 survey by ICRW,[13] one in every five Indian men surveyed admitted to forcing their wives into sex and 65 per cent

---

12 https://www.researchgate.net/publication/265731948_Sexual_Assault_ Portrayals_in_Hindi_Cinema
13 International Center for Research on Women.

of Indian men surveyed believed that there are times when women deserve to be beaten.'[14]

HIS RIGHTS

Nothing depicts the mess that sex in India is where consent is concerned better than India's current status on marital rape and spousal sex. India's legal system largely models sex within marriage as a right, not choice.

Since marriage in India is perceived as a sacred union, marital rape cannot be brought within the purview of the law on rape.
—Haribhai Chaudhary,
Indian Minister for State of Home Affairs, 2015

As Flavia Agnes summarizes in one of her articles[15] on this matter, 'Hindu marriages ceased to be sacramental more than half a century ago and Muslim marriages were always contractual in nature.' However, the bigger problem with the two current legal provisions that grant men impunity on rape and forced sex within a marriage—exemption granted to husbands under Section 375 of IPC (exception 2: sexual intercourse or sexual acts committed by a man with his wife, wife not being under 15 years of age, is not rape) and the provision to restitute conjugal rights—is not only that it legalizes abuse under certain situations (within a marriage) but also that it reinforces 'consent' of the woman to be immaterial for sexual intercourse as long as it is her husband who is forcing himself on her. Let's take the lesser-known 'restitution of conjugal rights' matter. Section 376B of IPC does criminalize non-consensual act of sexual intercourse of a husband with his

---

14 https://www.icrw.org/news/gender-equality-Indian-mens attitudes-complex/
15 http://majlislaw.com/file/2015_06_06_Section_498A__Marital_Rape_and_Adverse_Propaganda_EPW_Jun_2015.pdf

wife who is living separately (whether under a decree of separation or otherwise). However, what essentially nullifies this protection is the fact that Section 9 of the Hindu Marriage Act (and Section 22 of Special Marriage Act) grants the right to either spouse to file a petition in a matrimonial court to restitute conjugal rights if abandoned by a spouse after solemnization of marriage.[16] It is worthwhile to note here that although in India such provisions remain valid under Hindu, Special and Muslim Marriage Acts, it has been done away with (in 1970) in the UK (feudal British legal system is quoted as the origin of the law in the first place). For legal disputes around this matter, including debate on the benefit and intention of this law (note: at the time of this writing, a PIL[17] was in progress to be heard by a special bench of the Supreme Court arguing for abolishment of the provision on the grounds of it being against Articles 14 and 15 of the Constitution), multiple articles can be found, including the few cited below.[18] But I believe that more useful information for analysing India's grasp of the concept of consent comes from reviewing the comments on articles reporting on a woman filing to block her estranged husband's filing of restitution of conjugal rights on her, like pictures that are worth a thousand words.

The woman in the case in point is living separately from her husband and has made it amply clear by the act of filing a plea with the Supreme Court that she doesn't want to have a conjugal relationship with her spouse. However, below are two examples (chosen from a *The Times of India* article[19] on the

16 P. Diwan, *Law of Marriage and Divorce* (Delhi: Universal Law Publishing, 2004).

17 https://economictimes.indiatimes.com/news/politics-and-nation/sc-to-decide-validity-of-provisions-governing-restitution-of-conjugal-rights/articleshow/68279688.cms?from=mdr

18 https://www.indianbarassociation.org/restitution-of-conjugal-right-a-comparative-study-among-indian-personal-laws/

19 http://timesofindia.indiatimes.com/articleshow/66074554.cms?utm_source=contentofinterest&utm_medium =text&utm_campaign=cppst

matter—representative of many other such)[20] of the what most men interpret as just in this case.

> Prenups should be made mandatory by law to secure men from greedy women who get divorce after few years of arranged marriage, get entitled for alimony and go live with their boyfriends without a matrimonial bond, and husband has to pay her alimony for his life.[21]

> Does sexual autonomy imply she can sleep with anyone she feels like. Gets divorce and alimony. And repeat the process with another man. It will be very good business model! Prostitution is at least honest![22]

The elephant in the room here is the fact that even if it is true that the woman's motivation in this (or in undertaking of similar actions) comes from a place of no particular grievance and is just a matter of not wanting to engage in a physical, or otherwise spousal, relationship with her husband, 'it is still her wish'. Forcing her consent through a state mechanism is still an assault on her autonomy and is not a viable position, no matter how wronged, a spouse should be seeking. Marriage doesn't grant consent for a lifetime, nor is consent a one-time matter. In libertarian civic societies, forcing anyone into sex is wrong, no matter what the reason is. The wronged spouse can file a legal suit to refuse alimony, nullification of marriage or even damages. But when a spouse (male in most cases) feels entitled enough to consider state-aided coercion as just mean to sex, there is a profoundly disturbing problem. This is in no way anything other than considering another human being inferior and equivalent to personal property. When

---

20 Grammatical and punctuation errors not corrected to keep the comments intact.
21 Commenter 1, *The Times of India*.
22 Commenter 2, *The Times of India*.

engaging in intercourse, such a person would be doing so knowing very well of the lack of consent of his partner, and yet wouldn't mind going forward. It is further problematic that this fact is lost on authorities and commoners alike in India.

To address the second commenter's question: Does sexual autonomy imply she can sleep with anyone she feels like? Yes. That is a lesser problem than him sleeping with someone who doesn't feel like sleeping with him. The problem is that most men feel that sex is something that is owed to them, and if they are virtuous, marriage is what it is owed to them through.

Furthermore, many men don't realize that pleasuring a woman might be more difficult than the pleasure they are getting out of the act of sexual intercourse. The biology of this is never taught to them and, therefore, they can't comprehend a woman having sexual urges that remain unsatisfied with her current partner. Thus, there are only two options to choose from when a woman is seeking out a different sexual partner, using other means for fulfilling her urges or is expressing unsatisfied needs: Either take it personally (I am not man enough) or blame it on her 'character' (she is a slut). The 2019 movie *Veere di Wedding*, for example, very genuinely depicts a woman's husband wanting to divorce her for her mere act of using a sex toy, for he considers it equivalent to adultery. However, in the kindergarten of mutuality when it comes to sex, this is far advanced a concept to grasp for men who have grown up without a healthy understanding of sex and gender equality in physical pleasure.

The more pertinent point made on marital rape by the supporters of it saying it is not a crime (also expressed in comments on social media but a bit more subtly than the entitlement ones) is on implementation and possible misuse for victimizing men. The abuse stories of Section 498A are often quoted on this (which will be tackled in detail in Chapter 8 through the exploration of men's rights movements (MRMs) in India). But it is important to recognize the preposterousness in the demands of decriminalization of a criminal act on the grounds of difficulty of implementation. Acid attacks should be legal then, for it has been proven that control of acid sales and prevention of access to acids is almost impossible a task in India, as should be mass murders during times of war, for war crimes are tough to trace back. Using the 'tough to prove' argument to legitimize coercion and assault celebrates the same mindset that causes the problem in the first place: tolerance of violence on women as a lesser evil.

R. Bose, a celebrated feminist, author and artist in India, is someone I have now known for quite a few years. She is the founder of a prominent women's site and has written explicitly on issues concerning women. She had shared accounts on social media of her two marriages in both of which she was raped by her spouse multiple times. What makes her account particularly pertinent is the fact that she, by no means, is someone who can be considered opportunistic or manipulative or naïve. The usual appellations attached to women when they come out and 'cry' marital rape can't apply to her. More importantly, after being a victim of domestic violence and marital rape in her first marriage, she had vouched to either stay away from marriage or find a man who by a long shot wouldn't disrespect women, let alone hurt them. However, her ending up in a second marriage where her spouse (dissatisfied with her decision to not try for a male child after she had had her daughter) rapes her outlines the need for legal policies of protection to safeguard women from domestic crimes. I had asked Bose to share her thoughts on the two primary arguments for decriminalization of marital rape:

- Sex in a marriage is a spouse's conjugal right. If a woman doesn't want to have sex, why is she married? What happens then to husbands who are taken advantage of by wives who marry them for alimony, then leave them or refuse to have sex.

- How will this be implemented? Women will just use this as a threat and use it against husbands just like Section 498A.

This is what Bose had to say. I use her own words to preserve the essence of her points which summaries the dichotomy quite well.

I can only speak for myself. Sex is a conjugal right for both the partners, so both of them have equal rights to either give consent or deny sex. In my case, I felt an emotional alienation from my second husband which slowly made me averse to sex with him, because I can't make love if I don't love the person.

My first husband, however, was more violent in bed, so I was saying yes to sex more out of fear than out of love. When I filed for divorce from him, I didn't ask for any alimony, all that I ever wanted from him was freedom. So it is hard for me to understand the reason why women may want to use it to extort money from their partners in the name of alimony.

My first husband never stopped me from working, so I was financially independent and there was no need for me to ask for financial aid.

With my second husband, he had forcefully stopped me from working; he hid my laptop, threatened to separate me from my children (since I have had mental health issues, I have tried to commit suicide twice and was on medication) using the fact that I am not fit enough to raise children. He demanded that I give my cell phone so that he can cut me off from my friends. His point being that as a mother, all I should do is raise kids and nothing else. My refusal for sex arose from these issues because I started to abhor him and could not stand him enough to let him touch me anymore.

I told him that he is free to sleep with anyone else he likes, and I don't want him in my bed anymore.

Now, here children are involved, and I have lost many years because of him in which I could have worked. So financially I am dependent on him. It is only now after 11 years of marriage to him I have found the courage to do something about it and have started my art centre. If I were to file for divorce now, then I will definitely ask for alimony to support the kids. You see, the two situations were different and thus the need for alimony too.

So, I guess, it will vary with every relationship. Coming to the second point, it is a very fine line. There might be loopholes in the legal system which may give women a chance to misuse it and demand unjust alimony. This is something that I can't really comment on.

But like I said previously, 'If the man has actively hindered his wife's attempts to be financially independent, then she should be entitled to alimony, and if the couple has children, there should be equal responsibility and the costs should be shared in case of separation.'

A CROWDED PROBLEM?

Let's move the vantage point from gendered consent and subjugation to the broader matter of personal space. The Internet has no shortage of articles on personal space being a problem in India (and for Indians)—from Quora threads on why Indians stare or push, to cultural handbooks on how the invasion of privacy with personal questions is not offensive, to scholarly and semi-scholarly articles dissecting culture vs necessity (the crowding experienced in daily life in India does necessitate operating in close contact, which is argued to be undermining the value and habit of privacy and space [literal and figurative] over a period of time). This is not unique for India and is well understood of several other nations and conglomerates. However, does this issue exaggerate the challenge of gender safety when combined with the lack of valuing of consent?

Yes.

First, it provides opportunities for violations. 'Personal space is a luxury urban elites enjoy,' author Jane D'Souza is quoted.[23] Whether its urban or rural India, from public transportation, walking the streets and residing in close quarters to having to

23 https://timesofindia.indiatimes.com/life-style/health-fitness/de-stress/the-great-indian-personal-space-mission/articleshow/70700270.cms

take desperate measures for relieving oneself (women who have to do open defecation are twice as likely to face non-partner sexual violence compared to women with a household toilet)[24]—too many instances of being exposed and surrounded happen to both men and women. Combined with the aforementioned factors, this results in women and children (including young boys) getting assaulted frequently. As shared in previous segments, almost every woman I know has encountered pinching or groping in public transportations. Also, sexual violence, like many other crimes, does have an 'act of opportunity' aspect that can't be nullified (but can definitely be minimized). The Japan public transportation harassment of women discussed in Chapter 6, for example, shows this to be not nation-specific.

Second, this necessitated living in very close quarters does play into development of tolerance for lack of physical space, which percolates into broader behaviours.

....

If you leave a space measuring more than your forearm—from the tip of your finger to your elbow—between you and the person just ahead of you in a queue, such a gap is just not feasible to sustain. It shall get bridged or occupied within five minutes.[25]

The reason why a gap is not feasible to sustain is not always a lack of space available. Developed behavioural culture plays a much larger role (in Bengaluru malls and airport queues, where there definitely is more than arm's length available to leave in between, I have consistently found people coming and inserting themselves in whatever dignified minimal gap available when they don't need to. Women and men, often women, push themselves into

....

24 https://www.ncbi.nlm.nih.gov/pmc/articles/PMC5100257/
25 Damodar Mall, *Supermarketwala: Secrets to Winning Consumer India* (Gurgaon: Random House India, 2014).

these gaps to make a point of upping one over the next person waiting). It is necessitated at times but is cultivated always, and the tolerance for lack of physical space easily extrapolates into tolerance of misdemeanours.

Several women surveyed for this chapter told me that not only were they often told by men stuff like '*haath lag gaya tha* (hands touched accidentally)' when they were sure that the act was intentional; there were women who said stuff like 'Don't come out of home if you are so delicate' or '*ab itna crowding mein aur kya hoga* (what else will happen in such crowding)?'

Now, instances of the opposite nature (public humiliation and bashing of offenders for touching women inappropriately) are also aplenty and are worth mentioning, but what is important to note is the connection between development of tolerance for violation of personal space plus increased opportunities of violating and getting away with such violations furthers the already minimized need of seeking consent. This makes a non-consensual touching the path of least resistance.

WHEN YES MEANS NO: AZIZ ANSARI AND THE TRUE GREYS

Before we conclude, it is important to talk about the cases where lack of consent is not obvious. There is an impactful training that I had attended (almost accidentally) during my very first year at Cornell. At 23, I was still so naïve sexually that not only did I not understand the nuances of pleasure, but I also didn't understand that even during the process of lovemaking, it is OK to change your mind. Till then, I hadn't engaged in a sexual relationship beyond fondling and didn't understand the steps and the stages leading to penetration and climaxing. My exposure to porn (the usual mode of understanding sex in the late teenage and early 20s) was zero at that time. So I was very confused when the first-year undergrads enacted a sex scene on stage to drive home the point of consent (campus rape has long been an issue North American universities were grappling with).[26] The play was scandalous to sit through, and I made mental notes of things I would need to remember to look up or ask about. But one thing that got etched in my mind was that a ńo can be said at any point—or might not be said at all.

'Did I say no when you were inside me?' The girl playing the part asked.

'Yes...,' the boy remembered after persistent denying (the screen-play had the otherwise caring boyfriend demanding that he hadn't raped her while she had felt otherwise and had, therefore, ended the relationship). 'But you didn't say that before we started....'

'But I said no. And I said no before. I just didn't speak it. You would have known if you had paid attention—to me.... But I said no when you were inside me. You heard. Why didn't you stop?'

The play had ended reinforcing two key messages:

- A no is not always obvious. So paying close attention to your partner is vital.

- No matter when a no is heard (or sensed), the act needs to be stopped.

Another fellow author and women's rights activist whose columns I follow regularly has written about her growing up years. She has said that she had felt compelled to play along even when unwilling out of the fear of losing love. I know the same to be true for many other women, and possibly men. But a key distinction does need to be made here, and I attempt to do so below.

1. In the first case, if a no has been voiced, no matter at what stage (or there have been real, strong, non-verbal signs of discomfort), the leading partner needs to stop the act. On failing to do so, he or she needs to face consequences.

2. In the second case(s), if a partner was reluctant during the act but had not signalled discomfort through reasonably apparent

---

26 Hirshman, *Reckoning*.

queues, it can't be pursued as a matter of justice. The incident, albeit unfortunate, is an opportunity for education on the need to ensure that discomfort is voiced, and expectations are managed. Men (and women) need to be further educated on 'enthusiastic' sex and non-verbal signs of coerced or compelled participation. But they also need to learn to voice discomfort or not go along if they are not into it with full consent. The consequences of not doing so are on them.

For understanding the pillars of consent in as simplified a manner as possible, I turned to the Internet. In my scouting, a plethora of resources showed up. The four pillars published here are compiled from what I found to be most effective yet comprehensive.[27]

First, consent should be enthusiastic. It is often, especially for Indian women, a hard bridge to cross and a prime reason for perpetuation of misinformation. Women are trained to repress their sexuality and are shown to be desirable only if coy by the media. Both real and cultivated reservations come into play for a woman to be able to express if she really is into the act. Therefore, this is also the most important one. It is needful to enforce that if enthusiastic consent doesn't exist yet, it is required to hold back from the act.

Second, consent needs to be continuous. A yes can change to no at any point, even during the act, and a one-time sexual interaction doesn't amount to lifelong permission. This is a matter which is again used more as an excuse than a tool. Many men I interview on their view on consent failed to recognize that even though they had kissed the girl one time, or she had engaged in intercourse once, they didn't—through the mere enactment of the act—get a lifelong card of consent.

'Well, she has been OK with sex I know. So I didn't trust her when she said that she didn't want to do it anymore with me. She

27 https://feminisminindia.com/2016/07/26/sexual-consent-in-india/

was simply just mad.' It was a real answer from a friend who had confessed to coercing one of his girlfriends into sex multiple times after she had ended the relationship. 'We were like bunnies—we kept coming back to each other for sex.'

'So, she wanted sex? Even after you broke up?'

'Well … she always said no and tried to push me away, but she never said no to meeting. Why would she come to meet me in a private place if she really didn't want to continue the sex?'

I asked this friend the following: 'If she really wanted sex and she had had that relationship before—so obviously there isn't a shyness factor—she isn't a woman who needs to be convinced of her sexuality. So if you are in a private place and she really wants it, why wouldn't she just say yes instead of no?'

The thing is that it is time for men to stop interpreting the non-verbal cues of a yes when a woman says no and to concentrate on the non-verbal hints of a no when she is saying nothing. This brings me to the third point on consent: Consent can't be coerced.

The romanticized celebration of persuasion by Bollywood needs to be de-celebrated. This is where social movements like #MeToo play a role. For example, the famed Christmas song 'Baby It's Cold Outside'[28] was criticized post #MeToo for the coercion that is happening in the song. The woman, who wants to leave, is being forced to stay and eventually engage in physical lovemaking. In 2019, the song was remade with new lyrics, where the man deliberately voices his hearing, and appreciation, of the not so strong discontent expressed by the woman as she insists on leaving. He says that it is OK if she wants to leave, and he will love her anyway.[29]

---

28 https://en.wikipedia.org/wiki/Baby,_It%27s_Cold_Outside
29 https://www.billboard.com/articles/news/holiday/8543129/baby-its-cold-outside-2019-lyrical-transformation

Lastly, consent needs to be informed. Both partners need to be fully cognizant and aware of not only what they are getting into but also of the consequences of engaging in the act.

I asked a few teenage boys what they thought about this. 'You are scripting lovemaking' is what their opinion paraphrases into. 'I mean, if you love someone, why would you think of so many things?' said a 15-year-old from West Bengal. Love, therefore, needs to be not only dualized but also equalized for the next generations in India.

As we build towards a solution path with our understanding of global movements, national history and current on-the-ground realities, understanding and celebrating consent will be the foundation. Here are four prime reasons which emerge for India largely ignoring or misunderstanding consent.

1. **Historical:** Controlling women and viewing them as beings who shouldn't be in control of their own sexuality have been designed as a virtue for both men and women.

2. **Perpetuation of incorrect information (scriptures, symbolisms, popular narrations and Bollywood) combined with rigid family decorum that discourages dissent and dialogue:** Along with what was elaborately discussed above, most Indian families don't talk about sex, hide symbols of sexuality when it comes to the woman and suppress questions on sex.

3. **Lack of personal space and tolerance for invasion into privacy.** The concept of personal space is still quite foreign to indigenous societies and is quite so for India. More often than not, the need for privacy and boundary, therefore, is not comprehended or appreciated (Figure 5.1).

He went on to explain his logic. "I believe this is happening because our youth is being wrongly influenced by cinema and TV. I think that girls should be married at the age af 16, so that they have their husbands for their sexual needs, and don't need to go elsewhere. This way, rapes will not occur," said Singh. Notice that nowhere is the man responsible for raping a woman – it is

Source: https://www.youtube.com/watch?v=Pgom8LRF8hQ

Figure 5.1: Snapshot from Quint Video: Haryana's Rape Culture

4. **Reinforcement and legalization of entitlement.** Men believe sex to be a right, while women are providers who can want sex only within the boundaries of a marriage or when coerced by the right man.

Although connected and interdependent, an action plan targeted to each of these needs to be designed for the path forward.

CHAPTER 6

AFTER MeToo:
THE EVOLUTION

*On 15 October, actress Alyssa Milano suggested on
Twitter that anyone who had been 'sexually harassed or
assaulted' should reply to her Tweet with 'Me Too',
to demonstrate the scale of the problem. Half a million
people responded in the first 24 hours.*[1]

It is more than halfway into 2019 when I am starting this journey
of 'after MeToo'; the evolution of the movement would inevitably
have a year or more added to it. But I truly believe that from what
has transpired so far, the leitmotif will not change much. To explain
this, and to chalk up after MeToo as it stands in September 2019,
let me summarize the main points promptly and directly.

- #MeToo, three years after its breakout, can be called a global
  movement—yet not quite. A simple glance at the google
  trends data out of Me Too Rising[2] makes this abundantly clear.
  Although we will dive into the several adjacent campaigns
  (including #notyourhabibti (Palestine) and #BenDeNevin
  (Turkey)[3] and sub-movements around the world (e.g., increased
  awareness and uprisings against domestic violence[4] and gender

1 https://www.bbc.com/news/world-44045291
2 https://metoorising.withgoogle.com/
3 http://www.internationalviewpoint.org/spip.php?article5939
4 https://www.pri.org/stories/2018-07-13/he-likes-you-so-he-will-rape-you-paraguay-s-metoo

pay gap remedial actions), global MeToo is still very much in clusters and pockets. Countries such as Japan and South Korea lag far behind, while expansive segments of the world remain untouched and uninterested.

- #MeToo, irrespective of the country in consideration, is a segmented movement. Although there are quite some observations to be made on how the subsegments within the segment itself (aka Internet using, educated and predominantly working populations of the nations) vary, MeToo doesn't excite or effect all women of any nation even when taken out of the confines of its social media origin (referring to the #MeToo).

- Majority of #MeToo accusations, including the high-profile ones, will not be prosecuted. Or if prosecuted, it will lead to acquittals, except for the likes of Larry Nassar, where both the 'kind of harassment' and the 'number of accusers' (two key metrics that make prosecution of any crime easier) climaxed and converged. This is a key point that needs to be taught and talked about post MeToo, and I will do so with the help of experts in our action plan. But there is gold in the dust that is slowly settling. I have argued in the starting chapters that MeToo (and movements preceding or succeeding it) has a higher value for certain countries, and India is one of them. In this chapter, diving deeper into the distinction between the acquittals and dismissals, I will present this point again.

- #MeToo has increased dialogues on the prevalence of sexual harassment in the world either by creating awareness on how pervasive the issue is or by making the point that harassment is abuse and needn't be tolerated. It has shocked populations (especially men) in more developed and capitalized countries (including the USA and the UK), resulted in 'meh, everyone knows this so what's new unless you show me some action' for countries like India, Pakistan and Bangladesh (especially after the initial hype settled), and 'shit! this can be groundbreaking and life-ending at the same time' in the third group of countries

(Latin America, Lebanon and the Middle East). But it has brought harassment and gender gap in the 20th century to the forefront of global considerations. Backlash and follow-up actions line up, matching in intensity and temperament for each of these groupings.

• Last but not least, MeToo has many men questioning (with motivations ranging from true intent to drive change to merely self-preservation and staying out of trouble) on what they need to learn to avoid getting 'MeToo'd'. This again is quite segmented and can be grouped in national clusters (more in certain nations vs others) but should be seen as the real opportunity. After we review men's issues and MRMs (Chapter 8), the very vital need in this space (to not only ensure we prevent a backlash but also for social justice) will become apparent.

In a country where lodging a simple FIR is a cumbersome process, seeing a case on sexual harassment through is harassment in itself. Our government, laws and above all our society, don't make it easy.[5]

Let's tackle these points in the context of the two major fault lines of MeToo that were talked about right from its inception— the non-inclusion of all aka the 'evolution of the evolved' and 'the name and shame all you want but that's all you will be able to do' arguments. Both groups of nay-sayers do stay validated for the most part. But looking at the same Google trend report, of which there is a snapshot below, something else also becomes apparent. Two years out, MeToo has peaked from time to time, and cities with top hits have changed, but the baseline is still constant. There is no nadir to be noted yet. MeToo hasn't ended.

5 https://www.tribuneindia.com/news/spectrum/from-metoo-to-hetoo-not-guilty/807666.html

The Internet is teeming with articles from across the world on where MeToo stands today, and all of them outline sections (irrespective of the nation or region being discussed) that are excluded from the movement. So the point of 'non-inclusion of all segments' is like a dead horse in my opinion that needn't be beaten any further. Also, the point of 'limitation to certain segments of the population' about a movement originating via social media is like making a point on the ocean being wet. In Chapters 2 and 4, the segregation between segments in India, from ground realities to thoughts on MeToo (and gender rights in general), have been noted. The need here is to acknowledge this, not as a criticism, but as an opportunity, because this segregation is not because of MeToo. It has existed and is there despite MeToo.

Starting closest to home, in Pakistan, MeToo is criticized for not touching the most vulnerable of its segments,[6] including peasant women from Punjab, health workers (it is worth remembering that their vulnerability is comparable to that of social workers like Bhanwari Devi, minority sanitation workers, and domestic and informal sectors). Bangladesh is no different. Domestic workers, women in the ready-made garments sector, and other low-income segments, are the ones often abused and are at a higher risk persistently with no options. And they mostly lie out of the reach of MeToo till date.

Looking a bit farther into the continent of Africa, Lebanon outlines migrant domestic workers (especially those under the Kafala [sponsorship])[7] as especially vulnerable segments.

The theme that emerges of just these three snapshots, when overlapped over what we already outlined for India, is neither surprising nor hard to grasp. Socially disadvantaged sections are often the economically disadvantaged ones and vice versa. Lack

6 https://newrepublic.com/article/153355/making-metoo-work-pakistan
7 https://www.migrant-rights.org/2014/04/ethiopian-domestic-worker-disciplined-by-rape-in-lebanon/

of safety net worsens the problem of workplace sexual harassment (and this would be true of most socio-economic problems) for them, especially in nations trailing behind in resources. But what this also means is that solving a social problem and establishing protective infrastructure (even if the focus on the problem got magnified through a lens that had a limited field of view) have the potential to benefit those who are the most vulnerable. But it needs to be ensured that the sections are targeted through a granular understanding of the nuances that affect each subsegment. In the post-MeToo world, what is obvious but not acknowledged by the sceptics is that MeToo has helped in not only exposing the magnitude of the problem but also outlining the outliers. This presents opportunity for both global and local actions—an inadvertent but inevitable side effect of a global dialogue that sees such widespread interest. This is a key point, for this isn't easy to achieve and shouldn't be wasted.

Talking of outliers, anomalies and disappointments, another key theme that emerged for me while going through post-MeToo accounts and publications is the uncomfortable question of women supporting women. Should women be expected to support a cause merely on the merit of it being women-driven or about women? Why? Why not? We have visited this academically in the discussions on gender vs other (caste, family, political affiliation, religion, etc.) associations in previous segments. But there is need to explore this practically too. Sana Munir, the reclaimed author of *Unfettered Wings* (which incidentally was quoted by Sonali Bendre for having tales of women so inspiring that it helped her in her struggle with cancer), helped me understand how MeToo was looking in Pakistan vs in India. What she said about this is worth quoting here.

Women are encouraged to speak up, and they are supported by other women and some men. However, these women have to face a disastrous backlash from women and men as well, especially those who are clinging to a misogynistic mindset.

They demand 'proof', 'Why didn't you speak up earlier?' 'What are you gaining from it, money or fame?' 'Woman card', 'She is looking for attention,' whereas I feel that a moment of harassment is usually stolen in solitude, at a moment when a woman is not ready to film everything. A woman or girl touched inappropriately on the road cannot film it to gather proofs, nor can a woman in a meeting being stared at/touched gather proof. MeToo is a movement which allows women to vent, seek support and let other women know that it is okay to protest and talk about harassment. If the women speaking up late did not find a platform or the support to talk about it 'as soon as it occurred', then those women who are currently or might experience something later can feel that there is a support system to protest, speak up and get justice. It might expose what we all experience as women—gender-based harassment.

I cannot stress this enough. My book is full of examples, my interviews always have this statement in them: Misogyny and patriarchy cannot function and survive unless there are women to support it. Women must support other women, unconditionally. It's cliché and didactic maybe, but we desperately need sisterhood. A woman being battered at home cannot be beaten up if the other women in the house or the neighbourhood interfere. One knock, one report or one phone call to the police is all it takes. A woman in the office cannot be harassed if every woman working there stands by her. A man cannot touch, squeeze or grapple a woman on the road if she knows in her heart that when she screams and holds the man by the collar, she will be supported by other women on the road. We need to work on ourselves, and the men will learn to behave all on their own.

The point of women's role in patriarchy (and in the more defined context of backing women's movements or supporting women who come out) is a point to be pondered on (and does get pondered on with passionate arguments from both sides) in the larger context of feminism. It is not specifically related to MeToo. We will discuss in Chapter 7 if women can universally be expected to support women and the concept of 'covering' and 'co-opting' in the context of POSH. In the beginning chapters, through the recapitulation of history of women's movement, we have seen how women themselves have opposed the cause of women's suffrage and have time and again chosen other identities over gender. We have seen in earlier chapters how it happened again in 2020, thanks to socio-economic repression of certain segments of society dividing women's experience. But MeToo does offer the opportunity to look closely at the corollary of women not standing in support of the other women purely from the aspect of show of public support.

Let's take the examples of two very different countries on this point. In Bangladesh, when reality show participant Faria Shahrin came forward vocalizing how solicitation for sex is a routine ask in the entertainment industry,[8] an established actress came out with statements boxing Faria into a frame of 'why this could happen just to her' instead of offering a position of 'this should be looked into'. The point here is that although as many would argue, women shouldn't be expected to hold a 'female' position in female matters and rather a 'human' position for the sake of correctness and liberalization; they shouldn't be, by the same argument, obligated to take an 'anti' position either. They needn't come out, as they often do, as the prosecutor of the accuser. Holding a position of 'I don't know yet, but I will demand a probe into this and see through systemic improvements' or 'yes, this may be true or may be untrue, but that doesn't mean all men are bad or are abusers' is fair, neutral and rational. Faria's allegations (perpetuate 'the stereotype that women in the media industry have loose morals' and encourage comments like 'Who is this girl? Someone please give her some work so that this does not happen to her again') are not.

Similarly, in a heart-breaking account from Paraguay, Andrea Valobra (a singer, songwriter and victim of both IPV and sexual

8 https://www.thedailystar.net/star-weekend/opinion/news/why-metoo-not-happening-bangladesh-1648678

assault) depicts how she saw her mainstream career tank after she wrote and released a song called 'Ella' in an effort to use her platform for raising awareness on how common domestic violence is in Latin America. Andrea had grown up learning 'he likes you so he will rape you.'[9] Not surprising or shocking anymore to me as by the time I came across her account, women I knew and had talked to for this book from the region (e.g., Christie, who had been married into a Columbian family and has been quoted earlier) had made it abundantly clear to me that abuse by men is often not recognized as abuse (by men and women) and is rather seen as an essential part of cultural and societal functioning.

The result? As a blogger put in aptly in the context of the Faria account, 'When the women weren't standing up for their lot, the men too saw no reason to.'

It is abundantly clear in the after MeToo years that women issuing statements disparaging other women, staying silent or offering counter-argument defending abusers (I had the misfortune of listening live to such an interview broadcasted on NPR in the USA, where a close female friend of Brett Kavanaugh[10] gave an anti-account for Blasey Ford to support him) cause irreversible damage. As multiple bloggers outline, lack of support from women is a major cause of delayed systemic improvement or 'failure' of MeToo across the globe (Bangladesh, Pakistan,[11] the Middle East and Japan[12]). Recounting the Kavanaugh account, no one is

---

9 https://www.pri.org/stories/2018-07-13/he-likes-you-so-he-will-rape-you-paraguay-s-metoo

10 Associate Justice of the Supreme Court of the USA nominated by President Donald Trump and appointed in 2018. Christine Blasey Ford (and a couple of other women) accused Brett of sexually inappropriate conduct or assault. At the time of this writing, allegations remained unproven.

11 https://www.trtworld.com/opinion/metoo-a-failed-movement-in-pakistan-23030

12 https://www.pri.org/stories/2018-11-08/japan-sexual-harassment-isn-t-crime-women-who-say-metoo-are-targets

expecting women to be the judge, jury and prosecutor. The ask is not to believe that Kavanaugh is guilty before he is proven so. The ask is to say, 'It needs to be proven, but it needs to be looked into, for sexual and gender-based harassment is a widespread problem—a problem that is unacceptable and a problem against which we women at least will stand united.' The problem is that it's abundantly clear that even after MeToo, there are still a lot of women who need to be convinced of this. On the other hand, we have seen in the account of Bhanwari Devi (and the history of women's suffrage) what happens when women stand together and take public stances together.

Bringing the focus into the confines of a home, let's look at the other side of this coin. Often, the primary resource a victim (especially an under-age female victim) would confide in on abuse is another female. As we have discussed again and again, having women who either don't believe the accounts or believe the accounts but consider this justified and acceptable create new victims who will often either victimize or be okay with the victimization of other women.

Maitabi Banerjee, a blogger from Bengaluru I talked to, had put this well.

Chokhe dekheo kotha bole na, amar meye-r ki hobe (Even when they see it with their own eyes, they don't speak out (thinking) what will happen to my daughter). But the awareness, albeit in a limited sense, is higher now. My mother, for example, never talked about good touch, bad touch; I struggled all through it— dying again and again. Coming for family visits ... maybe I was fair ... or I dressed in shorts keeping up with my army colony ways even in Kolkata. It wasn't rape but definitely in Kolkata, during those visits, I was looked at differently. The abuse was galore and all coming from close quarters. See ... if you scream too close to a wall, it just hits you back. So there's no voice you know? No remedy. 'For Indian women, the biggest threat is their family members. Uncles. Cousins. And Indian women— mothers—are often the biggest propagators of abuse in the name of preservation of family honour.'

MeToo AND THE FRAMES: UNSEGMENTING THE SEGMENTS

Continuing the exploration of what lies excluded to identify opportunities through learnings, I want to cover next some elements that were a revelation—even surprise—to me (and to many others).

The nations which surprised the global community with slow or no participation despite the prevalence of sexual harassment, high Internet access and development (the combination otherwise deemed a winner for MeToo) are Japan and South Korea. I have visited Japan multiple times since 2014 for work (many times for extended periods), have very close Japanese friends and have multiple co-workers who are on an expat assignment in the nation. I am very familiar with Japanese workplace culture (my job was to manage Japanese corporate accounts my company sourced from). I also had Japanese men and women directly reporting to me (which made me privy to a deeper understanding of their lives, career aspirations and workplace challenges) and have professional close relationships with C-suite members of the corporate Japan community. Japan is a nation I deeply fell in love with. I was amazed at how people would carry trash with them for miles in crowded subways until a trash can is reached (post the nerve gas attack, Japan reduced trash cans and converted to mostly see-through bins) and how toilets play flushing sounds to ensure toilet noise doesn't reach the neighbouring stalls. But clichés apart, Japan and Japanese people also amazed me with the rare confluence of eastern priorities with capitalist principles in which the former drives forward efficiencies instead of inhibiting them. All that said, sexism did show up in many forms in the corporate Japan I experienced (e.g., tea and coffee server girls). Still, the fact that women would be socially boycotted, and that reporting sexual harassment would be criminalized, is not what I expected of a country that thrives on globalization and has law and order running like their superfast trains. But maybe I should have. I had come across the horrific account of Junko Furuta a few years back. What had happened to her is beyond comprehension, but what I should have noted is that it didn't give rise to post-2012-like movements in Japan. In fact, her family faced backlash for the social infamy caused to the assailant's families, and when I had asked one young woman I know closely (will leave her anonymous) on how something like this could have happened in Japan, everything in her response signalled an intent of preserving the polished, polite image Japan is known for and an embarrassment that I (a non-Japanese) had come to know of this event. There had been no pain, shock or shame. One read of Junko Furuta's plight (which I refuse to provide a reference to here but can be, of course, found easily on the Internet) will elucidate why this in itself is problematic.

Also, quite puzzling is the dichotomy in Japanese society around sex. There is enough out there for even the most disinterested of folks to be aware that Japan is one of the most sexless societies when it comes to marital sex. Yet it's one of the most extreme in experimentation and exploration of sex (from anime porn expressions and shocking viral trends of exposing random women by strangers pulling their skirts up to romantic date cafes where women can go just to be treated as dates by staff). There have been Netflix documentaries depicting how random and puzzling the completely contradictory subcultures around 'sex in Japan' are. But what about harassment? How does all this play into that?

Akemi Kannari (Akemi San to me) and Yajima Keiko are two senior women who have worked all their lives in corporate Japan. One of them is a mother to a teenage daughter, the other is childless by choice. The extent of discomfort around discussing topics concerning a sexual matter, even in the context of workplace harassment, is such that neither of them could even utter the words. We discussed gambling culture leading to children left alone in cars, vulnerable to attacks; groping risks in trains (well-known of Japan); and lack of any formal harassment prevention law and harassment being high in the workplace compared to the USA. All using indirect language, 'Men doing not nice things to a lady' and 'How can you tell your daughter something like this?' was Akemi San's genuine question to me when I discussed how I am teaching my daughter bad touch vs good touch—not very different from how my grandmother, or even my mother, would react in my childhood years if topics remotely sexual in nature got broached, even in most private of conversations.

Should it have been obvious that societies with such dichotomies would create the perfect storm of repression and objectification which could only result in 'hush' culture around harassment and rampant groping in trains? In retrospect, yes. I will explain why, when we deep dive into the factors that drive sexual abuse. But for here, this is another point to award to MeToo. Silence has hurt mostly females (that too vulnerable, underage females) for too long. As they dominate the Internet, movements like #MeToo serve to disperse shame with acceptance even in the most bashful of societies. Sex does exist. Human beings are sexual beings. Bad (or even good) men, and women, often do sexual things to unwilling participants. This needs to be acknowledged and addressed.

Another disappointing and discomforting learning for me was of the accounts of abuse by aid workers in the social work/non-profit segment. It is widely propagated that liberal thoughts and actions in one area promote overall liberal views. I have argued and cited references of this in earlier segments of this book, highlighting examples like the American Civil War and the fight for civil liberties leading to landmark victories in the USA for the women's rights movement. The history of social movements in India, up to the current discussion of how the 2012 gang rape served as India's MeToo and can be connected to several other signs of progress towards inclusion and equality (e.g., Section 377), supports this line of thought too. And it's believed to hold widely for the other side. Hard-line views are often harboured in groups. Although it doesn't mean that abusers are grouped into left or right, or can be found only in certain professions (we will come to this in detail in a bit), but I had assumed that at least people who choose to work in a segment that is low paying (and serve in high-risk areas) come with a certain level of awareness and decorum. I was once again grossly simplistic, uneducated and unaware. From reports of abuse by aid workers in Syria and Haiti to findings of systemic failures rooted deep within the biggest names in philanthropy, the segment is cluttered with abuse of the most vulnerable by the ones tasked to provide relief and rehabilitation.[13]

Japan and abuse in aid segment signal to the same thing: What triggers abuse, who is abused and who abuses are attempted to be framed again and again through findings, beliefs and perceptions. But it really can't be. The tenets of sexual harassment lie in two problem statements that are universal (sexual deprivation vs desire; and viewing of the opposite sex as inferior and/or merely objects). Through this work itself, while researching the past, present and future of harassment, diving into behaviours, studies and expert opinions across the world, I arrived at this unexpected (which some might call simplistic) realization on sexual violence. There are only two root causes. Everything else is a sub-modulator or an accelerator. And risk factors serve to worsen the statistics. The solution space, therefore, needs to have both universal and targeted actions through understanding of both the nuances and commonalities.

Talking of risk factors, in addition to bringing forward the worse affected, unexpected and excluded segments across the globe, MeToo has had the world wondering about the frames within a frame (e.g., a nation). India, possibly one of the most complex of nations in existence in the context of subnations within a nation, is the ideal candidate for studying this. The very precise to Indian factors (caste, class, mother state, Bollywood and such) have been dissected in detail in Chapters 4 and 5. Here, I present my findings on the more generic considerations applicable to any nation through India as a case in point, namely location, occupation, status (marital, economic and social) and age.

---

13 https://www.globalcitizen.org/en/content/sexual-abuse-aid-workers-syria-women-girls/

On location, comparing metros to villages or to second-tier cities, existence within an established and close-knit community seemed to emerge as the strongest modulator. Although cosmopolitan and globalized metros like Bengaluru do offer advantages (through infrastructure and freedom around certain choices such as exposure, clothing and mobility), what seemed to matter most is how close-knit, synergistic or evolved a community is.

For example, Mattie Milliken, a soft-spoken blonde woman from Tennessee, USA, who is residing in Bengaluru for fieldwork, says that most (not all) of apprehensions and words of cautions from her well-wishers about being a single woman in India stand dispersed, but she is aware that it is so because she is in Bengaluru.

> I have spent most of my time in Bangalore but also a few days in Delhi. Both cities are very modern and urbanized. I think my experience would have been significantly different in other parts of the country. I would not say that I have experienced any serious harassment in my time here, but I do feel quite vulnerable at times. Because I look different and I stand out, I am constantly being observed. I also feel that because I am a woman, there is added pressure regarding what I wear, where I go and who I am with. I have been followed a few times here and have had strangers (all men) come up to me on the street and ask me a lot of questions.

Piyusha Vir (also a single working woman originally from Delhi but working in Jharkhand at the time, teaching at village school) is someone I had approached specifically for my 'India vs Bharat' exploration with someone who has actually lived for extended time at the nation's capital and at a remote village. She had had this to say of location-based experiences of a single working woman.

> 'I felt safer in Jharkhand than in Delhi.' Maybe because it was a protected, or rather limited, environment. I mean, I can't speak of greater or entire Jharkhand, but this was a small village community where everyone knew of everyone. And my host family ... the street, shops there ... they were named after them.

So maybe that played into this. But no one looked at me when I walked the streets. I mean they will look once but they won't look at me or pay me attention to make me uncomfortable.

Maitabi Banerjee whom I have quoted earlier has had an upbringing in Army campuses. She has lived all around the nation but in a confined, protected atmosphere. Her experiences with abuse? At the hand of relatives, during family visits to Kolkata.

And, therefore, I re-state here the obvious, unfortunate, yet not surprising fact: Families don't offer the same protection within the confines of a home that communities offer out on their streets.

On coming back to the USA, within a month from my conversation with Maitabi, I had had a conversation with three of my close friends—all very independent, successful working women. The conversation had started around de-naturalization and demonization of sex by humans compared to what happens with animals. One of the women had shared her experience of a tour (which had showed breeding practices of seals) and asked if the higher amount of pain we humans attach to sexual assaults have to do with just higher intelligence, or is it because of a stigma attached through social conditioning. She had brought this up in the context of her experience with her cousin, who, when they were both young, had touched her inappropriately repeatedly. The other women had immediately chimed in. Although we all had varied opinions on the original point, we all had one thing in common—male relative(s) (or contact(s)) in our childhood who had been inappropriate and abusive. As one of them put it: '*Sab family mein at least ek kamina to hota hi hain bachpan mein*' (every family has at least one vile individual in your childhood).'

Another example on the point of microcosms of safety created by communities within a city, town or even village came forward in my conversation with Mr Roopinder Singh—a renowned journalist, author and senior associate editor at *The Tribune*, who has mentored me often. In a cordial catch-up session, it came up that he had grown up mostly in women's college campuses (from

Amritsar to Patiala), given his mother's occupation as principal and vice-chancellor of women's colleges in Punjab. I asked him about the life of a man in women's colleges and his opinion of women's status in India. He has said,

> I have given talks on this in the west and have argued with them. I have said to women there, *'Feminism aap ke yahan to kabhi aayi nahin; asli feminism is in India'* (You have never had feminism come here; actual feminism is there in India). Yes, we have problems. We have a frame we are boxed in because patriarchy is in our bones.

This is where I had to pause my notes to look at the man I respect so much and wonder, from how he said it, if he intends to consider patriarchy therefore as a norm. Accepted and acceptable. But that could very possibly be just my interpretation. He had continued,

> Caste is another big framework. *Abhi tak hum usse nikal nahin paye* (We still haven't been able to come out of it). Religious prosecution—legal gridlock—we have these. Still, 'we might objectify or deity-fy but we have vice-chancellors, prime ministers who are women for ages—*America aaj tak nahin kar paya* (American couldn't do it even today).' *Britain main academia mein upar aane hi nahin dete* (Britain doesn't even let women come up in academia). America does in academia but reluctantly.

Yes, I agreed with him. But is that enough to make a statement on the status of women and their societal position across the spectrum? Mr Singh was adamant.

> I can say absolutely so. Why do I say this? Because my mother was educated in the 1940s. She lived in a boarding school, studied in a co-ed college in Lahore in those days. So our tradition of women getting educated is an old one. Indian women have been able to carve out more room in domestic finances than in the West. But the beauty of our feminism is such that she lets the men think that they are in control. We don't go into direct confrontation.

What came about in my conversations with activists in India is shared in the other chapters, as have been accounts out of times of conflict. Before MeToo or after, the other side of community is when a community turns on women under the stronghold of misguided beliefs and loyalties.

I am not trying to make a point here on Mr Singh's views on feminism and status of women being right or wrong, or insinuate that his views are 'affected' because of isolation. Nothing can be further from the truth for Mr Singh, as through his occupation and his achievements, he has been privy to a global status and understanding which very few are. I am merely planting seeds here for considerations (upbringing, generation, gender and point of view) that are worth reflecting upon. Mr Singh has had a strong female role model in his mother; is a member of an elite, educated and economically privileged community; and is from a generation and religion of 'respect', pride and 'reservation'. He is also from Chandigarh, which is the city I will come to next.

Nonika Singh (Assistant Editor, in charge of *The Tribune Lifestyle*), Sarika Sharma (Reporter, *The Tribune*) and Geetu Vaid (Senior Editor, *The Tribune*) are highly accomplished women in the blessed city of Chandigarh. I call Chandigarh blessed not for the fact that Chandigarh is where my husband is from and where I enjoy the most peaceful vacation weeks seeping lassis, rolling in boisterous family gatherings and strolling by the Sukhna Lake with my father-in-law. It's because of all the places I have lived in my life across the globe, I have found Chandigarh to be the most sheltered. If an entire city could be a microcosm, Chandigarh would be it. 'Elitist' in a way as Nonika calls it, but not quite, for the sheltering here comes (in my opinion) more from the synergy between folks not very dissimilar from each other forming units, than from economic status. The latter does play a role, for poverty is not very visible in Chandigarh. Service sector city, the breeding ground of roadies and more traveling in personal cars (until the recent Uber expansion) vs in public transportation define Chandigarh.

I focused on Chandigarh to zero in on a baseline for women's safety (pin code wise) in India. In my conversations, I heard 'the South is safer than the North', 'don't want to ever end up in Bihar' and 'Mumbai is much safer than Delhi' again and again. I also heard that Chandigarh is really more a community than a city. Chandigarh also fits the bill of having both infrastructure and ecosystem (read a manageable amount of population, systemization and a higher-quality city living). Yet both Nonika and Sarika's responses when I asked about their experience with abuse in Chandigarh, surprised me. I had expected to hear 'less' maybe, but not 'none'.

Nothing happened to me. Definitely not in the workplace. See, Chandigarh is very close-knit and protected. Only four major English newspapers here and everyone knows everyone. Yeah, there are some matters we heard—like in *The Indian Express*, accusations against this one person. But definitely no personal experience.

—Sarika Sharma

Chandigarh is a little bit elitist. Things that are so common in Ludhiana, for example, are not common here. In the workplace also, I can't quote any personal experience. At best, harassment is someone liking someone ... maybe. Like the actress who said he raped me with his eyes. But see, I don't venture out exposed and have lived mostly protected. But I am fearful and protective for my daughter. I don't let her travel unaccompanied. I am sure in metros it will be very different. 'Figures tell a different story though, if you look at the crime statistics. So it's not that it's a very safe city for everyone, it's only for people who have certain power and privilege.'

—Nonika Singh

Nonika's last line has the most important nugget for me. To wrap up the location vs safety conversations, I present my discussion with Geetu Vaid to make my next point: Even within communities, in any city, a woman's experience is defined by her marital status.

Geetu Vaid (Geetu Di to me) lost her husband when her son was a pre-teen. She raised him as a single mother while raising herself through the ranks of journalism. I shared with her what Mr Singh, Nonika and Sarika had shared and repeated my question. Did she think it mattered, where a woman was?

Look if we are talking about MeToo or sexual harassment, this is one platform where East and West are the same—maybe barring the cultural differences. The point that everyone forgets, MeToo or no MeToo, is that the way the cases have been dealt with is not much different.

In a personal domain, *city (Chandigarh) ka culture matter nahin karta* (The culture of the city doesn't matter). Yes, of course, there have been advances. And the thing is that you can't call it out every day. 'That is the big problem with harassment. You get labelled. So when you speak up, you have to be ready that this is the first and last time you can speak up.'

In my personal experience too, I have observed this in every aspect of a woman's (and even a man's) being. This is not just true for harassment. You get labelled by calling out—'Feminist', *'Jhanda leke khade ho jaoge phir se'* (you will just be up in arms on anything) or 'has a problem of making a mountain out of a molehill'. But the kind of labelling Geetu Di was speaking of is a whole another game (and something I had missed to consider as a key factor for speaking out until she mentioned it), especially in the matter of workplace sexual harassment. In the Drew Dixon case study in Chapter 2, for example, Dixon experienced sexual harassment at two different companies with two different, extremely powerful supervisors. She wasn't someone who was powerless or without means herself. Yet she couldn't come forward until MeToo had happened. In the USA, MeToo has softened the ground enough that Dixon was believed both times. In India, MeToo has softened the ground too, but for a victim to be believed just once.

Geetu Di had added,

> 'The *Tehelka* girl, for example. She can't get the same mileage even if this happens with her the second time. No one can guarantee that second time this will not happen. But the second time she can't speak up. Because then it will be like why does it happen to only her? So when she speaks up, she has to remember that she has only this one chance.' Take the example of Monica Lewinsky or Rupan Deol Bajaj. See how things went for them. Deol Bajaj is still an exception and extraordinary and had quite some support and network ... but still.

At this part of the conversation, I was reminded of an earlier interview where it was anonymously shared with me that the reputation of K. P. S. Gill wasn't unknown in the least, both before and after Ms Bajaj's ordeal.

> *I had interviewed him, and I was instructed by the facilitator*
> *that* **shaam ko nahin milna aur ghar pe nahin milna**
> *(don't meet him in the evening and don't meet him at his home).*
> —*Anonymous*

As we have seen in the Bajaj vs Gill case study, Mr Gill, until and after his death, was treated as a hero, not an abuser. The punishment meted to him for the assault on Ms Bajaj was looked at as an unfortunate blemish (on him, and the nation). So well beyond the debate of 'proving' and 'due process' lies an entire battlefield of 'so what'. A mindset shift of 'unaccepting the unacceptable' is not guaranteed with process, prosecution or conviction. Additionally, we have already discussed some and will discuss more what a victory in court entails and why it is (as of 2020) near impossible in most of the cases. These two points are important to deliberate on again and again as we languish around the 'so what MeToo happened, people are getting off scot-free' thought.

The point on marital status in India was emphasized upon by Mattie too. She had shared how being a single woman presented her with additional concerns. She had said,

From what I have heard, it is quite difficult being a single woman in India due to societal pressure—especially if your family is of a lower socio-economic status. Most of the single women I know here still live with their parents and feel burdened to get married. I think my experience as a foreigner would be quite different, but I do think I would have less respect. One of my friends travelling with me is married and whenever someone finds that out, that automatically respect her and look at her as a "real" adult.

Next comes the employment sector question (i.e., safe vs unsafe professions). What came up again and again is how media, hospitality and entertainment are particularly 'bad' with objectifying women and therefore, expectedly, breeding grounds of both abuse and women who 'can be abused'. Transcribing these accounts (which I found to be primarily beliefs), I couldn't help but confront the question of academia.

I had grown up learning that teaching is a good, respectable and acceptable profession for women. My mother was a teacher and often during dinner table discussions, it would come up how aeronautical engineering or mechanical engineering would be disastrous disciplines to pursue as they would lead to unemployment for a woman, unless she was interested in teaching. My father, who retired as a senior official from Oil and Natural Gas Corporation (ONGC), often stated that he too wouldn't hire women field engineers in certain roles out of concern for their safety. And anytime there was a discussion on whether there could be a career from pursuing a subject, 'Well, you could always teach—that's a good profession for women everywhere' would be offered by mentors, professors and relations alike. But Raya Sarkar's list of folks in academia, and the debacle following, shouldn't have been surprising to anyone who has spent some years pursuing higher education in some of the most respected institutions in the country.[14] Female graduate students

14 http://theladiesfinger.com/raya-sarkar-list-of-sexual-harassment-accused-academics/

are easy targets, and those who criticize 'naming and shaming' for being anarchical and un-verifiable forget that most universities and academic institutions don't practise what they preach on due process. Neither do they put stuff on paper when concerns are bought forward to facilitate effective prevention or prosecution. As I have stated in earlier chapters (and in the K. P. S. Gill example above), the easier route is corridor know-how, avoidance, protectionism and tolerance. It is worth adding here that I don't think institutions elsewhere have a right to claim a higher ground either. It has been discussed in the context of the Larry Nassar example how premium universities fail their students again and again. On a personal front, one of the first things that shocked me in Cornell was walking in accidentally into the office of the then head of the Chemistry department and overhear him discussing the 'nice tits' of an undergraduate with an associate.

So a multitude of factors play into the drawing of a frame even within the 'narrowed' segment of urban working women: from skin colour and nationality (white), marital status, who knows you and how known you are in the community, to what she is expected to be based on other systemized segregations (profession, caste and class). And these play into not only who gets harassed and how, but also into the response to her harassment.

However, higher frequency of instances and behavioural expectations in the context of certain professions can't be completely discounted. One of the things that we all have heard I am sure on the Tanushree Dutta case, for example, is how being in the 'profession' requires some tolerance because of the expectation of exposure to certain behaviours. Piyusha Vir, whom I have quoted earlier, had posted post MeToo about leaving the field of hospitality and moving into teaching, citing propensity to harassment as the key reason. This is what she had to say:

The stereotype is more enhanced in the service industry (hospitality included). Women are expected to look a certain way and expected to be just that. Two examples come to mind, which, although not harassment, might help explain this point. One is from a male colleague, who, during my year of working at the front desk, had stated that all I need to do is just stand there and look good. Another is from another woman, during the days of my working in JW Marriott Mumbai, which exemplified how we women always pitch ourselves against each other, more so in certain industries than other.

The point of professional insecurities amplifying among women (and men—but we will come to that later) post MeToo is also universal. Quite a few senior women in my own network in corporate America have expressed the downside of this 'hype'. It would discourage men from mentoring or sponsoring women, they say, in an already-difficult environment for advancement. Geetu Di placed yet another consideration into this maze.

The other aspect to deal with is ambition. How are you going to deal with this in a scenario where others are willing to go along? Maybe even not for any agenda—maybe just because of higher tolerance. Or ignorance. *Bhai yehi joke to maine usske saath bhi crack kiya* (The same joke I cracked with the other woman too), she didn't have a problem.

She had hit a nail on its head. This was quite what my life had looked like right after MeToo in Chandler (Arizona) parties. My husband started a joke on 'HeToo' for any time someone would bump against him, and barring one male friend, no one else was sensitized to understand why I found it to be quite offensive when the men (and women) in the room trivialized non-consensual physical touch as 'no big deal unless it crossed a certain "base"'.[15]

In a workplace setting, many women don't find it appropriate to point out (let alone be offended by) insensitive or uncomfortable comments for the fear of exclusion. And exclusion is not just from

---

15 https://www.equalrights.org/legal-help/know-your-rights/sexual-harassment-at-work/

a path to promotion or from an opportunity. It can also be (and often is) from the network which more often than not is male dominated in sectors such as tech, pharma and finance (after work, happy hours and golf outings are not fun with a 'spoilsport' who is too rigid). As Gloria Feldt puts it: 'The danger of falling right out of sexual harassment into sexual discrimination is real.'[16]

While checking off the factor list, I found age—rather generation— to be playing a role. Through the conversations I had with men and women over 45 years of age, there was a definite emergence of the theme of higher faith in Indian feminism in the older age groups vs that in millennials. The prevalence of dialogue seems to be mostly appreciated however, with a caution on 'too much feminism' and 'Western feminism' taking over.

These sentiments matched what Mona Sengupta (previously a journalist with *The Telegraph*, *The Statesman* and Singapore Press Holdings, currently an entrepreneur and socialite, and one of the rare women I spoke to who had said that they hadn't faced sexual harassment, either through personal experience or of others) had to say:

> During our youth, women were definitely not forthcoming, and talking about sexual harassment was a taboo or women were embarrassed to speak about these issues. So it's good to see MeToo taking off but frankly, I have no personal expectation other than women finding a platform to speak about their plight.

MEN GETTING MeToo'D

After MeToo, more and more men are asking questions about sexual harassment and appropriate behaviour at the workplace and beyond. Whether this is here to stay only time can tell. But for now, this is a fact. A lot of the 'real good' (for those who are counting measurable actions out of the movement) comes

---

16 https://time.com/5120607/companies-leadership-metoo-era/

from endeavours that stem out of increased male intent towards solving a predominantly gender-biased problem, especially at workplaces around the world. As Akemi San had put it: 'Yes, there is no police to go to, but I work now for a very Japanese company, and now even we have to take training every year on appropriate behaviour. On moral behaviour. Men take it. So it is getting better.'

Another aspect of increasing male awareness is the trickle-down reduction of objectifying behaviour. As one article puts it, 'Most men are not abusive, but most have probably engaged in sexist, inappropriate jokes and banter and in behavior that perpetuates the objectification of women because they couldn't see how it is harmful.' As more and more men ask questions of their own behaviour, even if in clusters, culture change is initiated.

It's much easier to change laws than to change the culture.
—*Gloria Feldt*

However, a lot of questions are yet to be answered, especially in a way in which it'd make sense to a wider audience of men coming from varied experiences, social conditioning and levels of gender sensitization. It's not an option to leave them behind. And really, they are the ones who should be talked to. As mentioned earlier, I heard many senior women in corporate America express views on how MeToo will hinder career aspirations of young women (even in public events, my non-profit organized or participated in on workplace sexual harassment). It was also expressed that women mostly use such advances for convenience until it's not convenient anymore and that this factor is not getting acknowledged anywhere. Some men said that they were just going to stay clear of women in the workplace (reminding me of the IIT faculty who refused to take female graduate students in his group fearing unnecessary 'trouble' and the friend whose law-enforcement male colleagues joke on how they don't want to be 'MeToo'd—examples that I have discussed in previous chapters).

One school of thought looks at this to be a simple problem. For example, Gloria herself, who is developing a workplace programme that is getting adopted by corporates on language and dialogue and is the founder of Take the Lead,[17] didn't think that this was rocket science.

'What do you think is a path forward to ensure objectivity (not all claims of 'too far' or 'convenience' or 'misunderstandings' are outrageous maybe) and education and to be an effective counter towards workplace sexual harassment?' I had asked Gloria.

Her answer was:

'Let's get real. All men need to do to avoid being "MeToo'd" is to remember what they learned in kindergarten about how to treat every one of any gender.' Be respectful of other people's property, listen when they speak and keep your hands to yourself for example. How hard is that?

But is it really that simple? No. 'Undoubtedly the workplace is better for women than it was three or five years ago,' MSNBC quotes,[18] speaking primarily of the USA. In India, and in many parts of the world, there are mountains to be moved before such a conclusion can be arrived at. But the same article goes on to report on a Match.com survey which had found over 50 per cent of the men surveyed in the USA quoting that they have changed their behaviour post MeToo and had become more mindful. And this, I found to be mostly true for India too—whether for the wrong or right reasons (i.e. 'yes, women are worth respecting' or 'I just want to stay out of trouble and not get caught')—when it came to actions in the workplace. Listing case-by-case instances and devising behaviour guideline for men (and women), gender interaction trainings (starting with pre-teen and teen males) and

---

17 https://www.taketheleadwomen.com/
18 https://www.nbcnews.com/better/lifestyle/men-sound-metoo-i-definitely-look-back-cringe-ncna1054886

continued sensitization of the legal systems should be focused on as next steps. But the biggest challenge that India needs to tackle to set itself on a post-MeToo success path is of balancing its own expectations out of MeToo.

We Indians are impatient and quick pessimists. It was abundantly clear in the conversations I had with men and women from across the length and breadth of the country that India didn't have the same enthusiasm about MeToo in 2019 as some of the other nations of the world. Indian onset (or rather peaking) with Tanushree Dutta coming out was late, but the interest seemed to have fizzled already. We went from despair to hope and back to despair fast. Although accusations against Anurag Kashyap in 2020 brought the words (MeToo) back again, it didn't necessarily bring back the momentum. For that, the Hathras gang rape can be credited, just like Nirbhaya in 2012, and Priyanka Reddy in 2019. What happens in the following years needs to be seen before we can conclude.

In India, celebrities have a stronger voice than intellectuals or academicians. 'SRK (Shah Rukh Khan) coming out and saying one line will have more effect than Indira Jaising screaming for a month.'
—*Maitabi Banerjee*

Let me quote Arpita Banerjee, a tech professional in Bengaluru, for example. She said,

'Just like any other thing, this will be abused. And just because we know it will be abused—judges, everyone, knows it will be abused—judges will take longer to deliberate.' So, on a discussion level, it is good. And good that it has come out of the closet—but it will always be more for the power corridors.

Maitabi, whom I have quoted earlier and who had been elated about MeToo until the news of investigation being dropped against Nana Patekar broke, was visibly dejected in just a few months. Her words were:

'Yes, initially I too thought why is she coming out now? Why after so long? But then I could see my thought changing to "at least she came out!"' So you know, yes, something must have built up. Her coming out, it offered ... it led to a route out for the suffocation that had built up from not being able to speak up for so long on sexual abuse. Remember the Park Street victim? Was she drinking all day ... all those questions.... This suffocation propelled the movement. That I had had this happen to MeToo, but I couldn't come out.

Mattie, who had said that she had felt her life improving in the USA post MeToo (and saw the same with her friends too), had been somewhat awkward when asked about the same in the context of MeToo and India. She had said,

The MeToo movement was very powerful to me as it opened my eyes to how big the problem of sexual assault is in the USA. The MeToo movement has also been labelled as a leftist topic, which has limited the impact on the overall society. I don't know if India is different before and after MeToo, I guess I don't know much about MeToo in India.

The contrasts in her answers when asked about MeToo and its effect on her life (which would be mostly in the USA) vs MeToo and India stood out to me. And let me recapitulate that although Mattie isn't Indian, she has been living in India and interacting regularly with Indian women in a city like Bengaluru where platforms, dialogues and events on gender and MeToo are a galore.

Some of these opinions and the underlying pessimism about whether MeToo (or anything really) can ever be effective in ushering in gender parity in India have valid reasons of being. The deep-rooted patriarchy safely guarded by propping up of 'culture' bamboo poles around it; and women doing the propping in the name of culture is the major one of those reasons.

Think about *Kabir Singh,* the movie. I wrote criticism for that and women in scores came after me. *Matlab kya nikale isska* (What should we make of this)? That relationship! And people are liking it. Maybe they are like that or they are caught in relationships like that? In general, we say Indian men are better, no? They care about family. But maybe the man–woman relationship in India is still skewed? Maybe women place much more value on relationship vs anything else?[19]

—Nonika Singh

India, fiercely proud as a nation even of its shortcomings, wanting its own revolution, is another.

The framework we have for reference for feminism is a Western one. There needs to be a counter for that through our culture. What changed the conscience of the country is not MeToo. The only 'movement' I have seen really is in Delhi. After Nirbhaya. I remember, we were there—and early morning—in a bus stand, there were these young boys really holding placard. That is what mattered.

—Roopinder Singh

I do wholeheartedly agree with Mr Singh on the significance of the Nirbhaya case for India. As stated earlier, the ground building that the civil rights movement is often credited with for wake of feminism in the USA should be attributed to the Nirbhaya incident for India (and on that note, we should stop referring to the same as the 'Nirbhaya' incident and start mentioning 'Jyoti Singh Pandey'). But the hopefulness around MeToo is not as low, nor were people as dismissive, in the USA. In my daily speaking to the women here, the disappointments around the acquittals are lower compared too 'thank god this happened' and 'this will reveal cracks that need to be fixed to disprove wrongful accusations' sentiments.

19 https://www.tribuneindia.com/news/movie-reviews/movie-review-kabir-singh/791060.html

The most important reason, however, lies within the dismissals/ acquittals themselves which show the higher inefficiencies in the Indian handling of sexual harassment accusations and the resulting lack of faith in law and order. Let's contrast the Nana Patekar 'clean chit' reports to the 'Kevin Spacey acquittal'. Up to the time of writing this (few months past the reported closure report filing),[20] all I could find on the 'why' for the Nana Patekar case dismissal was 'lack of evidence and hence inability to continue the investigation'. On looking up Kevin Spacey, however, in a few seconds, it comes out that the key witness claimed the fifth amendment of the US Constitution (which grants the right to not self-incriminate) following the disappearance of the cell phone which would be a piece of key evidence. One read through even the most basic of the reports available on the case makes it evident that reasons for dismissal could be quite valid. Such satisfaction, alas, is often not an option for cases in India. Reports and statements, whether by committees, bodies (e.g., CINTAA) or the police, often don't include confidence-inducing specifics that show due diligence. Of course, every nation has its missteps (let's remember the Larry Nassar first-time investigation 10 years prior to his getting indicted which was discussed in Chapter 1). But our systems and infrastructure have wider rooms for improvement and higher loads—another area that can benefit from a global movement that offers opportunities for direct comparisons.

MeToo AND THE MEAT

In the world post MeToo, acquittals are to be expected, dialogues are ongoing and interest is still on (globally). Both the lines that divide and the points that unite lie exposed across the world on sexual harassment. This offers tremendous opportunities. But what are some specific achievements that can be quantified and listed?

---

20 https://economictimes.indiatimes.com/magazines/panache/tanushree-dutta-nana-patekar-case-police-files-closure-report-saying-not-enough-evidence-against-actor/articleshow/69770176.cms

- 'Even the nations lagging, disinterested or disenchanted already have their success stories.' In Pakistan, for example, a first of a kind policy against sexual harassment was put together for the educational institutes through the collaboration of multiple women's rights groups[21] as a direct result of increased dialogue and outrage post MeToo. Similar examples emerge out of Japan, Latin America and the Middle East.

- Workplace policy refinement, training, sensitization programmes, and diversity and inclusion initiatives are getting speared off in most global corporations, either as directly sponsored initiatives or in support of government-issued polices.

- Time's Up,[22] as of 2018, had raised more than $22 million for the legal defence fund and more than 800 volunteer lawyers. Advocacy for policy change and funding for legal battles are key enablers of prevention and prosecution. This is not an achievement to be discounted, even if mired with execution road bumps.

The indictments, downfalls and exits (from resignations to expulsions) have been catalogued and discussed in detail in earlier segments and hence are left out of the list here.

For summing up the concerns, considerations and potential of MeToo, I had posed the question whether MeToo is destined for greater things or is it on death leg already (to myself and to many others). However, before and after are nuanced and fluid, and waves are continuous.

Do you think MeToo will live and if yes, how?
Or is it on its death leg?
It all depends on us.
—Gloria Feldt

---

21 https://newrepublic.com/article/153355/making-metoo-work-pakistan
22 https://en.wikipedia.org/wiki/Time%27s_Up_(movement)

CHAPTER 7

THE ALL OR NOTHING GAME

To meet the legal definition of harassment, the conduct in question has to be severe or pervasive, it doesn't have to be both.

—*Workplace harassment, USA*

In 2012, in a lawsuit filed in San Francisco County Superior Court, Ellen Pao[1] (investor and activist, former Reddit CEO) accused Kleiner Perkins, her former employer, of sexual discrimination. The case generated unprecedented interest. The parties involved weren't trivial (Kleiner Perkins is one of Silicon Valley's most famous venture capital firms where Pao was a former partner and Pao's clout wasn't insignificant either). The Valley (and corporate ecosystems all around the USA) held breath. The outcome was expected to be groundbreaking and trendsetting, no matter which way the verdict went.

Possibly, a bit more context on this and corporate America is needed here to explain the 'why so' and, more importantly, the relevance of this case here as a case study. In very simple terms, forsaking all diplomacy, gender bias and discrimination is commonplace, despite all kinds of diversity initiatives and inclusion goals in corporate America (and the world). However, it is impossible to prove legally. Reason?

1 https://en.wikipedia.org/wiki/Ellen_Pao

Most 'laws' in the corporate workplaces for hiring, retention and advancements are actually guidelines. Having been a manager myself here, I can outline this first-hand—most actions can be justified in retrospect. In this chapter, starting with discrimination and then moving on to harassment, I will attempt to establish that the letter of the law can be taken care of easily. And the spirit? Well, that's good to debate but hard to prove. Silicon Valley is notorious for gender un-parity—from Uber[2] to Google[3] to Facebook.[4] Most of the tech industry, especially tech C-suites, are male-dominated,[5] and problem statements such as sexual harassment and sexual discrimination are too subtle and subjective.

It's not always targeted malice that is behind behaviours and practices. Habit, culture, lack of consequence/call-out and, there-fore, ignorance, are the beasts leading the charge with real culprits (relatively lesser in number if I may dare claim) riding the flux. Let me explain with an example.

Say in a Fortune 500 company, there is one woman in an otherwise all-male team. She misses most of the social networking opportunities either due to a difference in preferences (she doesn't do locker room talks or Sunday night football) or because of personal obligations (she needs to be home at happy hour, golfing or late dinner times). She slowly realizes that even though her co-workers are cordial and accommodating, she doesn't share the same rapport they have with each other. She continues to perform well, however, gets appropriately rewarded and, in general, finds no reason to complain. She chooses to ignore (or, more accurately, has no choice but to ignore) the tad bit of sadness she feels during

2 https://thinkprogress.org/uber-diversity-problem-7cf5e164f528/
3 https://www.nytimes.com/2017/08/07/business/google-women-engineer-fired-memo.html
4 https://www.cnet.com/news/facebooks-so-white-and-male-leadership-highlights-bigger-diversity-issue/
5 https://www.forbes.com/sites/naomicahn/2021/02/19/womens-status-and-pay-in-the-c-suite--new-Study/

non-work conversations in which she feels her participation is superficial.

Then, she and her co-worker (male) get into a disagreement with their senior director (let's assume it to be just a difference of opinion—no right or wrong). While she follows protocols and uses learned behaviours (constructive confrontation, bringing it up in meetings, sharing her opinion one-on-one, using factsheets, justifications and 'influencing language' taught for corporate effectiveness), her male colleague just knows (like you would for your best friend) how to place his opinion in the director's ears without having to go through such pain or, more importantly, without needing to shine an unfavourable light on himself. He is successful in this because both he and the director speak the same 'language'.

A note here for clarification (because I have seen this getting confused): I am not claiming here that no female can know this 'language' because of her gender (many females do). Or that the 'language' by the virtue of being one that the male characters in this example speak is a 'male' language. Neither am I placing an argument on the 'language' being right, or wrong, or more, or less effective for corporate functioning. I am merely establishing that there is a language of the band that most (but not all) members of the band tune in to and use more effectively. Several factors play into this (including demographic and behavioural similarities) which are outside of available scripts. You either fit in and have higher ease with difficult conversations and situations or function well but have only guided protocols to abide by. This language is inherently not diverse in most corporate work environments—certain segments like C-suites being worse than others—and that puts women (and other minorities) at a disadvantage.

So the director decides to follow his own path on the given matter. But in the days to come, the woman senses things getting a bit more difficult for her. She is not able to put an actual finger on it. On asking for official reports on say a position that she gets passed for, she finds smoking guns but none with bullets. 'The job was awarded to the better candidate following corporate guidelines, candidate fit was assessed on not just hard skills but also soft ones—like ability to influence.' In her performance reviews, she might find things like 'developing a better rapport with stakeholders will result in achieving results more effectively' suggested or 'needs to continue developing people and influencing skills' documented—nothing punishable by the law or nothing to even raise eyebrows, but severely disadvantageous to her career.

This example has multiple variations that most women have experienced. From getting a job, performing in a job and handling confrontations in the job to advancing in a job and getting sponsored for upward positions. Women have said that they believe that their male counterparts are forgiven for gaffes and career blunders easily while they have an impossible time re-establishing confidence and trust. Most women don't understand how to remedy these situations. If they confront, they are called confrontational. If they conform, they are labelled weak or impassionate. Discrimination is real, so is retaliation, and more often than not there is a gender component.[6] This is why, as we have seen in the earlier chapters, and will see in the next, that POSH comes under the equal employment opportunity scope and is handled under civil rights or labour laws. Discrimination (and/or retaliation) is mostly impossible to prove though—in a court and otherwise (read internally)—but is common. In the Drew Dixon account shared in Chapter 2, Dixon said that discrimination and retaliation, post sexual harassment and her rejection of the advances, caused her to realize that she couldn't have a career and she left the industry altogether.

---

6 On discrimination too, as we have seen, intersectionality and other variables playing a bigger role (e.g., caste or religion in India and race in the USA) comes up as a point. But gender remains the biggest common denominator that both differentiates (women vs men) and groups (behavioural expectations and experiences) the global human population.

*They literally have to grab your breast to be fired or
even censored for wrongdoing.*

*—Heather Mattisson, Corporate HR Worker,
USA (speaking on retaliation and harassment)*

In the Pao case, for example, her accusation of 'sooner promotions of male colleagues with a similar profile who had joined the firm after her' is not illegal and could be perfectly justified by a well-prepared corporate legal team. The 'joining later but getting promoted sooner' could be rightfully blasted with the meritocracy argument, and 'the similar or equivalent profile' would fall under 'soft skills' or 'hard to objectively measure but they had it' explanations. It is not discrimination just because it happened. It is discrimination only if it can be proved that it happened to her because she is a woman. What can be proved under most circumstances is that it happened to her and that she is a woman or, at most, this happened to only her, a woman. Besides, as it happened in the Pao case, it can be proved more often than not that there were other women to whom this didn't happen at the same company.[7] This might sound familiar as a popular argument touted in defence of individuals (or institutions) accused of sexual harassment. 'I have known him long and he was never inappropriate with me.' Or 'there are so many other women who work here to whom such a thing has never happened.' Several chapters in this book outline many such real-life examples used to challenge the MeToo accusations.

Pao's case also had the matter of an affair with a married junior colleague and alleged retaliation. Pao claimed that she had been pressurized into entering a sexual relationship with Ajit Nazre,[8] a partner at Kleiner at the time, and was retaliated against for

---

7 http://www.mercurynews.com/business/ci_27779413/kleiner-perkins-discrimination-trial-nears-end-closing-arguments
8 https://fortune.com/2015/03/27/man-at-center-of-ellen-pao-case-still-working-in-vc/

breaking off and complaining. This brought under the microscope other allegations and speculations. The long-known reputation of Nazre, potential out of court settlements, mysteriously missing administrative assistants and the hush-hush departure of Nazre from first the firm and then from the limelight altogether were all reported upon. These are all familiar narrative arcs for workplace sexual harassment and harassers: a reputation yet nothing proven, alleged out of court settlements, debate on consensual, consent, and coercion, and departures without legal consequences (the Chapter 4 and elsewhere discussions on academia culture and reaction to LOSHA and Chapter 6 examples are worth remembering here, as are the cases of K. P. S. Gill, M. J. Akbar and Larry Nassar, which have been discussed as case studies). Just like Nazre, CEOs of well-known companies have resigned or have been ousted, but is anyone in jail? The answer is no in most cases. For sexual harassment, the stakes are higher. The defendants, even one's like Pao, must face questions that are hard to face and even harder to answer.[9]

Ellen Pao captivated the nation's attention. If she could successfully prove in a court of law that there indeed was discrimination, harassment and retaliation during her employment at Kleiner and caused her eventual dismissal, it would be unbelievable and of unprecedented consequence to corporate America. If she lost, it would affirm the complexities surrounding 'due process' which is so often offered as the only way to go, as if it's an all or nothing game. 'Don't accuse someone if you can't prove it in court. Naming and shaming are anarchic, take them to the courts instead.'[10]

....

9 https://www.usatoday.com/story/tech/2015/03/10/ellen-pao-kleiner-perkins-discrimination-bias-gender-trial/24697491/

10 Pao lost her case against Kleiner Perkins. Accusations against Kleiner and Ajit Nazre remain unproven at the time of this writing (https://www.nytimes.com/2015/03/28/technology/ellen-pao-kleiner-perkins-case-decision.html). This work makes no claims of guilt on part of the accused and merely presents facts and reports publicly available in the context of the broader challenges around gender-based discrimination and harassment.

Of 2,000 US employment discrimination cases, most were thrown out or settled, the cost of litigation and adversarial process proving too big a barrier for employees. Only 6 percent of cases went to court. Two-thirds failed.[11]

Ellen Pao lost her case two years before the breakout of #MeToo. Two years after the breakout of #MeToo, in India, police have dropped the Nana Patekar investigation, citing lack of evidence; M. J. Akbar has filed a defamation case against Ramani;[12] and Ranjan Gogoi has in effect exonerated himself.[13] Hopefully, it's clear now why the Ellen Pao case is of relevance here. It demonstrates clearly how:

- Sexual harassment in the workplace is no different from sexual discrimination when it comes to proving—yes, surprising prima facie but true.

- Sexual harassment is often used for discrimination and vice versa.

It is not just in the fields or the fringes but in global, international corporations too. Also, on a separate note, this speaks to the grit and strength of Ms Bajaj in the 1990s India. Yes, her plight had eye-witnesses. And yes, she wasn't trying to prove the nebulous gender discrimination, but still. She was persistent, as was Bhanwari Devi and the supporting activists which led them to their civil victory.

Pao alleged coercion and retaliation for calling off of an affair (causing deliberation into the matter of consent for workplace 'consensual' relationships). She accused her employer of enabling Nazre's sexually predatory behavioural pattern. Harassment at the workplace has both a cause and an effect relationship with sexual

11 Ellen Berrey, *Rights on Trial* (Chicago, IL: University of Chicago Press, 2017).
12 https://www.indiatoday.in/india/story/priya-ramani-to-court-in-mj-akbar-case-sexual-harassment-case-1597366-2019-09-09
13 https://mumbaimirror.indiatimes.com/mumbai/cover-story/spectacle-fit-for-a-kangaroo-court/articleshow/68972786.cms

discrimination. Since without safety there can be no parity, as the economy shifts from brawn to the brain, sexual harassment—a prime modulator causing loss of women from the workforce globally—becomes not just a social but also an economic problem (with the cost to businesses—as noted in Chapter 3—estimated at over US$6 million per Fortune 500 company per year).[14]

- Pao vs Kleiner Perkins exemplifies how a legal victory is tough to impossible and, therefore, the legal route unviable (read not advisable) for most (the resources Pao had at her disposal for who she is, and the 'salacious details' available as most reports called it, made this case as fortified as any such litigation can be expected to be; yet she lost).

- It shows that the playing field is level globally. Legal proceedings are messy, resource-intensive and a gamble for anyone, anywhere.

- It also reinstate that a court victory is not everything (even failed cases seed movements) boosting arguments in favour of 'name and shame' as a technique. The case during its course and post verdict created movements of inclusion across the Valley and highlighted real time the issues around proving discrimination or harassment in court.

- Pao vs Kleiner proves that retaliation and backlash are real consequences not just for the concerned parties but also for the broader population (Pao's defeat was seen to be a major setback, and venture capital firms were known to hire fewer women secretly, as a result).[15]

Now that the broader environment is established, let's dive deep into the specific-to-India facts. In India, for the 'due process, don't

14 https://openknowledge.worldbank.org/bitstream/handle/10986/29865/126579-Public-on-5-30-18-WorldBank-GenderInequality-Brief-v13.pdf?sequence=1&isAllowed=y
15 https://www.vox.com/2017/9/19/16330682/maha-ibrahim-technology-sexism-venture-capital-investing-mark-recode-decode-kara-swisher-podcast

call out names' route of redressing (workplace) sexual harassment, there are now two options: A criminal complaint under IPC and internal committee (IC) redressal using POSH. It's important to note that our reason for choosing POSH is not just India. It is indeed quite comprehensive in a number of areas and, therefore, serves as a good model case to study.

POSH (Sexual Harassment of Women at Workplace (Prevention, Prohibition and Redressal) Act, 2012; enacted December 2013), on the surface, reads excellently. Not only does it establish an actual legislative Act in place of guidelines for workplace sexual harassment (Vishakha), but it also widens the definition of 'workplace' (a common grievance with Vishakha). It envelopes hostile work environment, a promise of preferential treatment (coercion) or threat of detrimental treatment (retaliation) as adjacencies (as outlined earlier, these concepts are entangled with sexual harassment at the workplace and play into discrimination/gender un-parity) and attempts to provide the committees (ICs) with more teeth than ever. It imposes fines on institutions for failing to comply and on individuals for violation of confidentiality. However, so far, it is overwhelmingly underwhelming in achieving results.

Despite the globally true problems, some of this might be extraordinarily excruciating because of the India factor and not POSH itself. As Dr Reicha Tanwar (an author; women's rights expert; Director, Women Studies; and Head of the Department, Kurukshetra University) states, 'India has no shortage of laws when it comes to sexual harassment, but the question is, how many people have access to legal machinery and how efficiently does the machinery run to instil confidence, let alone justice?'

Professor Tanwar has drafted the policies on sexual harassment and has served on numerous committees since Vishakha, investigating complaints. For years, she has also run a training programme on how to understand, unravel and prevent sexual harassment at workplaces. According to her, the Indian society doesn't have the mindset to be able to take sexual harassment seriously, let alone condemn it. Therefore, laws are rendered meaningless. This corroborates what other activists and social workers, including Renuka Pamecha, had said. But the point here is that it's not just heartlands or rural ecosystems. It is the environment everywhere, including second-tier and first-tier hubs. My personal journey of learning (for this book and my activism) has led to this conclusion again and again. This is why I continue to place the claim that MeToo (or movements like MeToo) is more important for India's gender parity than policy upheavals (which the nation has seen quite a lot of, most recently post 2012) and actual convictions.

POSH is not the only way for redressing sexual harassment, neither is it intended to be the 'legal prosecution' way. As noted by Devanshu Sajlan (a litigating lawyer at the Supreme Court of India, Delhi High Court, Tribunals and district forums), POSH was put in place to give workplace harassment victims a way of immediate and easier redressal of their concerns. IPC Section 509 and Section 354 (which was bolstered into 354A in 2013 to specifically call out and criminalize sexual harassment) do criminalize sexual harassment with definitions broader than most international laws (i.e., on what can qualify as sexual harassment) and did so before POSH and 2013. POSH doesn't link directly to the IPC, nor is there a threshold above which incidents merit as a criminal complaint under IPC. The processes can run in parallel, and the complainant has every right to lodge a criminal complaint in addition to taking a matter to an IC. As we have seen in Chapter 2, Renuka Pamecha also calls this out in her statements to Amit Shah's committee. She is all in for maintaining a civil redressal mechanism for what she has called 'safeguarding the workplace'. But it is important to note that in some other matters (e.g., for Section 498A in India), having multiple redressals is what drives a lot of the anti-sentiment. We have discussed this in quite a few places in this work.

For POSH, a few things need to be brought forward as areas of opportunities.

1. **Low implementation and adaptation:** POSH outlines consequences (a debatably minimal fine of ₹50,000 on failure to implement or comply for workplaces employing more than 10 employees) and as previously stated, widens the definition of a 'workplace'. But who is keeping track and who has the infrastructure needed to keep track, let alone impose penalties for failure to comply, in a country like India?[16] Just like the measure to counter acid sales for prevention of acid attack (where the block development officer is assigned responsibility without the manpower to support it), POSH implementation is lagging because of an impracticable implementation plan. One example is that global companies in top metros will, and do have, POSH posters displayed in their cafeteria boards (e.g., Intel Corporation), but in my limited personal investigation visiting small to medium-size workplaces across the nation (including reasonably prominent publication houses given that media was at the epicentre of India's 2018 MeToo breakout), I found no committees established or POSH publicized as required by the law at the time of this writing.

2. **Subjectivity:** POSH leaves several things to interpretation which POSH (or even India) can't be necessarily singled out for. Every nation is struggling with this, including the USA, the UK and Australia. In addition to extending the definition of the workplace and including other adjacencies previously mentioned, it mostly uses the definition from Vishakha for sexual harassment but widens it. The definitions are therefore quite broad (e.g., it includes showing pornography or sexually coloured remarks), and this possibly seems to be a merit as it places POSH as a stronger law in terms of offering protection. For example, the 'gross and/or repetitive' criterion in the US workplace sexual harassment guideline does not apply to India. Even a single instance can attribute to sexual harassment. 'Anything that makes a woman

---

16 https://www.dw.com/en/indian-firms-take-little-notice-of-law-against-sexual-harassment/a-17298779

uncomfortable in her workplace, if proven to have happened, can merit a decision by the committee that sexual harassment has occurred,' stressed Devanshu Sajlan. Unfortunately, this is not a good thing. Not only does this open a Pandora's box of misinterpretations and mis-accusations putting the men at higher risk, but this also disservice the women. More often than not, thanks to societal tolerance and the mechanism relied upon here, the definition fails to offer any real protection while creating discrimination. As Professor Tanwar explains,

Most evidence is circumstantial, and a high amount of discerning judgment is needed. And even if there is evidence, India has a high tolerance for sexual misconduct. So, what if something can qualify as harassment? Most acts are trivialized and minimized by the committee members.

3. **Authority:** As Devanshu Sajlan puts it,

Article 21 of the Constitution protects life and liberty. These can't be taken away without state sanction (read legal proceedings by a judiciary body). The ICs tasked with addressing complaints in POSH are not judicial bodies, they are still private bodies, and the status meted to them as civil courts are only for recording of evidence, not adjudication. They can't, therefore, recommend punishments beyond the termination of employment, suspension, penalty (aka any recourse that would impact liberty or life is out of scope for the committee), for criminal punishment can only be handed out by a judicial body after indictment and prosecution.

However, Devanshu doesn't see this to be a disadvantage or limitation for POSH.

Even though POSH doesn't link to the IPC, the wronged can pursue a criminal complaint in parallel, and if found to be guilty of criminal misconduct—remember, the definition for harassment is wide and therefore doesn't exclude any incident or set any threshold—sentencing will happen.

The problem is that if POSH was designed keeping in mind the hassle of going through the Indian legal system, it is an alternative, not an addendum for those who chose to redress their concerns without having to file a criminal complaint. POSH leaves them hanging as the committee's job ends on recommending action to the institution and leaves it to the institution to punish and/ or report to authorities. The institutions, as Professor Tanwar and Devanshu both agree, could choose to act very differently if they chose to act altogether (as noted in point 1, penalties are provisioned but can't guarantee implementation).

4. **The IC problem:** This is the point on which all experts agreed: Reliance on 'ICs' which are to be appointed by the institutions themselves is the single greatest flaw POSH suffers from. It's already proven to be an ineffective methodology and is rendered further useless, thanks to well-meaning but inept criteria. Professor Tanwar says it better than I could, so I quote her below.

Which organization in the world will select a committee that will cause trouble? Most organizations find people like me trouble. They don't want liability or liability (read cost) causing committees, let alone the entire problem of patriarchal conditioning and lack of training. Even senior women in legal positions say stuff like 'so what, *rape to nahin huya*' (So what, it wasn't rape) or '*senior aadmi hain, unke to betiyan hain*' (He is a senior person and has daughters himself), as if that is the proof of innocence in itself.

Having been part of several corporate investigations and having talked to counsels and diversity experts in Fortune 500 companies, I couldn't agree more. Human resources in corporations are primarily tasked with minimizing liability and exposure, not pursuing social justice. Of course, the Ranjan Gogoi modus operandi cited earlier is therefore expected to happen often.

Devanshu Sajlan reinforces this further by bringing in additional concerns and considerations.

Say I am an employee of the company and my CEO is implicated. The company's performance depends on the CEO, as does my earnings, and I know that. How objectively and truthfully will I choose to act, provided I choose to act at all? Applies whether I am chosen to be on the committee or if I am brought in to testify.

What can render this methodology successful is objective and effective 'dos and don'ts' on who can be in the committees. POSH tries but fails in this miserably. It is an improvement no doubt from Vishakha and an attempted step in the right direction (specifies the need for training, stresses the importance of having the right committee and provides guidelines on membership) but is set up to fail nevertheless, thanks to the quintessentially flawed assumptions.

> The IC (independent committee) shall comprise a senior level woman employee as the chairperson or presiding officer, a minimum of two employees committed to upholding women's rights, and another member from an NGO or an association dedicated to women's welfare or conversant with issues of sexual harassment. It is pertinent to note that where an employer or organization has multiple locations, with each location having 10 or more personnel, it is mandatory to set up an IC in each such location. The term of IC members shall not exceed three years and a minimum of three members, including the chairperson, are required to conduct an investigation into any complaint. The Act has afforded the IC the status of a Civil Court and is empowered to summon or enforce the attendance of any person, order the production of documents, and perform any other matter(s) as may be prescribed.[17]

What constitutes the championing of women's rights? The actual language says, 'preferably committed to the cause of women', which is even worse.

17 https://www.accdocket.com/articles/india-posh-act-a-snapshot.cfm

We mentioned earlier that we will talk of 'covering' or 'co-opting'. Internationally, 'covering' or 'co-opting' are known issues for women who have struggled to put their women band forward. In layman terms, covering and co-opting are behaviours in which women chose to either hide their support or support men over fighting for, or associating with, other women, or even sympathizing with women's causes and rights. Many factors play into this, and women can't be singled out for this behaviour either. Studies have shown that African-American men in white-collar jobs in the USA shy away from socializing publicly with African-American men in custodial jobs for the fear of detriment by association (automatic dismissal of their credibility) but do so freely with white men in similar blue-collar or custodial jobs. Similar behaviour is known to have been observed (and famously showcased in movies like *Article 15*) by lower-caste men in India who have risen the ranks. The same applies to religious minorities who are widely prosecuted or fearmongered against (e.g., Muslims). Benazir Bhutto is widely criticized for regressing the women's causes in place of advancing. One personal example that comes to mind is that of multiple American women who are close friends expressing to me at the time of Hillary Clinton vs Donald Trump campaign, 'I love Hillary, but I don't think a woman is ready for Presidency. That's a man's job and I don't want to be seen supporting someone just because I am a woman and she is a woman. That typecasts you.' And, of course, in the introduction, we have discussed women not wanting to be typecast as feminists, thanks to careful manipulation of the image and years of conditioning of women on what their role should be.

Although women or Indian women can't be singled out for this behaviour, India (and any highly patriarchal nation where oppression and marginalization have had a long history) can be expected to have an exaggeration of such behaviours. Earlier, the role of Indian women in forwarding and exacerbating the Indian patriarchy has been discussed under different contexts. But to explain the impact of social conditioning on confidence and identity, in brief, I will use the baby elephant analogy made famous in TED talks. Elephants, even when full-size adults, believe that the small pole they are tethered to is strong enough for restricting them and therefore make no attempts of overstepping their boundaries. This sums up the point on years of conditioning, leading to beliefs contradictory to reality. Such social conditioning has effects that can't be overturned. Assuming women to be advocates and allies automatically, or to have expectations of sympathy or sensitivity just because they are women, is an illusion India chooses for convenience. It's a tool for strengthening patriarchy and the easy and ineffective way out.

The LOSHA examples and toothless committees before POSH responsible for rendering Vishakha Guidelines useless have been showcased already. POSH, unfortunately, makes the same disastrous mistake. In the next chapter, we will look into other options (e.g., EEOC model, the USA) and their pros and cons.

Let's now come to legal recourse through the filing of a criminal complaint. As Professor Tanwar and Devanshu Sajlan reinforced (along with academic papers on the matter I have quoted earlier), India doesn't have the problem of lack of laws. Contrary to what most believe (strong laws and policies need to be in place to usher in women's safety in India), Indian laws don't lag. Many other nations, including the USA, have bigger problems in this matter.

I had visited the US sexual harassment guidelines and the matter of criminal prosecution for sexual harassment in the USA with Susan Blount[18] (previously executive vice president and general counsel, Prudential, who is recognized as one of America's 50 Outstanding General Counsel by *The National Law Journal* and has received recognition from organizations such as the National Association of Women Lawyers, National Organization for Women-NYC, the New Jersey Institute for Social Justice and

18 https://law.utexas.edu/cwil/directory/susan-blount/

the New Jersey Law and Education Empowerment Project), and she had agreed.

I too struggle with the gross or repetitive. As if a single instance can't be a crime here unless it's proven to be gross—which is subjective. But the bigger question is, is sexual harassment a crime or a criminal offense in the USA. The answer is that it depends.[19] I myself have to find out for you and it's not easy.'

This is the reason why I had stated Susan's bio elaborately. If she struggles with it, imagine a woman without a legal background risking her employment or advancement opportunity trying to decide if a legal recourse should be followed. And now put that together with the case study we started this chapter with, caste studies in Chapter 4, and the statistics presented earlier. The answer will be clear.

Coming back to India and the legal recourse route here, what is terrible is the implementation which is crippled by corruption, incompetence and lack of infrastructure for due process. The subjectivity (that exists in general and is often used by intention) that is used to dismiss cases (e.g., in plausibility arguments) has already been discussed in detail, as have been other matters such as a statute, witness tampering and evidence tampering.

I brought up the matter of due process and the lack of details in the closure of the Tanushree Dutta case with Devanshu Sajlan.

Police has to file either a charge sheet or a closure report with a magistrate and the report, in either case, has to be detailed and satisfactory to the magistrate for him or her to accept it. The complainant can again (like Tanushree has) file an appeal as long as a prima facia a case can be made out for the police to have to investigate. She can appeal if she feels she has done that against closure reports. The veracity of the witnesses, etc.,

19 https://www.criminaldefenselawyer.com/resources/is-sexual-harassment-workplace-a-crime.html

is not her responsibility and is not needed. However, the matter of statute also applies here. Statute of limitation applies to anything that will have criminal punishment of fewer than three years. For her case, this problem does apply.

Although I haven't tabulated it above, the statute of 90 days (plus 90 days extension if seen fit by the IC) is noted to be a key issue with POSH by many, including Devanshu, as is the fact that POSH didn't come into effect until 2013. But the key point he stressed brings us back to square one. Laws must rely on people doing their jobs honestly and with the best skills. I will just wonder out loud here, without overstepping the boundary of making a statement on an unproven legal matter, that there are countless cases (from Maya Tyagi to judgments handed by judges on cases of 'restitution of conjugal rights'[20]) which have been dispositioned atrociously.

Magistrates and judges are not immune from the conditioning, external corruptive influences and implicit biases that affect IC members and senior officials. So what guarantees justice? As Susan Blount and Professor Tanwar had both said, 'Laws can't do anything until mindsets change.'

Pao was quoted in an article (where she stated that the fight was worth it and the dialogue her case has created on diversity in Silicon Valley is rewarding enough[21]), giving permission to anyone who doesn't feel like coming forward (going to the authorities or courts) to not do it. She can't be blamed for this. Nor is she alone. Several mentors, activists and trailblazers across the globe resonate with her in sentiment. The women are stuck (globally) in the perfect catch-22 under the current legal systems. You can't just name and shame: You should take legal action and prove in court. But realistically, you won't be able to prove in court. Professor Tanwar summarizes the 'why' that I have cross-sectioned for so long, best. 'Most evidence is naturally circumstantial or

---

20 Gangoli, *Indian Feminisms.*
21 https://www.ft.com/content/9fc459da-2f7a-11e9-80d2-7b637a9e1ba1

non-existent; otherwise, there wouldn't have been an issue in the first place.'

The second catch-22? When you fail to prove it in court, there is a cost (defamation suit and damaged reputation) and if you stand a chance of proving, that comes at a cost too (the recent case of former Union Minister Chinmayanand[22] and his accuser getting counter-accused is all too common and doesn't need an analysis).

Lastly, let's look at MeToo analytically as a technique for redressal and recourse. There is no doubt that many 'gives' surround the 'gets' of 'name and shame' as a redressal methodology. Having spent months reading accounts of MeToo accusations, there are cases that stood out to me for having a stronger possibility of a prima facie case existing. Some of the links[23] here provide good summaries which readers can avail and make their own inferences on which cases stand a higher chance of being smudges that are unfortunate, collateral or completely untrue, damages. I don't intend to chronicle them here and to prevent playing judge, jury and executioner on who is guilty vs who is innocent. The cases I choose to showcase are either proven or have been highly chronicled. I also want to make it clear again, in addition to the disclaimer provided earlier, that the intention is to review them as case studies, not make legal judgments on guilt. There is undeniably the factor of making inferences on the likelihood of feasibility based on the number of details available and what those details are—irrespective of the legal outcomes—that I have used while deciding what to talk about. But that doesn't prove or disprove a matter legally. What can be showcased similarly is the ancillary undesirable effect of MeToo, for example, getting named

---

22 https://www.indiatimes.com/news/india/bjp-leader-swami-chinmayanand-arrested-in-up-law-student-rape-case-376181.html
23 https://economictimes.indiatimes.com/magazines/panache/2018-the-year-when-metoo-shook-india/varun-grover-sham-kaushal-piyush-mishra/slideshow/66345999.cms; https://timesofindia.indiatimes.com/india/me-too/metoo detail/66215419.cms

and associated, causing damage higher than the act that needed to be repudiated. Let's take the examples of Tanmay Bhat, AIB ex-CEO, and Aziz Ansari of the 'Patriot Act'.

Irrespective of whether the accusations against Utsav Chakraborty get proven, Tanmay's role in missing to take appropriate actions have been established by his partners. However, does that justify his career tanking for life or should his removal from the CEO post of AIB suffice? Or should it have been some other form of corrective action—sensitivity training, disciplinary show cause—that should have been meted out instead of ousting? The problem is that no one knows. As outlined in the laws themselves, what extent of harassment (or failure to deal with harassment) deserves what punishment remains subject to judgment and is highly variable. Besides, during the time of this writing, it was also a possibility that the AIB YouTube channel would possibly not emerge again—another potentially overextended consequence.

Similarly, there was an accusation that surfaced against Varun Grover[24] which lacked details and had the additional problem of being from an entirely different time. The USA has debated this particular aspect (whether a past mistake, especially from formative/reckless years should matter) in the Brett Kavanaugh[25] case and this, even at the risk of being called out for, I do think is a valid point for differentiation. Factors like these have some nations putting 'repetitive' in the definition and others leaving it up to committees to decide. However, there are other matters too which can be considered for making inferences (e.g., how the accused chose to behave, whether they demand a fair and independent investigation, how many other threads start emerging around the

---

24 https://www.ndtv.com/entertainment/varun-grover-accused-in-metoo-writes-believe-all-women-but-differentiate-from-believe-all-screenshot-1932876
25 https://www.factcheck.org/2018/11/ford-did-not-recant-accusations-against-kavanaugh/

accusation). Varun's case, in my humble opinion, is quite likely what Varun calls it himself: 'collateral damage'.

Revolutions are beautiful. They are cathartic,
powerful, necessary, and like #MeToo—inevitable.
And revolutions, inevitably, have some collateral damage too....
Revolutions can be messy, but they can't be perceived as unjust.

—*Varun Grover*

Unfortunately, Varun's last line needs some modification or, rather, clarification. What a movement gets perceived as is very important. But there is no movement that is, has been or can be just for all. MeToo is not just for all either.

The Aziz Ansari account, as noted in some reports, has been a 'flashpoint' for conversations surrounding the 'power and limitations' of MeToo. Not only does it outline the complexities around consent, but it also is a tale relatable to women and, unfortunately, men. Feeling pressurized into voicing consent and going along while uncomfortable, and missing to note discomfort and dissent, both happen and can keep happening—colouring the grey areas a darker grey. In a name and shame narration, Ansari will not come out unscathed even if he genuinely had had no malice. The Ansari case is discussed in further detail, for when a yes means no is an area worth evaluating and acknowledging for training and learning.

By definition[26] 'name and shame' is a tactic used most when 'official channels are unlikely to be (or have already proven themselves not to be) sympathetic or responsive' and is 'useful when a community has an informal or undocumented structure, such that there is no central authority who can enforce anti-harassment norms'. As presented in this chapter, all of these are applicable to sexual harassment (even post MeToo) globally. MeToo is, therefore, a valid,

26 https://geekfeminism.wikia.org/wiki/Name_and_shame

acceptable and necessary route for countering sexual harassment. However, being primarily a name and shame technique, it has a high cost to not just the perpetrators but also the accusers. Thus, it's important to know what the pros and cons are. I summarize them verbatim below as obtained from one source.[27]

Benefits of name and shame:

- may result in an organization or community warning, condemning, or expelling of a harasser where they would not have done so otherwise,

- may result in public pressure on an organization or individual to stop harassing/enforce anti-harassment norms where private pressure did not,

- may result in opponents of harassment organizing within a community where they had not previously done so,

- may result in additional documentation of harassment in a community (although identifying information on harassers is not always necessary for documentation to happen),

- may reveal other victims of a harasser, and thereby identify a serial harasser who may have been repeatedly assumed to be a one-off harasser,

- may help other people who've experienced harassment and abuse to find support or justice or identify themselves as victims of a systemic problem rather than having invited or encouraged their harassment or abuse.

Costs of name and shame:

- may result in condemnation of the namer-and-shamer for any perceived or actual bad consequences to the harasser,

- may result in loss of the namer-and-shamer's job (if complaining about a colleague or perceived to damage their employer's interest) or membership in a community

27 https://geekfeminism.wikia.org/wiki/Name_and_shame

(if complaining about a fellow member or perceived to damage the community's interest)

- may additionally result in further harassment of the namer-and-shamer from previously uninvolved third parties,

- the reaction may demonstrate that the community (or sections thereof) is divided on the issue of harassment or at worst is uncaring or actively supportive of it,

- may discourage any further reports of or action against harassment or abuse within a community,

- victim-blaming may be widespread, analysing whether the namer-and-shamer 'deserved' or 'invited' harassment,

- the ensuing discussion about whether harassment is bad, the harassment was bad enough for naming-and-shaming, whether naming-and-shaming is ever OK may be divisive and give rise to a harming the community accusation,

- may result in legal action against the person who spoke out. The truth is not a defense against libel in all jurisdictions, and even where it is, the threat of legal action or the early stages of legal action may be distressing or costly.

In summary, for gender parity and gender violence prevention, with the odds stacked high against a feasible courtroom victory (or even opening of prosecution), there is no way around naming and shaming which in turn will have unintended consequences and collateral damages. There is a cost to be paid for playing the all-or-nothing game, and there are gains to be made even when the battle is lost in court.

CHAPTER 8

THE REAL RISK

By now, we have hopefully established what fosters gender inequality and violence against women. We have also looked at #MeToo as a movement and other movements before, after and around it. But women's rights and safety concerns and movements concerning them don't exist in a vacuum. Therefore, men's movements (especially MRMs), alongside men's issues and viewpoints, need to be critically evaluated. We did a bit of that in the earlier chapters, but we didn't quite collect everything which would allow us to compare men and women. Beyond being comprehensive, understanding the modulators and the mechanisms (factors and movements) helps us devise a path forward. Identifying the risks helps safeguard the same. Outlining the threats to movements like #MeToo (and by extension, to the women's rights movement) is not possible without an understanding of men's issues, the men's rights scenario and the impact of all these on social reforms. In addition, alongside theoretical and factual deliberations, showcasing voices and opinions (of the men and on the men) is also important. We will do so here and end with making a case—again—for gender justice.

Men who commit violence against women
feel that rights for women mean the loss of rights for men.[1]

---

1 Ravi Verma and Sapna Kedia, 'We Need to Talk about Men', *India Development Review* (2018). https://idronline.org/need-talk-men/

First, let's start with the question: Are men suffering? As a close friend correctly says, in a country of one billion, everyone is suffering in one way or another. Issues of air quality, lack of opportunities, discrimination, lack of access to infrastructure, shrinking GDP, delayed justice, and physical and mental health conditions don't affect just women. Neither is this suffering limited to India. So this will seem to be a loaded and possibly irrelevant question. However, the question intends to understand if men are faring worse than women? Can that be determined as a fact through quantitative metrics (GDP, healthcare statistics, crime statistics, etc.)? For example, it is quite established indeed that black men fare worse in the USA than black women in terms of life expectancy, education and incarceration rates.[2]

So the question is: Does gender outrank caste and economic status as a differentiator of well-being in India? And why India?

Well, India ranks terribly for women in most global studies including a particularly controversial one by Reuters.[3] So apart from our interest in a solution space for gender in India, India would also serve as a good corner case candidate out of the democratic nations where women have equal rights under the Constitution.

Given the scope of the topic at hand, we will need to break this into subsegments: 'economy', 'crime' and 'opinion' (health will come about too, but not quite as directly and elaborately).

Labour force participation, employment, economic security and advancement status of men vs women in India are summarized well in the paragraph below from the World Bank. In Chapter 3, additional economics of gender discrimination and harassment has been discussed. So this summary should be enough for the purpose here: 'establishing that women, currently, are not faring

---

2 https://www.census.gov/prod/2005pubs/censr-25.pdf
3 https://www.reuters.com/article/us-women-dangerous-poll-exclusive/exclusive-india-most-dangerous-country-for-women-with-sexual-violence-rife-global-poll-idUSKBN1JM01X

better than men in India economically, and this is largely agnostic to caste, class, region or religion'.

India ranks 120 among 131 countries in female labor force participation rates and rates of gender-based violence remain unacceptably high. It's hard to develop inclusively and sustainably when half of the population is not fully participating in the economy. At 17% of GDP, the economic contribution of Indian women is less than half the global average, and compares unfavorably to 40% in China, for instance. India could boost its growth by 1.5 percentage points to 9 percent per year if around 50% of women could join the workforce.[4]

Summarizing a definitive gender statement on crime and violence, the next focus area is not easy and by the time we end this segment it will be clear why. Although certain conclusions are published by quite a few global agencies and are widely known—there is a lot of counter popular opinion that is out there too. The data is consistently challenged, and many caveats need to be considered. Therefore, instead of starting with summary statistics, I decided to build the case up here, taking the readers on a journey parallel to my own in which I dug deep and built it brick by brick, arriving at a place where passing a high-confidence judgement on the summary statistics out of the global reports would be possible.

Also, as expected, several reports and studies have the sample size and target populations selected based on the focus of the study[5] and, therefore, cause data integrity pitfalls (like confirmation bias, biased sampling and incorrect extrapolation) if we attempt to generalize the conclusions (which is what, as I will show, is often done). Therefore, this segment can be meaningfully tackled only by breaking it down further into subcategories: intimate partner/domestic violence, violent crimes, sexual assault, acid attack and such.

4 https://www.worldbank.org/en/news/speech/2018/03/17/women-indias-economic-growth
5 https://www.ncbi.nlm.nih.gov/pmc/articles/PMC6437789/

For example, the Rohtak study cited above (on domestic violence) does note a whopping 52 per cent of men surveyed to have experienced violence from women; however, the study focuses on Haryana—Rohtak to be particular—and a specific demographic. Besides, there is no equivalent survey done on the female population for us to be able to compare directly between the genders. The cited study does compare against other such studies (including one by Sarkar, Dsouza and Dasgupta[6] and one from the UK and Canada[7]) and attributes the discrepancies (which are quite large) to differences in methodology and target population selection. It also acknowledges an important second point: It is not known how much of this is counter-violence or if self-defence and other such factors play a part. This issue will come up again and again in the references we will cite through this chapter.

On the matter of intimate partner (or domestic) violence, however, a few things can be established. Bi-directional violence is prevalent (in India and globally), and men do experience physical violence (the most common form noted in multiple studies out of India is slapping). However, experiencing sexual violence from a partner is predominantly a gender-based experience (women experience sexual violence in much higher numbers). It is important to note here that marital rape not being a crime in India seriously complicates this because the entire concept of 'sexual violence' being a form of domestic violence gets negated. In the case of other intimate partner physical violence, aggression from Indian women is noted to be much less than from men.[8]

---

6 S. Sarkar, R. Dsouza, and A. Dasgupta, *Domestic Violence against Men: A Study Report by Save Family Foundation* (New Delhi: Save Family Foundation, 2007).
7 http://www.dewar4research.org/DOCS/websiteGovtStatsonDV1995-2013.pdf
8 A. Nadda, J. S. Malik, R. Rohilla, S. Chahal, V. Chayal, and V. Arora, 'Study of Domestic Violence among Currently Married Females of Haryana, India', *Indian Journal of Psychological Medicine* 40, no. 6 (2018): 534–539.

Gender symmetry does not exist in India for physical violence.[9]

The scenario seems to be a bit different for countries like the UK and Canada. For example, a *Psychology Today* article[10] cites a study from the later noting equal prevalence of perpetration of physical domestic violence between men and women. The same article also cites the famous BBC documentary 'Abused by My Girlfriend', which portrays violent assault on a male partner by his female partner.[11] Most importantly, the article brings out the more pertinent points on men's suffering when it comes to IPV: emotional trauma, shame, stigma and lack of support owing to expectations of masculinity.

'Emotional violence on a male partner', in mid-2020, came to a boiling point in India with Sushant Singh Rajput's suicide.[12] Sushant's death became the centre of a national storm with accusations of bullying of the actor by mainstream Bollywood, accusations towards his girlfriend of abetment of suicide (and mis-appropriation of his finances) and murder speculations (yes, several parallel conspiracy theories on how he might have died emerged too). In October 2020, the cause of his death was ascertained again as suicide with an AIIMs report.[13] What Sushant's death had also brought to the forefront (albeit not as much as it should have) is the matter of mental health of men and emotional abuse of men, both worsened by expectations of masculinity and strength. Out of the issues affecting men, this emerged as an important one in my research—not just for India but also the world, although it has

9 https://journals.sagepub.com/doi/full/10.1177/2631831819894176#bibr2-263183
1819894176
10 https://www.psychologytoday.com/us/blog/talking-about-men/201911/
domestic-violence-against-men-no-laughing-matter
11 https://www.bbc.co.uk/bbcthree/article/81a8f303-5849-45b8-85a0-
e8532b5d948b
12 https://www.bbc.com/news/world-asia-india-53655118
13 https://www.deccanherald.com/national/aiims-panel-says-sushant-singh-
rajput-died-by-suicide-submits-report-to-cbi-896746.html

a discerned manifestation due to cultural and geopolitical antiquities. We will cover this in detail later in this chapter.

For domestic (aka intimate partner) violence research, I was fortunate to chance upon the Partner Abuse State of Knowledge (PASK) project study directed by John Hamel, Editor-in-Chief of Partner Abuse (a Springer publishing company).[14] Despite some reservations shared by domestic violence activists I spoke to regarding the study,[15] I found the study to be a genuine attempt and an interesting approach. The concerns with the study, as I understand and agree with, lie with how the summary and findings are misconstrued and overextended by certain groups, not with the study itself. The study compiles and compares research published (mostly other studies) between 2000 and 2010, applying inclusion and exclusion criteria to eliminate bias (e.g., it notes to have excluded studies in which participants were sampled from identified domestic violence victim population like a women's shelter for domestic violence). It looks into heterogenous partner abuse only, but given its span (it notes to have covered all primary literature databases, retrieved 750 articles after elimination of replicates, performed data cleaning, and had 42 scholars at 20 universities and research centres participating to cover 17 areas of domestic violence research) and due diligence (reports methodology including comparison and grouping mechanism, has been peer-reviewed), it seems to live up to its claim of being extensive and 'most' comprehensive.

....

First, we conducted a sweeping review of scholarly articles published in peer-reviewed journals and by government agencies outside of the United States and English-speaking developed nations that provided quantitative data on physical, psychological, and sexual abuse of intimate partners, as well

....

14 https://www.springerpub.com/partner-abuse.html
15 http://www.prweb.com/releases/2013/5/prweb10741752.htm

as consequences, risk factors, and attitudes. Most of the studies reported on female victimization only, but 73 reported on both male and female victimization. Second, we conducted an analysis of data from large community and national surveys, including from one multi-country study of dating violence, to determine the relationship between prevalence of abuse, social factors and women's empowerment.[16]

The core methodology of the study is a compilation of instances of occurrence rates reported in the individual studies to arrive at aggregated male vs female victimization and perpetration rates in large populations, nations, demographics and such. Therefore, the summarized data can be taken as a mark of prevalence or occurrence, but not as a direct quantitative comparison.

The conclusions out of the study, if one takes the time to read the report fully, are the following:

1. In a significant number of the population groups studied, male and female perpetration of domestic violence is comparable in rates. However, this excludes sexual coercion. Additionally, victimization rates remain higher for women: 'Across all studies included in this review, approximately one in four women (23.1%) and one in five men (19.3%) experienced physical violence in an intimate relationship.'[17]

2. The risk factors and motivations for domestic violence are the same for male and female. It notes domestic violence to be an emotional and relational matter, not a sociocultural evil. However, this conclusion, expectedly, has a high geo-subjectivity. For example, some nations like Nigeria and India had much higher social acceptance of domestic violence on women by men (among both men and women). We have talked in depth about some other nations in the earlier

16 http://ww1.prweb.com/prfiles/2013/05/16/10741752/PASK%20Overview. pdf
17 Ibid.

chapters to point out the effect of cultural conditioning on gender equality.

3. Worldwide, the study acknowledges what I have stated above: Research and statistics are lagging. The study summarizes 162 articles reporting on 200+ studies that met inclusion criteria publishing tables for Asia, the Middle East, Africa, Latin America, the Caribbean, Europe and the Caucasus. It also compares and summarizes some multi-country studies. 'The findings, contrary to what a primary MRM site insinuated, doesn't show men to be victimized at higher rates globally by domestic violence. Counter-violence, initiation, self-defence and other such factors can't be extracted from the summaries in the PASK study without going into the individual articles.'

In 11 countries women were found to be predominantly victims and males were found to be primarily perpetrators. There were 14 countries in which rates of partner abuse from larger populations were found to be symmetrical across gender: China, Hong Kong, Philippines, Thailand, Botswana, Namibia, Swaziland, Zimbabwe, Barbados, Brazil, Jamaica, Trinidad/Tobago, Portugal, and Ukraine.[18]

The key point to be noted out of the PASK study, in my opinion, is it's finding of high male victimization due to arbitrary and incorrect law and order proceedings—from arrests to convictions.

Men are not only disproportionately arrested in domestic violence cases, but sometimes arrested for arbitrary reasons, citing, for example, that police often arrest the bigger and stronger party in cases where the perpetrator is unclear. 'Such policies are not only ineffective but violate people's civil rights.'[19]

18 Ibid.
19 http://www.prweb.com/releases/2013/5/prweb10741752.htm

In conclusion, domestic violence (physical and emotional) on men does need to be considered in redressal mechanisms and intervention techniques and included in awareness and sensitivity training to prevent incorrect arrests and prosecution.[20] Studies like these should be talked about (which also serves to disperse hegemonic masculine portrayals) but shouldn't be overextended to overshadow the impact and risk to women.[21] Geo and demographic-specific factors, which we will deliberate further when we come to conviction rate statistics, make this a matter that is not a one size fits all.

Sushant Singh Rajput's suicide also brought to the forefront the matter of androcentrism and patriarchal bias in the subcontinent. We will discuss this a couple of times in this chapter, including public opinion and media trial of Rhea Chakraborty, the deceased's girlfriend. For now, let's move on to other forms of crime, especially sexual crimes.

There is zero to minimal official data available for 'sexual harassment' for men out of India. What is available mostly, again, is in the form of survey statistics (e.g., a Centre for Civil Society survey[22] is referred to in several articles on the topic and reports 18% of the men surveyed noting forced or coerced sex, out of which 16% note their perpetrators to be female). When talking about sexual harassment and the grey zone of consent and coercion that we have been discussing in the previous chapters, this could be significant. But lack of laws that allow the inclusion of male adults as victims, along with shame and stigma, preclude such surveys from becoming vetted crime statistics. The legal definitions used in this space are extremely problematic, including existing terminologies (e.g., eve-teasing). How rape is defined in the IPC results in the complete exclusion of adult male victims. Current Indian legal standards for what constitutes 'rape' (vs physical assault vs

20 https://domesticviolenceresearch.org/
21 https://www.ncbi.nlm.nih.gov/books/NBK499891/
22 https://ccsindia.org/indias-law-should-recognise-men-can-be-raped-too

sexual assault vs penetrative sexual assault) create exclusion of all scenarios except for the cases in which the perpetrator(s) are male and victims are female. For example, as a Centre for Civil Society article[23] rightfully points out, a female perpetrator penetrating a female victim with an object—like what had happened in the Nirbhaya case—wouldn't constitute rape or penetrative sexual assault in the eyes of law. In simple terms, the IPC (Section 375) understands rape to be an act of violation of a female by a male.[24] Attempt(s) of modification included the stop-gap Criminal Law Amendment Ordinance which changed rape to sexual assault, broadening its scope and allowing for gender neutrality.[25] However, the omission of the word 'rape' in doing so was rightfully criticized. More damaging was the women's rights backlash (where activists expressed rape to be primarily patriarchal and, therefore, objected to gender neutralization of rape), ultimately causing a reversal in the actual act.[26] This is quite unfortunate and a valid grievance. As noted by several concerned groups, this is not only incorrect but also excludes adult males from viably achieving justice against sexual assault perpetrated on them. The Protection of Children from Sexual Offences (POCSO) Act[27] does recognize sexual assault on male children, but non-inclusive definitions of what can constitute penetrative sexual assault or rape plague this space too.

As it is well known from the Aruna Shanbaug[28] case (whose attacker wasn't charged with rape as sodomy wasn't even considered so at the time), misclassification, or exclusion of intent statements, can cause serious harm as it limits both the punishment meted in the specific judgment and the setting of precedence. Sodomy and rape of male children are prevalent problems. An Indian

23 https://ccsindia.org/indias-law-should-recognise-men-can-be-raped-too
24 https://blog.ipleaders.in/critical-analysis-of-rape-of-male-in-india/amp/
25 https://www.vifindia.org/sites/default/files/Criminal%20Law%20Amendment%20Ordinance.pdf
26 https://ccs.in/indias-law-should-recognise-men-can-be-raped-too
27 https://www.jurist.org/commentary/2020/05/mayank-tiwari-posco-act/
28 https://www.bbc.com/news/world-asia-india-32776897

government report of 2007[29] notes 57.3 per cent male against a 42.7 per cent female ratio for severely sexually abused children surveyed. However, knowing whether the rape of adult males is equally prevalent through published statistics, right now, is virtually impossible in India because of how rape is defined. We must infer. In doing so, despite the concerns and considerations we have captured so far, it can indeed be concluded that females are victimized sexually in much higher numbers across the world, including in India. Several academic and mainstream references support this, but possibly the most comprehensive one-stop shop is the Wikipedia page 'Rape by Gender',[30] which has connecting links, allowing a nation-by-nation review, and includes excellent supporting references.

In understanding what constitutes rape, international law has evolved from viewing it just as penile-vaginal to penile-orifice and then to penetrative-orifice, all within a non-consensual context.[31]

An excellent study depicting the other side (sexual victimization of men) in the USA was published in *The Atlantic* in 2016, just a year before #MeToo, challenging the long-standing definition of the Federal Bureau of Investigation (FBI) of rape as gendered (male against female).[32] However, female victim numbers were noted to be still higher, victimized by both male and female perpetrators.

BEYOND STATISTICS AND SURVIVING SEXUAL ABUSE

Statistics tell us a lot, but not everything. Real voices, albeit subjective and not too different from surveys, need to be considered

---

29 Indian govt. 2007 report on child sexual abuse
30 https://en.wikipedia.org/wiki/Rape_by_gender
31 https://ccsindia.org/indias-law-should-recognise-men-can-be-raped-too
32 https://www.theatlantic.com/science/archive/2016/11/the-understudied-female-sexual-predator/503492/

too, especially when statistics are lacking. True, this is not the route to making data-validated quantitative conclusions. But that's not the goal here. There's a common saying in engineering: What we measure, we improve. What is critical about this statement is that it intends to emphasize the thought that should be put in deciding exactly what to measure. Because that is what will be taken forward. Meaning, if we care about a matter enough to measure it, we will work to improve the same. The problem of sexual harassment or assault of men hasn't become (yet) a matter in which shocking incidents come cascading, forcing measurements and reforms. So we need to go deeper to make a case for that for some of the blatant issues (like the lack of inclusive definitions and reporting mechanisms, and sexual abuse of male children).

For men's experience with sexual violence, the agonies, at the very basic level, are no different. But there is an added nuance of hard-line gender expectations that delegitimize their experience further. Two close friends of mine who have teenage boys at school had brought forward two similar instances that can help demonstrate this. In one case, the boy—an introvert and in no way an aggressor—was showing signs of demure on return from school. After a couple of evenings of his mother's prodding, he revealed that a girl in his class had been touching his genitals as a part of a dare with her girlfriends (made apparent apparently through their giggles and comments). His discomfort with the actual act was compounded by his dread: He would be the one punished if this came forward to school authorities, especially since it had been tutored consistently to the boys in the school that respecting women is key and all interactions (even borderline inappropriate) would render severe consequences. His dread unfortunately isn't unreal. As discoursed above, men can't be 'raped'—especially by women. This is a topic of turbulent courtroom debates. Whether or not men can be assaulted by women (sexually) is also often debated. The legal definition, matching the outlook towards sexual crimes that consider such crimes to be exclusively patriarchal, makes this battle impossible for men in India. Now, of course, as we have discussed in most of the past chapters, this space is loaded against women too, but differently. We will touch upon the same later in this chapter when we discuss androcentrism.

I spoke to several men over two months, reaching out to friends and family and strangers alike. Most didn't want to speak about 'such a matter', especially to a woman, that too an Indian woman. But almost all of them eventually opened up under the condition of anonymity. They shared that uncomfortable touching (or 'exploration' as some called it) had happened to them (Note: for all the men I spoke to, it was a male perpetrator—either another boy or a man). Every one of them also added that they considered the matter(s) to be trivial, at most uncomfortable. There was a definite sense of shame in being thought of as the victim. A distinctly different kind of shame from the multitude of women I spoke to who shared experiences of being groped or pinched (all by men).

The second account I would like to share here is extremely personal and, therefore, quite difficult for me to disclose. But as the author, I feel a personal responsibility nevertheless to not shy away from doing so. My husband was abused, by a male servant, for over three years. The abuse had begun when he was merely four years of age. The incident, which came forward after over 10 years of our marriage after intensive counselling (such was the extent of the trauma which was not only from the abuse but also from the sense of self-loathing that he had imbibed within for failing to live up to the male strength expected in Punjabi families), has had a tremendous effect on our married life. His family is still unaware, although he has been able to share the matter with his friends. It will take years for him to be able to address this fully, moving from his current mode of dismissal (which, although incredible progress from denial, is not ideal). The day he had shared this, at last, it was as if a fog had been cleared. From anger and impulsive acting outs to downright depression cycles lasting months, the act of childhood abuse had shown a full spectrum of side effects inside my own home. Most of it had come from the fact that the abused child in this case was male, who, even with the best of resources at his disposal, was ashamed of being abused as a man, forgetting that a man child is still a child.

Indian (and most) societies associate a high amount of strength to the male gender. Expectations of breadwinning, protection (of sisters, mothers and wives) and emotional stoicism are bored into a male offspring from birth. I have written previously (here and elsewhere), as have other experts, on how the inflexible definitions and the good son model disservice young boys of India, which in turn compounds gender violence (from honour killings to domestic violence and violent and sexual assaults). It causes men to role-model unrealistic control (over self and others) and being in control (of situations and happenings), which manifests in continuous viewing of women as secondary and lesser beings. We will discuss this in detail. However, the point I am trying to make here is not a behavioural or theoretical one. Boys and men not having ways of addressing sexual violence occurring to them in India while it remains commonplace (especially for younger boys) is a fact.

As *The Boston Globe* made it internationally famous through its reporting of the cover-up of the Catholic Church scandal, male children are abused rampantly throughout the world, including in the most sacred and celebrated of places. It is not an India-only problem. Pakistan's hidden shame—as it is commonly referred to after the 2014 documentary on the same—speaks to the issue of homeless and orphaned boys getting prostituted and raped continuously.[33] In global studies published on sexual violence on young men and childhood sexual violence for boys, it's widely acknowledged that although the matter is quite prevalent, evidence and statistical reports are hard to find.[34] In one such study encompassing Haiti, Kenya and Cambodia, the prevalence of percentage who have experienced some form of sexual violence

33 https://www.dawn.com/news/1129614
34 https://pubmed.ncbi.nlm.nih.gov/17531768/

goes as high as 25 per cent.[35] No discussion on male child sexual abuse can be complete without a deep dive into the Catholic Church scandal mentioned above. First instances of abuse are centuries old (Wikipedia traces it back to the 11th century), but the matter came to the forefront only in the 1990s. Also, despite the high focus on the US scandal in the 2000s,[36] following *The Boston Globe*'s reporting and the movie *Spotlight*,[37] the scale and spread of the issue (from the USA and the UK to Chile and even India) is colossal, which means that there can be no better case to study for child sexual abuse (not just male but also female). The Catholic Church sexual abuse scandal establishes more than any other example of how sexual abuse is covered up rampantly, in every nation. It isn't just a matter in developing countries or for ecosystems that lack infrastructure. Like academia, which we have talked about in the context of LOSHA and sexual abuse in the US universities, prestige is guarded preciously at a high cost to the society by all institutions, not just families. And that is how it's always going to be. That is why no policy can do what awareness and outrage can. Abuse of young men—a global issue—suffers from a global denial to date. As recently as in 2018, Pope Francis had responded to accusations of a cover-up against Bishop Juan Barros[38] in Chile by calling it a slander, a decade plus after *The Boston Globe*'s Pulitzer Prize-winning coverage and publication of the John Jay report.[39] In the year 2018 itself, Washington D.C. Cardinal Theodore McCarrick resigned from the College of Cardinals, and additional revelations of systemic cover-ups (of abuse by more than 300 priests) surfaced in Pennsylvania.[40] What

35 https://pubmed.ncbi.nlm.nih.gov/27244799/
36 https://www.bostonglobe.com/metro/2018/11/03/bishops/qVYEiZ5SY5w VzCgA3gvN5O/story.html
37 https://en.wikipedia.org/wiki/Spotlight_(film)
38 https://www.bbc.com/news/world-latin-america-42949250
39 https://www.usccb.org/
40 https://wgntv.com/news/catholic-archdiocese-of-chicago-targeted-in-lawsuit-over-records-on-clergy-abuse/

was happening in India at the time? Through 2014–2018, Catholic priests, just like godmen and gatekeepers of other religions, were being arrested for rapes of minors,[41] which had been happening over long periods of time.

Yes, the Pope changed his tone (with the changing climate, let's dare admit). Victims were invited to the Vatican. Investigations were launched by the Church. But it's still a long road ahead. Because the Pope's first position, despite all the revelations up to 2018 which makes such a matter quite plausible, was not a position of neutrality. It is critical to keep talking about the 'position of neutrality' for devising a path forward, and we will do so again in the last chapter. But for now, let's review the basic tenets of sexual abuse on males which we claimed earlier aren't too different.

- **Shame:** Exaggerated by the expectation of strength (like it's exaggerated by expectation character for women)

- **Fear:** Of retribution, further damage and being disbelieved

- **Trauma:** From the event itself and from the inability to attain justice

Some nations fare worse than others, and differences of course exist in the nature of the crimes. But like in sexual abuse of women, the characteristics are universal.

In systemic abuse, often the perpetrator is known and is from a position of trust. In the Church scandals, they are the respected individuals hailed to save the communities. A common modus operandi in the Church scandals (especially in the account of John J. Geoghan)[42] is for the priest to offer help to struggling single, often socio-economically disadvantaged, mothers with childcare and then preying upon the grateful and submissive child. Victims, in adulthood, are quoted to be struggling with depression and alcoholism, a lot of

---

41 https://en.wikipedia.org/wiki/Catholic_Church_sexual_abuse_cases
42 https://www.bostonglobe.com/news/special-reports/2002/01/06/church-allowed-abuse-priest-for-years/cSHfGkTIrAT25qKGvBuDNM/story.html

which has been traced back to the feeling of shame, powerlessness and fear. It's also from the feeling of betrayal from being violated by men and institutions looked up to as protectors. As one article quotes, the records are slim on these matters because of court-ordered confidentiality seals granted to church lawyers. So just like in the Larry Nassar case, what is more haunting than what happened is that it took a succession of officials (3 cardinals and many bishops) 34 years 'to place children out of Geoghan's reach'.[43]

To find out later that the Catholic Church knew
he was a child molester—every day it bothers me more and more.[44]

Shame and fear keep the victims from coming forward and when they do, doubt prevents action, which allows for trauma to accumulate and the cycles to continue. We spent extensive time elaborating in the earlier chapters why, therefore, a culture of belief matters more than proof and prosecution for prevention. A culture of belief creates a position of neutrality. It is not any different for male victims, who are also disbelieved when abused than it is for females. If we need more convincing on what can awareness do, one search today on 'Catholic Church sexual abuse' offers a plethora of results, resources to reach out to and reports (commissioned by the Catholic Church itself). Prevention and awareness materials are abundant. Training programmes can be looked up on sites like United States Conference of Catholic Bishops (USCCB),[45] and active participation is pursued in many churches for their clergy.

Just like in the case of abuse on women, there are valid arguments on prevention efforts needing to be prioritized. The most obvious, it would seem, would be to identify root causes and eliminating them. However, as one report (John Jay, commissioned

---

43 Patrick McSorley, Boston Globe report.
44 Ibid.
45 https://www.usccb.org/news/2011/john-jay-college-reports-no-single-cause-predictor-clergy-abuse

by USCCB) finds, some correlation can be marked with social influences, but common suspects like celibacy, or homosexuality, didn't necessarily correlate as a clear cause for the perpetration of abuse. Besides, the report quotes: 'Priest candidates who would later abuse could not be distinguished by psychological test data, developmental and sexual history data, intelligence data, or experience in the priesthood.' Although I couldn't quite agree with all statements on this particular report[46] (and had to wonder alongside other critiques[47] if there were motivations behind some of the conclusions cited), the obscurity around what causes such behaviour is a fact. Meaning, it would be quite impossible to prevent abuse by clergy via prediction and root cause elimination.

The other common prevention measure—extremely popular as we know when the abused are women—is elimination (or reduction) of opportunity and exposure. This would also not work in this case without essentially putting the church out of business. Clergies will continue to have (and need to have) private access to their parishioners.

However, thanks to the noise that has been made, the culture of belief has been established on the matter of abuse by priests. Example? Imagine yourself to be a devout practising Catholic who believes the Catholic Church to be the most supreme of institutions. Even in the early 2000s (post the 1990s scandals but pre *The Boston Globe* and *Spotlight*), if you heard of abuse by clergies on underage boys, you would vehemently protest such defamation. Today? You will stay silent and will possibly start believing in

---

46 https://www.usccb.org/issues-and-action/child-and-youth-protection/upload/The-Causes-and-Context-of-Sexual-Abuse-of-Minors-by-Catholic-Priests-in-the-United-States-1950-2010.pdf
47 Additional reports including critical analyses of the John Jay study published on some sites (e.g., the National Catholic Register) seem to have their flaws motivated by bias (e.g., towards homosexuality). As of the time of this writing, finding an independent peer-reviewed study on causes of abuse by clergy wasn't available. https://www.reuters.com/article/us-church-usa-abuse/critics-slam-study-that-u-s-priest-abuse-in-the-past-idUSTRE74H6YA20110519

your heart that it might be true. True, every accusation should still be investigated fairly and from a position of objectivity, but the belief that it might be true goes a long way for precaution, faster intervention and, therefore, prevention.

Of the other crimes, 'acid attack' merits a closer look for men as victims, because acid attacks do happen on men. This was a shocking discovery for me during my engagement with Acid Survivor's Foundation India in Kolkata (ASFI)[48] because, predominantly, acid attack is noted to be a crime against women. The leading cause of acid attack on men in the subcontinent is noted to be land, business or professional dispute, while that on women is noted to be rejection of sexual or romantic advances, domestic discord or jealousy.[49] In the UK, which has one of the highest rates of acid attacks per capita in the world (Acid Survivors Trust International [ASTI]), four out of five victims are male.

However, barring the UK and Africa, acid attack remains primarily a crime against women.[50] Out of 1,500 attacks happening world-wide per year (ASTI estimates), 80 per cent of victims are women (excluding the UK and Africa). In addition to the numbers, the geographical and causal differences in acid attack on men vs women mark it as a predominantly patriarchal crime.

The crimes of domestic violence involving physical assault, sexual violence and acid attack as we have found above are prevalent primarily against women. However, it'd be a blatantly incorrect statement to make that violence and crime affect women more than men. It's quite the contrary. Comprehensive data out of India that would offer a gender lens into general violence victimization rates remains problematic because of data integrity issues (sample size, bias, baseline comparisons, incorrect classifications and

48 https://aswwf.org/; https://www.huffpost.com/entry/acid-attack-in-india-wher_b_9559790
49 https://www.herrights.website/resources
50 https://www.asti.org.uk/a-worldwide-problem.html

incomprehensive reporting). But a gender lens can nevertheless be applied based on global studies (and for the most part extrapolated to India). One report[51] out of the USA notes the FBI's findings from 2007: 78 per cent of murder victims are male. The same report cites another study out of the National Crime Victimization Survey, which notes men to have higher victimization rates than females for all types of violent crimes except rape/sexual assault.[52] Certain categories like gun and gang violence affect men disproportionately and in certain nations (e.g., the USA, Afghanistan, Turkey and India), segment (race, ethnicity and economic placement)-specific differences dominate the statistics.

It will be imprudent to not add here that the perpetrators of violent crimes are also mostly men, and factors like 'incarceration rates' or 'conviction rates' don't tell the whole story of 'which men' are especially bad. A plethora of resources is now emerging on how socio-economic factors and historical contexts affect crime rates. For the sake of brevity here (we need to not digress too much from the gender issue we have in hand), a deeper dive into race, the 13th amendment in the USA[53] and an excellent report submitted to the United Nations by The Sentencing Project[54] which tackles how the US criminal justice system is mired with systemic, designed injustice that results in black men dominating the numbers (from juvenile detentions and pretrial to sentencing and convictions) can be reviewed.

Data out of several other parts of the world (e.g., the Netherlands) reiterate similar conclusions (men fall victim to violent crimes at higher rates than women, except for sexual crimes which women are twice as likely to experience than men).[55]

51 https://www.bjs.gov/index.cfm?ty=tp&tid=955
52 https://www.bjs.gov/index.cfm?ty=pbdetail&iid=7046
53 https://en.wikipedia.org/wiki/13th_(film)
54 https://www.sentencingproject.org/publications/un-report-on-racial-disparities/
55 https://www.cbs.nl/en-gb/news/2018/51/fewer-women-than-men-fall-victim-to-violence

In essentiality, I vetted if the classification of GBVs (classified so because they overwhelmingly have a gender component, i.e., happens mostly, and in most places, to women—even at times of peace) is valid. I wanted to make sure that the concern 'it happens to men too, but no one talks about it' is addressed fairly. And I needed to make sure that GBV classifications don't overreach or obscure issues that affect men. It's appropriate now to look at the summary report data on gender and violence that I alluded to at the start. Following is an excerpt from the United Nations 2016 report on VAWG.

Violence against women and girls (VAWG) is one of the most pervasive human rights violations occurring in the world. It happens in every country, not only in situations of conflict or crisis, but in contexts others call peaceful, and in both public and private spaces.

Figures around the world demonstrate the gravity of this scourge.

- 35 percent of women have experienced physical and/or sexual violence in their lifetime.

- Globally, 47 percent of murders of women are committed by an intimate partner or family member, compared to less than 6 percent of murders of men.

- Women represent 55 percent of victims of forced labour and 98 percent of the victims of sexual exploitation.[56]

The goal of this chapter is to evaluate where men stand in terms of suffering relative to women, not just how certain crimes affect women vs men. It is important to do due diligence here, for an anti-MeToo (or more broadly, a backlash to women's rights as

56 https://www.unwomen.org/en/news/stories/2016/9/speech-by-lakshmi-puri-on-economic-costs-of-violence-against-women

some scholars like Susan Boyd[57] would argue) would be more appropriate in one case vs the other. Therefore, moving up from the subcategory of violence—specifically sexual and physical violence—let us look at all matters affecting men.

Men's issues, like women's, have a high amount of overlap irrespective of socio-economic differences. If women's issues can be broadly grouped (into discrimination, GBV and lack of access to resources), so can be men's. As collected from several national and international sources[58] (which include large studies and reports, and MRM-backed resources like International Conference on Men's Issues), men's issues group into the following categories:

1. Expectations of masculinity (or more broadly, discriminatory expectations)

2. Disposability (drafting into war primarily) and higher exposure to violence

3. Lack of support for mental (and physical) health issues

4. False accusations and lack of protection

DECONSTRUCTION OF FAMILY DYNAMICS AND POLITICS

Women are overwhelmed everywhere, trying to bear the load of child and elder care because societal expectations and support ecosystems didn't keep up with women entering the workforce in large numbers. Working women are stretched thinner than their male counterparts in most workplaces. Also, with systemic prioritization of resources for men in some societies, many women find themselves in lesser occupations with unsatisfactory jobs and lower pay. In other cases, as discussed in Chapter 7, they find themselves outnumbered and struggle to advance. The fact

---

57 https://en.wikipedia.org/wiki/Susan_Boyd
58 https://goodmenproject.com/featured-content/talk-men-top-10-issues-today-gmp/; https://menscenter.org/issues-that-affect-men/; https://icmi2019.icmi.info/index.html#about

that caregiving is overwhelmingly a responsibility women find themselves in (either by choice or compulsion), not men, makes having a choice to not work seem rational. Many women also make arguments of preference and skillset to justify this ask. Women's incomes are also, more often than not, considered disposable. So investing a lot of heartache and feeling stretched for something that can go if it has to is difficult.

When two partners look at who should take home to take care of family, it's usually the one who is making less. Systemic education and pay gaps determine this— so it's more often than not the woman.[59]
—Lorraine Hariton, President and CEO, Catalyst

Understandably, women feel frustrated. 'But the core argument that it should be a viable choice for women to not work and they shouldn't be made to feel bad about it is invalid.' The argument has the same fatal flaw as the androcentric ideas that fuel the MRM. This has been called out by MRMs too (Note: I find this point to be one of the few valid points made by some of otherwise highly misogynist organizations).[60] 'Because women's equality and men's equality are after all two sides of the same coin.' So to be a just argument, the narrative requires a counter-consideration: Do men also get the same choice?

I don't want to imply this as a generalization, but more and more what I am seeing for married men like me, all around me … I guess what is happening with Indian men … is that there is an expectation that they will slog to bring the bread home, no matter what, but there can be no counter-expectation. I guess what were previously unfair expectations on women—that they

59 https://www.drnancyoreilly.com/level-up-the-diversity-womens-business-leadership-conference/
60 https://gynocentrism.com/2019/12/01/anti-gynocentrism-is-the-only-anti-feminism-that-matters/

have to wash and cook—are now eased with maids and services available, but the pressure on men can't ease.

—Rajarshi Bhattacharjee, IT Professional, Chennai

Every time a man gets looked down upon for not providing for his family or doesn't get to choose what the society segregates as 'homely' (e.g., a primary caregiver or homemaker role), we are making a statement. The question becomes: If a man is less of a man for staying home or rearing children, is a woman less of a woman for stepping into a boardroom? The argument of equality and the right to choose can't be won at the same time except in a facile way. Economic sustenance is key to human survival. Both genders getting to choose to not work is not a feasible scenario. Anuja Chauhan,[61] one of the spunkiest women I have ever met, said this to me on the matter and it stuck with me: 'There's one thing my mother taught me from childhood—every human, man or woman, needs to have two things. They need to know how to cook. And they need to have a source of income.' I have a personal story too on this—from my mother—but I will save that for later.

One of the grievances expressed in MRM charters is around alimony and the burden of support. Men feel slighted to be stuck with the burden of paying for expenses of an ex-spouse, specifically when the marriage was short-lived, doesn't have offspring or was terminated owing to a reason outside of the man's control. We have deliberated on some of the points around alimony earlier, but the specific point to stress here is that women not being self-sufficient makes them vulnerable to others in all stages of their life. Economic prowess controls social voice. Therefore, forcing men to be the breadwinners and bearers of expenses creates a problem of unequal social currency. And it goes further, for it also creates a lack of representation. If more and more women choose not to work, those who do would be outnumbered, courts won't have female judges, and governments won't have female policymakers.

61 https://en.wikipedia.org/wiki/Anuja_Chauhan

For many women in this world, it's not a choice to work. My argument is for them—not towards them.

Ladkiyon ko self-sufficient banate nahin hain. Parivar unko padate nahin hain. To bas, bad mein dhamki de dete hain ke case uthalo, ya phir police ke pas jao hi mat, khilayega kaun? (They don't make the girls self-sufficient. The families don't get them educated. So that's it. Later they just threaten them: take your case back or don't go to the police. Who will feed you otherwise?)

—Renuka Pamecha, Social Worker and Activist, Rajasthan

MASCULINITY AND MAKING OF VIOLENT MEN

Apart from not being fair and creating an unequal socioeconomic infrastructure that would result in further limitation of opportunities and propagation of injustice, gender-differentiated expectation creates societies in which men commit grievous crimes against women—and other men. The Save Indian Family Foundation (SIFF)[62]—the primary of the Indian MRM groups—has landing and FAQ pages that would shock feminists and non-feminists alike (e.g., image below). However, there is one point on their FAQ page that holds merit. In answer to the question 'Do men commit a greater number of crimes?' they cite the assignment of 'violent protector' roles to men as the reason. Expectations of masculinity plague men and harm women all around the world. But in extremely patriarchal societies like India, this manifests in violent ways. The harmful reinforcement of 'culture' (which is sometimes labelled as honour and at other times as values), without understanding and acknowledging how and why such was designed, has been criticized in several places in this manuscript (e.g., in Chapter 4 through the case studies and in Chapter 5 in the context of consent). Conclusions are not hard to draw. But concluding and comprehending are two very different things, so as

---

62 https://www.saveindianfamily.org/

we near the end of this work, I will do a deep dive here into gender role assignment and its effect on violence.

To err is human. To flex is male. To rise is un-female. The Indian society, for the most part, believes women to be not only honour bearers and in requirement of protection but also the ones less effectual in maximizing returns. Practices like dowry further worsen a woman's value, for she is seen as a nuisance who'd need to be protected, can bring dishonour to the family and will cause a drain on the family's finances on growing up. This is not just a tale out of the villages of Rajasthan and Haryana, but a reality that is true for most Indian homes. In the 2010s, the Indian government had to run regular campaigns to convince its citizens to keep their girl child (alive) and invest in them.[63] Women are more often than not the brunt bearers of inequality when resources are limited. In my own extended family, for several of my neighbours back in India, and many colleagues here in the USA, economic discussions involve conversations on daughter's wedding expenses. Their education is mandatory these days (at least up to college), but there's no expectation that they'd bring in income that'd supplement the family's income, especially after marriage. So in families with lesser means, the boys go to school if only one can. In families which can educate both, more expensive degrees are reserved for the male children, who, in turn, are under a disproportionate amount of pressure to succeed.

Apart from education and skills, the personality traits of men are also made to develop in line with the expectation that they would need to be the gatherers, the protectors, the iron shields. We have talked about atrocities against girls because of this differentiated upbringing, which ranges from putting them in an earthen pot in shallow graves[64] to saving the best meals for the boys.[65]

---

63 https://www.pmindia.gov.in/en/government_tr_rec/beti-bachao-beti-padhao-caring-for-the-girl-child/
64 https://www.bbc.com/news/world-asia-india-50668883
65 The latest instance of this that I have witnessed has been in a diaspora family in the USA we are very close to, where the glass of milk kept out for

Humne to ghar pe yehin dekha, bhai ka tabiyat kharab ho to turant le jaate hain doctor pass (What we have seen in our homes is that if it's my brother who is ill, they will take him to the doctor as soon as possible).

—Kamini Shukla, Activist, Rajasthan, quoting girls from families she works with

But what happens to the boys is not pretty either.

- They are taught to be strong and shamed for crying. It's drilled into them that they need to be the breadwinners and the protectors.

The insecurity I have ... I had ... has been there from childhood. When we were young it was because the family wants you to be something, but you want something else. Social structure is such that the pressure is on men that men have to study, have to excel. Because you have to make your family proud. If you want something else ... if your personality is not that ... even if you have confidence that you are on the right track, you will be ok, no one listens.

—Rajarshi Bhattacharjee, IT Professional, Chennai

- In the same years where their interests and hobbies are channelled to make sure they stay male, their libidos are ignored. No conversations or acknowledgements happen. However, allowances are made (for boys will be boys after all) while their sisters are projected as coy and 'need'-less (pun intended).

- The way of life demonstrated to them has tasks; for example, cooking meals, cleaning dishes and washing clothes are taken care of for them primarily by the women in the family.

---

longer is handed to the female twin, while a fresh glass is always put out for the male child.

- Stories are selectively picked from the epics to celebrate male virility and female sacrifice. And while stories of war front valour by men are showcased, discussing matters that show female endurance is shied away from. There are no talks to boys on menstruation, pregnancy and childbirth. Mothers hide their struggles from their sons, raising males who are either awkward and impassionate or are abusers, for they see these as weaknesses, not strengths.

- In Hindu tradition, sisters tie bands on the arms of their brothers to seal the promise of protection. Similar traditions exist in other religions, subcultures and marriage vows, where protection is promised and, in exchange, they trust the men (brothers, husbands and fathers) with decision and power.

- Backbench giggles and 'talk' in locker rooms are allowed for boys, as long as they act proper in family functions. But for their sisters, they are appointed as moral censurers and wingmen.

I grew up in a bubble, between two brothers. I was very protected. Live-in or boyfriends are far-fetched, my elder brother won't even let me answer the doorbell if I was wearing sleeveless. I love him but was terrified of him. Still I am.

—A close friend, 2020, anonymous for she doesn't want her father or brother to read this and think that she's ungrateful

For me, growing up, my 11-year-old brother had needed to accompany 19-year-old me for short late-night walks back home from my uncle's house to mine. Safety? Yes, it can be argued at such, except that my cousin brother at 11 was a lankier, 'no way in hell can defend anyone' kid compared to my stout angry self.

- Lastly, the need to be respectful to women for social propriety is taught, but not enforced. It can't be enforced with the role expectations that are defined. It can't really be reasoned for that would require unravelling of what has been conditioned.

Their sisters, friends and neighbours—the ones who are lesser, weaker, the ones who are allowed to, and in fact expected to, cry, the ones held to lower economic but higher moral standards—suddenly need to be placed as individuals who should have equal say in matters of family, have the right to reject their advances and can choose to leave them. This is a hard and sudden pill to swallow. So respect for women is taught as the 'right thing to do' (read 'the honourable' thing to do), not the 'right thing'. The condescending undertone of 'real men don't rape' campaigns and Bollywood tag lines of heroes who don't hit women don't celebrate equality. They celebrate masculinity.It is not surprising therefore that Indian boys grow up trying to, but never really comprehending, gender equality. Following are some quotes I picked from Quora and other public opinion forums from Indian men noted to be between ages 25 and 40:

Yes, I do want to give my daughter the same liberties as my son—but it's just so much more unsafe for the girls.

A woman brash and stupid enough to want to party among hooligans and male drunks deserve to be molested. We are not against equality, but we are for common sense.

We discussed in previous chapters surveys that showed that Indian men overwhelmingly believe that women, at times, deserve to be beaten. It shouldn't be surprising that the impossible, unreal men, who have grown up hiding their fears and doubts, when shoved around by life, expend their pent-up aggression on the ones they believe are weak, which is mostly the other sex, who have been conveniently conditioned to be ready for the same. In times of crisis or conflict or when faced with rejection, most men are ashamed to ask for help. We will go more into this in our discussion on men and mental health and as we discuss Sushant Singh Rajput's suicide, but it's not just self-harm that's an outcome of this. Violent acts like the throwing of acids, gang rape, rioting and public lynching have a component of claiming back power. Inadequacies, inabilities and rejections don't matter as much in the anonymity of a crowd.

A clear sex difference has been documented cross-culturally in the way men and women display aggression.[66]

On men and violence, statistics are indeed available worldwide to mark distinctly that a much higher amount of violent crimes is committed by men than by women (United Nations Office on Drugs and Crime has published some pretty comprehensive reports). Now, as mentioned above, SIFF reasons that this is because of the role men are put into, and if the roles were reversed, the statistics would be too. But is it completely so? Most reports available at the time of this writing summarize the reasons to be a combination of biological—primarily, testosterone and predisposition to certain mental disorders (like anti-social personality disorders [ASPDs] which men are three times more likely to have than women)—and social (adherence to masculine ideologies).

When men hold onto a fairly narrow view of what it is to be a man, challenges to this masculine identity—such as when a partner who doesn't wish to play the housewife or a gay man who doesn't act as a man 'should'—can lead to feelings of intense anger, ultimately resulting in violence.[67]

Narrow definitions of what it means to be a man, although not as exaggerated with cultural reinforcement as in India, exist throughout the world. In the West (read the USA), these are often expressed through popular culture, mostly for corporate

66 https://nypost.com/2019/01/16/the-scientific-reasons-why-men-are-more-violent-than-women/
67 https://nypost.com/2019/01/16/the-scientific-reasons-why-men-are-more-violent-than-women/

(read sales) benefits. 'My mother raised me to be a man' is not an uncommon phrase to hear. Aisles in department stores in the USA can be identified from miles as boys vs girls. Pink, crafty, dolls and dolling-up sets are the toys placed in front of girls from infancy, while guns, trucks, building blocks and tools are given to boys. 'Daddy's little girl whom daddy will always protect' and 'Daddy's princess whom daddy will give away'—fathers take pride in such lines and daughters gush. In a popular matrimonial show in the USA ('The Millionaire Matchmaker', Bravo),[68] the matchmaker, a woman herself, repeatedly asks the women to dress for the men in a way that'd get their juices going and to not have too much 'masculine' energy.

It is important to note here that I have had some experience with a European upbringing and found it to be quite gender-neutral in comparison. I had the privilege of questioning Joacim Mattisson (a close friend's husband who left his job in Switzerland to be able to marry my friend in the USA and has no problem earning less or even sitting idle while she remains the primary breadwinner) about gender roles in upbringing in Sweden—his native land. 'It doesn't exist,' he had said. 'It is only on coming to the USA I had realized that girls and boys are supposed to play with different toys. That girls and boys are supposed to be different.'

But all European nations are not the same. Maxim Kostylev is a close friend I met in graduate school. His parents moved to the USA to escape communist Russia when he was 11, and he has had a mostly Russian, some American upbringing. 'No, my parents never discriminated. But yes, they brought my sister up to be a woman and me up to be a man.' Maxim had said adamantly. 'What will you do for your boy? Do you believe there is a need to bring him up to be a man? Or can he be just brought up?' Maxim, who is an ultra-liberal woke in most matters, a hippy almost, didn't quite answer.

---

68 https://en.wikipedia.org/wiki/The_Millionaire_Matchmaker

The relationship between testosterone and violence is noted to be quite complicated. Although some clear correlations of testosterone spikes with violent behaviours have been established, the effect of testosterone has been found to have a range of responses and is not consistent across the male populations. Also, gender discussions now challenge the notion of by-birth gender-differentiated character traits. We will come to that in a bit, but it can be concluded that at least 50 per cent, if not more, of the blame lies with hegemonic masculine ideologies that are ingrained into men. American Psychological Association's practice guideline for men and boys[69] (released for the first time in 2018, reportedly after 13 years of work) guides mostly against the traditional masculine ideologies.

Note: The one for women and girls was published in 2007.

The notion that men and women are different is behind gender roles and gender-differentiated societal expectations. So it needs to be mentioned here that this notion itself has been challenged quite a few times. A 2005 analysis, which in turn is a compilation of 46 meta-analyses over two decades on the topic,[70] found only a few main differences that appeared with gender. It noted gender to have none-to-minimal effect on most of the psychological variables examined. This study's multiple citations and other independent studies on brain composition support this claim. Besides (and more importantly), assigned gender roles and social context had more to do with a person's actions than their actual gender—in other words, being told whether to be a man or a woman and how that decided behaviours, not preferences that are thought to be inherent to each gender by birth. So is it the years of living the 'differences' that have convinced us that we are different? Or has being different led us to prefer (and be good at) different things?

---

69 https://www.apa.org/about/policy/boys-men-practice-guidelines.pdf
70 Janet Shibley Hyde (American Psychological Association, October 2005).

It is not possible to conclusively comment on these questions at the time of writing, for as many would argue, irrespective of what some published research says, different behaviours are observed in women vs men, and physiological (hormonal) differences that lead to this have also been widely researched and published upon. Some studies also argue that gender itself is a spectrum.[71]

It must be noted, however, that masculinity (like femininity) does have a spectrum. All men are not alpha men, and men who are not alpha men are equally victimized by expectations of hegemonic masculinity, possibly more than women who are ridiculed and challenged for being unwomanly.

Whether we believe gender to be a social construct, biological and binary, or a spectrum, the harm caused by gender-differentiated role scripting to men, women and society is not debatable. Therefore, these are questions worth keeping in mind. Physiological differences needn't be worsened with sociocultural exaggeration.

MEN AND MENTAL HEALTH

According to the National Institute of Health, USA, the prevalence of mental health issues is lower in men than in women.[72] But men are less likely to have received treatment for mental health. Centers for Disease Control and Prevention report[73] (2018) showed men more likely to die of suicide than women, and suicides increasing for both men and women. Most of the matter around mental health for men lies with the stigma which is worse for men than for women. Men having mental health issues, and needing to seek help, is seen as a lack of strength, while for women, excuses can be made blaming hormones (moods). This prevents men from

71 https://www.usd.edu/diversity-and-inclusiveness/office-for-diversity/safe-zone-training/spectrum-model#:~:text=The%20Gender%20Identity%20Spectrum,considered%20to%20be%20non%2Dbinary
72 https://www.nimh.nih.gov/health/topics/men-and-mental-health/index.shtml
73 https://www.cdc.gov/nchs/products/databriefs/db330.htm

seeking help.[74] It is interesting to note that awareness around post-traumatic stress disorder (PTSD) and trauma in general is owed to men—the soldiers in the Vietnam War in particular—and is still largely viewed as a war veteran condition. PTSD was referred to for long as 'shell shock', stressing it's connection to war.[75] Global studies note men to be predispositioned to have a higher occurrence of certain mental health disorders like ASPD, while women are predispositioned to disorders such as depression and bipolar disorder.[76] The reasonings for the same, however, remain unclear and are left at being the interaction of complex genetic and environmental factors.

Searching for mental health statistics for men specifically out of India expectedly leads to mostly dead ends. One fairly comprehensive report published in *The Lancet Psychiatry*[77] appraising the same period as in the US study found anxiety and depressive disorders to have a higher prevalence in women in India, and mental disorders increasing in adults steeply between 1990 and 2017. Another Lancet study found men to women ratio for suicide death rate in India to be 1:34.[78] One report that cites and analyses this study notes women to be suicidal in higher numbers, owing to biological susceptibility to certain conditions and high prevalence of post-marriage emotional and physical abuse (domestic violence, dowry abuse and emotional abuse by in-laws).[79] Despite expert testimonials, it is very hard to ascertain if such assertions are facts because of two reasons. One, high integrity quantitative data is

74 https://www.healthline.com/health-news/how-can-we-reduce-mens-mental-health-stigma
75 https://www.verywellmind.com/ptsd-from-the-vietnam-war-2797449
76 https://www.womenshealth.gov/mental-health
77 https://www.thelancet.com/journals/lanpsy/article/PIIS2215-0366(19)30475-4/fulltext
78 https://www.thelancet.com/journals/lanpub/article/PIIS2468-2667(18)30138-5/fulltext
79 https://www.theweek.in/news/health/2019/12/23/anxiety-and-depression-more-prevalent-among-women-than-men-in-india-study.html

rarely accompanying or available (e.g., experts quoted in the report mention studies that show that women have more suicidal thoughts and attempts but the actual studies are not cited). Second, bias can be high, even among regarded medical professionals (e.g., in an *The Indian Express* article I was interviewed for, a credited expert provided the opinion that post-partum depression has to do with women not wanting to be mothers when research repeatedly discredits such assumptions).

Reasons aside, the reports quoted here do suggest that suicide and affectation rates are higher in women in India. In my opinion, although it might seem prima facia that this can be attributed to either life being harder for women in India or to women being biologically predispositioned, or both, there isn't enough data that I could chance upon at the time of this writing to conclude on the root cause. For example, life could be harder for men in India than women for completely different reasons (while women are discriminated against, abused and side-lined, men have no choice but to be breadwinners in a developing economy, bear family responsibilities in a low-infrastructure nation and live with higher pressure of expectation). What is more important to note is the fact that both male and female suicide death rates in India were found to be significantly higher than the global average.

Now the tough question: If women are more affected by mental health disorders and suicide remains significantly higher in Indian women than in both Indian men and global women, why the plethora of articles suddenly on men's mental health and mental health awareness? Well, women committing suicide is an easier-to-accept concept in India. Historical and cultural references are aplenty—from Jauhar and mass suicides post partition[80] to women killing themselves in scores in movies on being violated or tormented. Women—submissive, softer, weaker, having a more

---

80 https://www.researchgate.net/publication/304222881_Women_as_ Martyrs_Mass_Suicides_at_Thoa_Khalsa_During_the_Partition_of_India

difficult life in India—are expected to kill themselves. Men are not (unless they are students appearing for high-pressure exams). Second, awareness of mental disorders in men (and, therefore, acceptability) has indeed been zero to minimal in India.

Let's take Sushant Singh Rajput's suicide for example. On 14 June 2020, Sushant Singh Rajput was reportedly found hanging in his Bandra, Mumbai, home.[81] His death came as a shock to the nation, as most celebrity deaths do. However, the reaction to Rajput's death was unprecedented.[82] Coming in close succession to other celebrity deaths (including the likes of Irrfan Khan and Rishi Kapoor, both of which saw expected bout of sadness from the nation for a limited amount of time, Rajput's death started dominating the nation's headlines and, as of the end of September 2020, continued to be an unbelievable saga of media manipulation, social media domination and public rage (first against Bollywood heavyweights for allegedly having driven Sushant to suicide through bullying and exclusion—Sushant being an outsider allegedly had had to fight harder for opportunities competing against celebrity and insider youngsters—and then against his girlfriend for pushing him towards suicide). Although reports surfaced of him being depressed and bipolar, including chats with his sister that ascertained their know-how of him being on medication, #JusticeforSSR trended higher than any other matter of pertinence (from the COVID pandemic and shrinking GDP to Indo-China conflict), and conspiracy theories obscured the airwaves.

India, for the most part, refused to believe that Rajput could have taken his own life without provocation. He either was murdered (as per one group of speculators) or was pushed and manipulated to kill himself (through drugs and emotional abuse by his girlfriend). It is worth noting that Rajput did have a story that is expected

81 https://www.nytimes.com/2020/06/14/world/asia/sushant-singh-rajput-death.html

82 https://www.scmp.com/lifestyle/health-wellness/article/3095335/sushant-singh-rajput-suicide-bollywood-actors-death

to resonate strongly with the common man India. A brilliant student and a philanthropic individual who was able to break into Bollywood and raise to the heights of stardom is someone for whom a great amount of sympathy should exist. However, his death by suicide continues to be challenged by India as an incident that is impossible not just because of who he was or his popularity.

Let's look at two other celebrity deaths for a comparison. Irrfan Khan,[83] who died a little over a month before Sushant of a terminal 'physical' illness, was also an outsider who had made it in Bollywood and debatably had demonstrated much finer acting skills. Irrfan was also an international actor who had starred in British and American films. His death had saddened the nation, but there were no denial or conspiracy theories. Actress Sridevi,[84] who had dominated Bollywood for over five decades and had risen to legend status, was reported to have died of 'accidental drowning' in her bathtub in her hotel room in Dubai. She was said to have gone into the bathroom after having chatted with her husband, who was waiting in the same hotel room and found her a bit later unresponsive in the tub. At first, her death was reported to be due to sudden cardiac arrest. Later, that reasoning was retracted, saying that no signs of cardiac failure were found. Her getting drowned suddenly in a bathtub with no intoxication or incapacitation, or any other reasoning provided, was mostly accepted. Conspiracy theories did float around for a brief while (not much in mainstream media, mostly on YouTube) about her possibly being on anti-depressants and such, or her husband having had something to do with her death. But for the most part, there wasn't much resistance. Similar after-stories had followed the deaths of actresses Divya Bharti[85] and Parveen Babi (the latter was accepted to have had long-term paranoid schizophrenia).[86] Sushant's girlfriend Rhea,

83 https://en.wikipedia.org/wiki/Irrfan_Khan
84 https://en.wikipedia.org/wiki/Sridevi
85 https://en.wikipedia.org/wiki/Divya_Bharti
86 https://en.wikipedia.org/wiki/Parveen_Babi

against whom his father had filed an FIR for misappropriation of funds and abetment to suicide, had been taken into custody for trafficking marijuana, was refused bail, was interrogated non-stop for days, was slut-shamed in all major social media platforms (with memes of her as a witch or a black magic practitioner trending) and was hounded by the media. Images of her getting pushed, shoved and manhandled by the media while she was in visible disarray had surfaced as had troubling details of her interrogation, but for the most part, Indian sentiment stayed the same—she deserved to be witch-hunted and punished for Sushant's death. Note: after three-plus months, charges that could be brought against her, despite the involvement of multiple government agencies, were not related to Sushant's death but in connection to recreational drug use and distribution. India finds the blame to lie with Rhea for Sushant, a 34-year-old, using marijuana.

This had happened after the 1990 suicide of businessman Mukesh Agarwal too, following which his wife, Bollywood star Rekha, was turned into a national enemy overnight. Rekha was called a murderer and a vamp, even though she was out of the country when Mukesh took his own life.[87] Just like Sushant's father, Rekha's in-laws, particularly her mother-in-law, had blamed her publicly for her husband's suicide.

Indian women, no matter how successful, can get sad, depressed and schizophrenic and can take their own lives. Indian men have to be manipulated, emotionally abused and drugged to get there.[88] Bollywood is just a microcosm mirroring a society. Blaming women for all the misfortune that befall men (and women) is a consistent narrative which, disregarding what is found to be the truth in Rajput's case, is disserving the nation. Particularly, channelling the dialogue away from mental health like it has been

---

87 https://www.idiva.com/entertainment/bollywood/rekha-a-murderer-blamed-for-mukesh-aggarwals-death-by-suicide/18013149
88 https://www.womensweb.in/2020/06/depression-and-suicide-real-illness-we-need-to-talk-jun20wk3sr/

post Rajput's death is a tremendous missed opportunity and a dangerous precedence to set.

MEN AND SEX: OR SHOULD IT BE INDIAN MEN AND SEX?

Another common narrative—immortalized through proverbs and sayings and such—is that male is the gender with higher sexual urges. Combined with the 'men are takers' angle, it is made to seem inevitable that men will have to engage in sexual coercion and assault. September 2020, like many of the preceding months, saw another high-profile incident of gang rape happening in India in which a 19-year-old,[89] raped and grievously injured by four assailants, succumbed to her injuries. Allegations of corruption, gross negligence and cover-up, and caste oppression by an upper-caste nexus (including the government and law-enforcement agencies) are strong in this case, very akin to Bhanwari Devi's account in Chapter 2 (from discounting of the victim and victim's statement to the possible destruction of evidence and citing of dubious facts), indicating that heartland India has been stuck for 30 years. But possibly most pertinent out of this incident was a statement from former Indian Supreme Court judge and Chairman of Press Council of India—Mr Markandey Katju, in which he had called sex to be a natural urge for men and, therefore, rape an expected outcome with rising unemployment among youth,[90] who would need to a have a release. Understandably, his statement created a firestorm (worsened by the fact that his word choices and how the sentences were formed in his tweet didn't do justice to any valid point he might have had on the male sexual urge, and instead read like a justification for young men to rape).[91]

---

89 https://www.bbc.com/news/world-asia-india-54370087
90 https://www.deccanchronicle.com/nation/current-affairs/011020/hathras-horror-markandey-katjus-post-linking-unemployment-to-rapes-i.html
91 https://www.scoopwhoop.com/news/justice-katju-what-s-wrong-with-you-there-is-no-other-reason-for-rape-than-a-rapist-period/

But does Katju have a point? Do men have higher sexual urges which worsen with socio-economic stress? Of course that can't justify rape, not by itself. For rape to happen, unsatisfied sexual urge and increased aggravation have to meet objectification and disregard of the other person's humanity. But even as a co-factor, that'd be a strong argument for healthy and regular release of sexual tension, which is lacking significantly in India.

Although a significant amount of available research does ascertain that men indeed have stronger and more persistent need for sex than women,[92] counter-views on this matter are also aplenty. The most comprehensive (and easiest to follow) article I could find in this matter is by Professor Roy F. Baumeister of the University of Florida.[93] The piece (which does cite counter-views, articles and books and also explains the rationale and methodology behind its conclusion) concludes that men have a much higher sex drive than women. Men and women are also noted to have different kinds of sex drive.[94] Works on this topic also point out the difference in the state of arousal behaviour in men vs women.[95] It is also known that decision-making in a state of arousal is significantly poor and affected.[96]

These, when combined with a lack of avenues of healthy and frequent sexual release, do create a build-up effect and contribute to increasing rates of sexual misdemeanours against women. As we have been discussing, for Indian men, there is an aspect of sociosexual expectations which, when combined with factors

92 https://www.psychologytoday.com/us/blog/dating-and-mating/202003/how-high-sex-drive-differs-in-men-and-women

93 https://www.psychologytoday.com/us/blog/cultural-animal/201012/the-reality-the-male-sex-drive

94 R. F.Baumeister, 'Gender Differences in Erotic Plasticity: The Female Sex Drive as Socially Flexible and Responsive', *Psychological Bulletin* 126, no. 3 (2000): 347.

95 M. L. Chivers, G. Rieger, E. Latty, and J. M. Bailey, 'A Sex Difference in the Specificity of Sexual Arousal', *Psychological Science* 15, no. 11 (2004): 736–744.

96 D. Ariely, *Predictably Irrational* (New York, NY: Harper Collins, 2008).

discussed above and in the earlier chapters, add towards the objectification and dehumanization of women.[97] Thinking of women as lesser and objects, and with deviant sexual urges, worsens with both socio-economic repression and deprivation. Indian men have to repress sexual urges and expressions and are largely in spaces where sexual escapades become difficult. But what causes them to rape, unless they are sick with a disorder, is that they also believe that they should be able to, and can, control women who they believe to be lesser.

World Health Organization's report[98] on sexual violence provides as conclusive a statement as possible in the matter of whether or not sexual deprivation or socio-economic stressors increase the occurrence of violence against women. They conclude that the factors at play here are additive and can only be looked at as increased risk factors.

I wanted to interview sexual offenders for further insight. What drove them to do what they did? There is excellent work done on this already by some BBC reporters, and getting interviews with incarcerat:d folks got difficult as COVID broke. So I talked to Nicki Bartram, a clinical counsellor who has been working with sex offenders in the prison system for over a decade, instead.

According to her, it is not about sex—unless there is a disorder. For every one of her patients—from college dorm rapists to the ones who had attacked women on streets, and from juvenile offenders to adults—there is a component of control that had come into play. She directed me to the wheel of control, which covers the entire spectrum of abuse—from emotional to physical to sexual.[99]

---

97 https://homegrown.co.in/article/802495/the-sexual-insecurities-of-indian-men
98 https://www.who.int/violence_injury_prevention/violence/global_campaign/en/chap6.pdf?ua=1
99 http://www.ncdsv.org/images/PowerControlwheelNOSHADING.pdf

It was about control. For all of them. They were trying to take control back somehow—somewhere in their life, they felt they had lacked it.

—Nicki Bartram, Counsellor, Phoenix

FALSE ACCUSATIONS AND MOTIVATED PERSECUTION

The pressure on men is incredibly high. Women can come dance in whatever way they want. They don't understand because they don't get turned on the same way, but then, if something happens, if I touch even accidentally, the responsibility is entirely mine....

—S. Bhagat, father to daughters, devoted husband, successful engineering professional, Jharkhand native, US resident

The quote above from S. Bhagat, one of the many men I interviewed for understanding first-hand concerns men have with #MeToo (or women's rights) in general is a perfect segue into the matter of false accusation. False (erroneous or motivated) accusations combined with lack of protection emerges to be 'the' key matter of concern, right after alimony and support burden, in all MRM charters. It emerges in both academic and non-academic debates around men's rights, and MeToo has expectedly stirred the hornet's nest further. Except for a small circle consisting of individuals who work day in and day out in legal aid and research, most city men I talked to have an overwhelming perception that men are powerless against accusations, and family courts are systematically biased against men. This, combined with stories of motivated accusations ruining reputations and preventing access to children that are found abound on the Internet, has them believing that they are one step away from a pitfall. We have talked about the grey areas in the earlier chapters, so we will focus here on motivated false accusations—data, opinion and impact on legal recourses.

False accusations and lack of protection affect men in two areas: family law (child custody, alimony and domestic violence) and sexual assault allegations (livelihood, social prestige and family life). In this manuscript, this matter has unsurprisingly come up again and again—from discussions on marital rape (as discussed, primary reasoning provided for the opposition of criminalization of marital rape in India is a higher risk to men for persecution with false allegations that will be impossible to disperse) to domestic violence (some reports, as noted above, show incorrect and erroneous arrests of men which affect their future significantly). Sustenance of financial responsibility of ex-spouses or partners through exaggerated child support or alimony, although not necessarily always a matter related to false accusations, emerges as another key grievance. Below are some examples lifted from the Internet which capture the sentiments.

Please stop believing these accusers!!! You have to do a
REAL thorough investigation. People are using
domestic violence as a weapon.

My life is in ruins I have not seen my children for
3 years and I am not guilty of anything. If I didn't have to
go through this nightmare I don't even believe it myself …
and my case is going through appeals … and my nightmare
continues and I miss my twins so bad.

Being a weekend father isn't enough. We are fathers full time. The
laws need to be changed or revised in a way that is fair for the chil-
dren and parents. Fathers shouldn't be forced to see their child one or
two days a week and paying child support for the other days that they
are forced to be absent. Equal rights are equal rights. Woman want to
be treated equally? Well so do men. Our children suffer the most.

All of these are comments on the website A Voice for Men (AVFM)[100] on an article on false allegations of domestic

---

100 https://avoiceformen.com/

violence,[101] lifted and used here as is from the website. And the like in the below tweet, calls for counter-movements are based on this more than anything.

It's so easy to take anyone's name publicly
and claim harassment.

We claim to want to be gender-neutral

If @anuragkashyap72 is found innocent,
will this woman be punished for publicly tarnishing
his reputation?#MenToo.[102]

Save Indian Family Foundation (.org) site directly alleges Section 125 of the Code of Criminal Procedure to be an extortion tool. In an article on the matter,[103] the author calls #MeToo to be a Western concept and, therefore, citing the Indian government's openness to the same, argues in the favour of spousal support law modification to match Western systems. The site's position on this is not just a grievance against the system(s) but a gross generalization of women to be gold diggers who run 'alimony rackets'. Another site with the same name: Save Indian Family (.in) has a document published for Indian men waiting to be married on how they can protect themselves (and their families) from disastrous false allegations and expenses post marriage.[104] The site (and the likes of it) also publishes regularly on events organized to create awareness on false accusations.[105] Similar documents exist on international popular MRM sites too (e.g., AVFM).

....

101 https://www.petition2congress.com/ctas/stop-false-allegations-domestic-violence

102 https://www.saveindianfamily.in/

103 https://www.saveindianfamily.org/already-paying-maintenance-to-wife-this-activism-will-end-it/

104 https://www.saveindianfamily.in/2018/05/21/warning-for-indian-bachelors/

105 http://www.saveindianfamily.in/2017/12/20/toi-on-valentines-day-activists-seek-justice-for-men-implicated-in-false-rape-cases/

Now, on the matter of false accusations and victimization of men by the legal system, valid concerns do exist. But it is flawed and distorted arguments like these that make the MRM sites appear misguided, ill-informed and misogynist. Let's take the SIFF article for examining this.

So, it is undemocratic and extremely unjust on the part of the Indian judges to order young men to pay lifetime maintenance to their estranged wives. Imagine, a 28-year-old man is getting divorced from his 26-year-old wife. If the wife is eligible to get maintenance, then Indian family courts order the man to pay maintenance to his wife for her entire life.

So, this 28-year-old man will technically end up paying maintenance for the next 50 years or so, if his wife chooses not to marry again or chooses not to do a job. This is almost like an infinite liability for the man. This literally signs men up for some kind of financial slavery, as they have to work for free and someone else gets a part of their income. Making men work for free for life is slavery.[106]

Section 125 of the Code of Criminal Procedure[107] is misconstrued quite a bit in this article and is not elaborately explained (possibly intentionally). The section is not just for spousal support but also for the support of children and parents. More importantly, the section orders a man to support his wife (pre or post divorce) only in cases where the spouse is unable to maintain herself but is either living with him or living separately for a valid cause, which from the way it reads has to be something that is not her doing or choice. She also needs to be not committing (or have committed) adultery. It clearly notes exception, even cancellation, of a previously issued

106 Save Indian family foundation.org
107 https://indiankanoon.org/doc/1056396/

court order if a spouse is found to be living separately by mutual consent, refuses to live with her husband without a good enough reason, or is or was involved in adultery.

(4) No Wife shall be entitled to receive an allowance from her husband under this section if she is living in adultery, or if, without any sufficient reason, she refuses to live with her husband, or if they are living separately by mutual consent.[108]

(5) On proof that any wife in whose favour an order has been made under this section is living in adultery, or that without sufficient reason she refuses to live with her husband, or that they are living separately by mutual consent, the Magistrate shall cancel the order.[109]

Therefore, even the points made on making proportionate adjustments to period and amount of payment based on the duration of marriage are worth deliberating. On the surface, it's only fair to ensure that a man is expected to bear this responsibility for a reasonable amount of time. However, most of the scenarios insinuated in the article where men are feared to have to bear expenses without reason are not as biased towards the woman as it's made to seem. The entire judgment rests on the premise that there is a valid cause for a woman to have separated or to be living separately from her spouse. There is also significant room for judicial discretion in determining what constitutes 'unable to maintain herself'. In simple terms, one merely choosing not to ever have a job is not automatically a good enough reason, for the section talks of inability, not unwillingness. Other discretionary considerations, like what artist and activist R. Bose said on this matter (a husband deliberately having limited his wife's ability to have an income), also need to be made. In such

108 Ibid.
109 Ibid.

a case, for example, if the husband's deliberate limitation of his spouse's ability to pursue education or employment continues to impact or reduce the prospects of the wife's earnings, and their separation was his doing, the merit of the 'duration of support needing to be proportionate to marriage duration' argument gets reduced. Let's also not forget what activist Renuka Pamecha had pointed out—in large sections of India, women's education and employment are not invested in; many women, therefore, once forced to separate from their husbands, are not left with viable means of sustaining a living. If the woman had invested in the marriage—supporting household responsibilities and bearing the load of chores which is often the case—it is cruelty to leave her without compensation if the marriage falling apart was not her doing.

On searching for national and international papers on this, I did come across quite a few which use court cases and legal statistics to disperse what men's rights groups claim.

For example, a work by Melville and Hunter[110] funded by the Commonwealth Attorney General's Department and Department of Finance and Administration out of Australia, analyses and cites several other contemporary and earlier works and looks into the accusations around women fabricating allegations to generate access restriction measures (apart from financial burdening, the second point made on this matter is that controlling and limiting access to the children as a revenge and control mechanism motivates women). It investigates whether or not Apprehended Violence Orders or Restraining Orders—as they are called—are pursued maliciously to limit men's access to children for vengeance or leverage, and family courts being rigged in favour of women allow this to be a mechanism for women abusing men.

The findings amount to what we have already stated: Equal prevalence of domestic abuse is possible in men and women, but

---

110 https://kar.kent.ac.uk/1719/1/R_Hunter_As_everybody_knows_2001.pdf

most studies concluding so have looked at the recording of the violence in isolation—aggression vs self-defence and other such confounding factors were not determined. The work also makes an additional point on the comparison of the severity of injury and harm caused.

On the other points, this work and other such discount the claims by using court records and judgment statistics. On the matter of false restraining order claims, for example, this work found that out of the 176 files examined, 54 per cent had the occurrence of domestic violence and 38 per cent didn't have a restraining order obtained. The work cites a few other studies of similar methodology and conclusion (including one on child sexual abuse allegations). The results presented amount to, at best, no evidence of the majority of cases filed being fabricated for control of access.

Another study provides alternative explanations for contact with children being denied to men like a breakdown of previous arrangements or repeat instances of violence posing risk to the children.[111]

Similarly, on the point of family laws being rigged in favour of women and court officials having a bias, the Hunter and Melville paper provides surveys conducted akin to articles cited above which generated comments in scores. The comments expressed the dismay of men against the family court system and overwhelming opinions that the system is biased. However, on comparison of actual court orders in the cases, evidence disadvantaging men because of bias wasn't found. In the majority of cases, fathers were allowed resolutions and in the ones in which they weren't, there were serious reasons. The dissatisfactions of the men were found to be amounting from several other compounding factors, including personal opinions on what is just.

---

111 https://www.csyw.qld.gov.au/resources/childsafety/practice-manual/prac-paper-domestic-violence.pdf

I talked about this to activists Renuka Pamecha and Kamini Shukla, people who have spent decades day in and day out in the criminal justice system in India (e.g., according to Pamecha, she has gone to court 180 times just to observe the criminal justice system in action and has studied and dispositioned over 13 years of FIRs file in Rajasthan). According to them, whether it's the police, court or society, gender violence is not accepted to be violence in the criminal justice system in India. The police work politically and even the administrative branches of government tasked with women's reform (like the Department of Women and Child Development and Social Welfare) would rather not have cases registered. According to Pamecha, she witnesses daily (her office is in a police station in Rajasthan) women getting disbelieved, coaxed and threatened. They are made to take back cases of domestic violence through trivialization, normalization and fear-mongering—often in the guise of well-meaning advice. This is because those she works with and around believe that, above all, families should be sustained and such matters (violence) are not a reason enough to split up families.

Hume kehta hain ke parviar todne wale auratein. Violence rokna unke language mein hi nahin hain (They call us the home breakers. The need to stop violence is not in their vocabulary).
—Renuka Pamecha, Activist, Rajasthan

Normally no one registers a case of even rape. *Dhamki milna regular baat hain. Gang itni strong hain inki ke koi register kara nahin sakta* (Getting threats is a regular thing. Their gangs are so strong that no one can register cases). *Women ko us trauma mein nahin jana hota hain* (Women don't want to go through that trauma). *Condition abhi bhi hain. Sirf rape nahin, cher char to aam baat hain* (Condition is still the same. It's not just rape, teasing and harassment are regular matters).
—Kamini Shukla, Activist, Rajasthan

Therefore, the concept of bias against men in the legal system, at least in India, is something they struggled to understand. What they felt is that some men, mostly urban, when dissatisfied with an outcome or served with an unfair experience (or just perceived to be unfair), start believing that theirs is the only narrative without taking time to consider the big picture. This is the point made in the Hunter–Melville paper too, which found that most men commenting on the bias of the justice system merely had received judgments they couldn't agree with.

The matter of perception also brings forward the issue of the Family Law Reform Act (and similar legislative modifications in other countries) brought about owing to resistance and popular sentiments generated by men's rights groups. The concern is that such modification(s) (made under the want of being unbiased and fair to men) endangers or ignores the safety and the 'best interest of the child'. Because they were changed to be in favour of contact with both parents to satisfy the need of the fathers not getting separated from their children.

Susan Boyd[112] in her publications argues the same to have happened in Canadian law, where social sentiments have affected 'legal knowledge in child custody law reforms'.[113] She argues that by overstressing the importance of a child's contact with both parents for his/her well-being and popularizing the idea that gender bias has operated to impact children's well-being negatively, men's rights groups brilliantly repurposed themselves as father's rights group (such as Fathers for Justice and Fathers are Capable Too) and were able to modulate child support and custody laws. The paper cites references to point out that in the matter of the well-being of a child, a well-functioning custodial parent and avoidance of parental conflict are equally important. These factors inevitably clash in some cases with the goal of continued contact with both parents and when such happens, legal systems are bound to lose sight of the 'best interest' of the child under the pressure of preventing bias against either parent.

112 https://en.wikipedia.org/wiki/Susan_Boyd
113 S. Boyd, 'Backlash and the Construction of Legal Knowledge: The Case of Child Custody Law', *Windsor Yearbook of Access to Justice* 20 (2001): 141.

Boyd's article also refers to other prestigious studies, like Dr Judith Wallerstein's, which found close relationship with a psychologically sound parent, whether or not the child comes into the divorce with pre-existing issues, and avoidance of exposure to the conflict to be more important than time spent with a non-custodial parent.[114]

Therefore, Boyd's article (and several other studies that research family law reforms) takes issue with such reforming. It further expresses that joint custody judgments more often than not ignore the matter of primary caregiving, nurturing and a mother's presence in the life of children being higher in most cases and, instead, 'focuses on the legal right to control women and children rather than the legal obligation to care for children'.

....

For a variety of complex socio-economic reasons, fathers rarely devote themselves to parenting the way mothers do. Most women would prefer that men engage in more parenting labor but achieving this result is easier said than done due to economic and social impediments. It is therefore inappropriate to introduce laws that overlook women's primary caregiving.[115]

There's also high precedence of judges awarding custody based on highly subjective sexist and moralistic personal biases (e.g., good mothers, despite being successful primary caregivers, lose custody for committing adultery or being a lesbian).[116] It is ironic that we are talking international courts here (and particularly, in this case, Canada) for I am sure that the readers recognize the similarity with the judgments dismissing gang rape and assault cases in India (Chapter 2).

....

114 J. S. Wallerstein and T. J. Tanke, 'To Move or Not to Move: Psychological and Legal Considerations in the Relocation of Children Following Divorce', *Family Law Quarterly* 30 (1996): 305.
115 Susan Boyd, Windsor Yearbook of Access to Justice, 2001.
116 K. Arnup, 'Mothers Just Like Others: Lesbians, Divorce, and Child Custody in Canada', *Canadian Journal of Women and the Law* 3, no. 1 (1989): 18.

As the Hunter–Melville work concludes, claims made in the matter of bias in family courts and malicious persecution of men by women with the aid of the legal system are hard to disperse with empirical evidence, but efforts (like the paper itself) need to be invested in that nevertheless. Otherwise, the signals are getting lost in the noise.

> *MeToo movement ka waise to koi fayda nahin dikhta: na to log jante hain, phir logon ke pass koi proof nahin hota par har jaga proof mangte hain, MeToo ke pehle bhi, bad bhi. To, us purpose se koi use nahin hain. Par han, misuse hain. Blackmailing ke purpose se use karte hain. Aadmi hi bata dete hain ke yeh karo* (There has been no specific benefit of the MeToo movement as such that I can see: People don't know about it, and then, people don't have proof but everywhere they ask for proof, before and after MeToo. So, in that way, there's no use. But yes, there is misuse. People use it for blackmailing. Men only tell them what to do). So the only way right now is gender training for boys.
>
> —Kamini Shukla, Activist, Rajasthan[117]

In summary, considering all that I was able to learn, there is subjectivity and bias that affect men adversely. Unfair and erroneous arrests, prosecutions and judgments do occur. In addition, bad actors (men and women) do use all mechanisms available with malicious intention (be it Section 498A, general false allegations or MeToo). 'However, what needs to be noted is that the same happens to women, has been happening for centuries, and in certain geographies happens at a much grander scale, tipping the scales completely.' The numbers are not comparable either (we will come to why MRMs and certain men believe otherwise), nor are the women solely to blame for the misuse and mistakes. 'Also, the issue of unfair prosecutions or abuse plaguing men, or any other

---

117 Shukla, recently detected with multiple sclerosis and wheelchair-bound, continues to be a part of SMILE and trains boys and men on women's rights. When we had this conversation, she had just finished one such training.

men's issue, is not what drives the popular MRMs, even though it's said so in most of their charters.'[118]

As we move from men's issues to MRMs, let's start with a quick look at their history and current status. First, what is the MRM? Simply an unstructured, generalized consensus in favour of men's rights? Well, no. MRMs are quite formalized, with origins traced back into the early 19th century. The groups from that time, mostly in Australia, had a basic agenda not too different from the popular groups today: opposition of spousal support, opposition of 'corrosive' influence of women's movements and general opposition to reforms citing damage to families and values. The next phase of men's movement is more or less universally attributed to groups emerging in the early 1970s in the USA (men's liberation groups) which often supported the broader social change and positioned them closer to feminist and women's liberation positions (including opposition to toxic masculinity). Academics have argued that these groups suffered from identity crises—facing scepticism from women's movements and ridicule from mainstream 'supporters of hegemonic masculinity'. In the late 1970s, men's rights groups re-emerged (post re-invention) in the USA—this time with a much closer charter to what is seen today. Some sources note this to be a split of the MRM into pro-feminist and anti-feminist groups. The later (newer) groups considered men's rights to be under attack and masculinity to be perishing, and therefore, not surprisingly, noted to be anti-feminists. Scholars identify this as a 'backlash' to feminism—not a movement arising with a central cause of its own.

Unlike the previous groups, the new ones didn't struggle to sustain themselves. With feminism and women's rights movements gaining ground, they found sympathizers who believed men to be at risk and suffering. The previously cited Hunter–Melville paper

---

118 M. Messner, *Politics of Masculinities: Men in Movements* (Lanham, MD: Rowman & Littlefield, 2000), 41.

makes a brilliant observation: These groups 'translated social issues into psychological issues' and, therefore, urged men to rise and be stronger by sticking to traditional masculine definitions while mostly ignoring the oppression of women. Another masterstroke, as noted by Susan Boyd in her articles on Canadian movements and mentioned earlier, was the extrapolation of risk to men to the plight of families (read fathers). The later strategy seems to be successful for MRMs in India too—with the primary umbrella organization Save India Family Foundation[119] stressing the premise of their origin to be the protection of families, rather than guarding of men's rights. Lastly, most Western MRMs are noted to have close ties with neoconservatism, including financial assistance and support from conservative and far-right groups.

Like for most things (including movements like #MeToo), the Internet and social media have helped significantly with increasing the reach and popularity of MRMs—primarily owing to the efforts of men like Paul Elam.

Paul Elam is the founder of AVFM (referred to by multiple sources as the largest and most influential MRM site). He is a prolific author in this space, is widely recognized as the founder of the modern MRM and has also been called a men's civil rights activist. Interestingly, even though AVFM (and other organizations they endorse like SIFF) has been avidly critical of #MeToo and the lack of due process in a trial by the Internet (it openly publishes on how to end #MeToo), AVFM opened a wiki page publishing personal details including addresses of women considered by the site to be false accusers of men. The page was shut down and then, at the time of writing, was back up again. The page had started with publishing details (including addresses) of women convicted of murdering or raping men and then extended itself to those they believed to be false accusers. Paul, in his own words, is not only anti-feminism but also anti-gynocentrism. He is, in

119 https://www.saveindianfamily.org/

fact, of the view that anti-gynocentrism is the only anti-feminism that matters, criticizing those who proclaim to be not feminists but believers in male chivalry and other such ideologies.[120] He is owed a lot to by the MRM, for he played a pivotal role in revitalizing the movement for the social media age, including effective use of shock and awe counter-tactics like the wiki page above.

Indian MRM started formalizing only in the early 2000s, with groups like SIFF getting founded. Despite the late start, the Indian MRM grew fast and strong, possibly not unsurprisingly given the increasing clash of patriarchal ideologies with highly public horrific incidents that have been forcing the nation to have gender at the forefront of discussion. Just in September 2020, Indian news had four incidents of violence against women or persecution of women dominating the headlines: Hathras gang rape,[121] 2-day-old girl child stabbed with a screwdriver over 100 times,[122] mass social media defamation of women by the government in power: namely, Department of Labour tweeting derogatory tweets for Deepika Padukone[123] and infant girl child buried alive in a shallow grave in an earthen pot,[124] not to mention regularly emerging reports of girl child deaths out of certain states (e.g., Madhya Pradesh, Rajasthan and Haryana). Such overwhelming emergence of gender violence causes a simultaneous rise in a counter-movement (the elaboration of 'the why' of the MRMs in the next segment will explain the why of this too). SIFF and other Indian MRM even find their images included in the Wikipedia page on MRM, are noted as

120 https://gynocentrism.com/2019/12/01/anti-gynocentrism-is-the-only-anti-feminism-that-matters/
121 https://timesofindia.indiatimes.com/india/cbi-files-gang-rape-murder-fir-reaches-hathras-for-case-file/articleshow/78610009.cms
122 https://www.independent.co.uk/news/world/asia/baby-girl-murder-stabbing-screwdriver-india-bhopal-police-b739816.html
123 https://www.freepressjournal.in/viral/d-for-depression-d-for-drugs-labour-ministry-rts-photo-shopped-pic-of-deepika-padukone-deletes-later
124 https://www.bbc.com/news/world-asia-india-50054875

important participants in the International Conference on Men's Issues[125] and have received an endorsement from Elam himself.[126]

> *You guys are lightyears ahead of us.... The Indian*
> *movement is setting an example for the whole world.*
> —Paul Elam, National Conference on Men's Issues,
> Hyderabad, 2016

THE WHY?

Some scholars of the matter such as Susan Boyd and Sarah Madison, in their studies of global MRMs, have stressed the matter of helpless anger originating from the belief that feminism and movements supporting feminist causes have caused real harm to men and their interest to be the driver. They have also called out the belief to be largely invalid. Some Indian researchers have argued that the issues around implementation of certain laws (primarily Section 498A), changing roles in marriage and multiplicity (both civil and criminal provisions of redressal) in means to justice, are driving the purpose of MRMs in India.

I read through multiple accounts and posts on SIFF's (official .org as well as .in which appears to be a copy) sites, reviewed case studies and papers on the matter (including the ones mentioned above) and talked to men—lawyers, professionals, activists and fathers (in the cities and the heartlands). As quoted earlier, I also spoke with women activists on the ground who spend their daily lives in the criminal justice system. Based on the same, I rest the case of male angst with the assignment of two primary causes to it.

1. The belief that supporting and taking forward women's rights causes harm (or will cause harm) to men

---

125 https://www.facebook.com/International-Conference-on-Mens-Issues-684011244952716/
126 https://www.vice.com/en/article/9b8akp/why-indias-mens-rights-movement-is-thriving

2. The lack of mainstream focus and (the more harmful) misguided focus on men's issues

Both above have the same sub-causes: androcentrism and ignorance. Androcentrism,[127] which we have referred to on and off so far, is defined as a worldview that puts men and men's experience in the centre. The below excerpt from Springer is a concise one I found that explains it in the context of patriarchy, misogyny and sexism (important for understanding it in the context of India).

Androcentrism is the evaluation of individuals and cultures based on male perspectives, standards, and values. The term refers to a male-centred worldview which does not necessarily present explicitly negative views of women and girls, but positions men and boys as representative of the human condition or experience and women and girls as diverging from the human condition. It is a complex, subtle, and often unacknowledged form of sexism, existing on a continuum which includes misogyny and patriarchal attitudes, but it is also informed by patriarchal cultures in which men are granted more power and influence, and thus the right to evaluate and interpret individuals and cultures.[128]

First, let's consider the point that MRMs and their protagonists vocally condemn gynocentrism (female-centric worldview), but instead of taking a neutral stance, they fall far and hard into the other end. Meaning, instead of being able to look at a matter objectively, they start with an androcentric (male-centric) outlook and, therefore, present arguments and evidence that are filled with fallacies (including ad hominem arguments, hasty generalizations, false dichotomies, circular arguments, appeal to ignorance arguments, citing irrelevant authorities and confirmation bias).

127 https://en.wikipedia.org/wiki/Androcentrism
128 https://link.springer.com/referenceworkentry/10.1007%2F978-1-4614-5583-7_16

On the topic of false allegations, let's analyse an article[129] from AVFM to demonstrate this through a case study. The article sites the PASK study on domestic violence that we have discussed earlier and uses it to make an argument that as is shown in the PASK study for domestic violence that men are the 'majority of the victims', majority of sexual assault claims against men are (and will be proven in due time to be) false. Since I had read through the findings of PASK study and its references in detail, spending hours to understand the comparisons and conclusions, and was satisfied with its comprehensiveness, I started reading this article with a lot of hope. I expected it to be a legitimate piece that would support its claim well. However, I was quite shocked that the article makes severely flawed arguments and is riddled with commonplace tactics used for fact manipulation.

- It grossly misrepresents and exaggerates the claims in the PASK study and omits critical points. For example, the summary of the study states that women are victimized more by domestic violence. The study never claims that men are the majority of the victims. As presented in detail earlier, the study merely talks of comparable rates of incidents of violence under certain conditions and the prevalence of erroneous prosecution of men.

- Shockingly, the author of the AVFM article decides that there are two categories of rape—trivial and violent—and claims that 'most rapes, as currently defined, are trivial affairs'. The author doesn't cite any reference or data on where this 'current definition' is coming from, or how he knows that most rapes as 'currently defined' are trivial.

- The article makes the circular argument that since most people will not report real rape (even violent rapes), most rape claims must be false (again, mostly as his inference and doesn't provide any reference).

129 https://avoiceformen.com/featured/flooded-by-false-rape-allegations/

- The article also makes assumptions on how (and why) statistics are generated, using it as the primary reasoning to substantiate his claim that most rape claims are false.
  - o It completely ignores the fact that many cases do lack evidence and are hence dismissed. Not having evidence might have other reasons than the story being false. Note: Low conviction rate is a commonly touted fact to discredit abuse complaints. The reasons for low convictions are aplenty and often have nothing to do with the claims being false. I will come to this again in the next example.
  - o It has a confirmation bias approach in offering testimony and examples. It can't be possible that the author didn't come across a single case of 'real' rape on the Internet against his two provided examples of false accusations (which he uses to substantiate his inference that the 'majority' of accusations are false). No reference is provided beyond anonymous hearsay that most police officers have purportedly claimed to him (secretly) that 50 per cent of rape allegations are false.

I have referenced the article so that readers can take a read of the entire document and decide for themselves. Since in this manuscript itself I have tried to provide a plethora of higher integrity articles which present the issues men face (including the discussions on the grey areas and harmful definitions which are real factors that can delegitimize the broader cause and damage a man's reputation), my conscience is clear as I call out grossly misinformative articles like these shamelessly used to manipulate opinions.

The second example I want to note here is of an email that I received in response to an article of mine on Women's Web, one of the many platforms I contribute to from time to time. The email is not unlike many emails (or tweets and comments) I receive, mostly from Indian men, who ask me why I don't see the grossly misrepresented statistics on women's issues for what they are: a

Western ploy to vilify India, a systemic bias against men by 'liberal' activists or a play by bad women for milking men out of their wealth. I respond to every single one of these after researching what they ask me to look into. But I never hear back (at least haven't to date). Sometimes, I get some propaganda videos sent to me, not as a direct response but I suspect as an attempt of so (e.g., last week I got some videos on China and the opposition's ploy of derailing Uttar Pradesh Chief Minister Mr Yogi's progressive agenda by 'creating' the Hathras gang rape). I dive into these too, going deep to identify the source and see if they hold merit. So far, none have.

This particular email, from which I provide a direct excerpt below, calls out India's Crime Bureau statistics[130] on low conviction on rapes and asks me to provide an explanation that if that's the case, how do I believe that rapes really happen in India to the extent (1 reported per 15 minutes).[131] Below is the email excerpt, provided as is (including the snapshot the author had included) to preserve the essence of the sender's sentiment.

3.) Having spoken about the forms of harassment experienced by men who are falsely implicated in a case of sexual harassment I shall now proceed to counter your argument

outraged about the possible few miss users than
the plights of the millions (and millions to come)
who are left scarred forever

You seem to believe that since a 'me too' campaign proves that majority of women active on social media have suffered from sexual harassment silently it also proves that the majority of males are sexual harassers and that the majority of complaints

---

130 http://ncrb.nic.in/StatPublications/CII/CII2014/chapters/Chapter%205. pdf
131 https://asiatimes.com/2020/01/a-rape-in-india-every-15-minutes-government-data/

that are made of sexual harassment stand to be legitimate with only 'the possible few miss-users among millions.' It is exactly this argument that I wish to challenge using legitimate and verifiable data from the National Crime Records Bureau (image attached below).

Disposal of crimes reported under crime against women by courts

There were 11,23,423 cases (consisting of 87,43,388 cases pending trials from previous years and 2,52,682 cases sent for trial during the year) were for trial during the year.

A total of 26,660 cases were convicted during the year 2014, showing a conviction rate of 21.3. Highest conviction rate was observed under the Immoral Traffic (P) Act (48.6)(75.7 under section 8 of this Act) and the Indecent Representation of Women(P) Act (46.7) whereas low conviction rate was observed in case under the Dowry Prohibition Act (10.2) and cruelty by husband or relatives (13.7). A total of 9,82,516 cases remained pending for trial at the end of the year 2014. [Table 5.6]

We have seen what Indian activists have had to say on this matter based on their daily experience. We have also reviewed what other researchers across the world have found. But since the matter of low conviction rates kept coming back, I went back and did a micro study myself. I reached out to lawyers and activists working in the courts and police stations, including organizations such as SMILE, My Choices and ASFI (organizations that work with specific crimes in the GBV domain such as domestic violence, sexual harassment, rape and acid attack). All of them confirmed what Renuka Pamecha had said. To keep the passion with which Pamecha spoke on this matter intact, I am putting her exact words below.

I have said already that I went to court 180 times just to observe and learn. I was part of the gender judges Sakshi study,[132] and I wrote my observations there too. I have written numerous letters—I used to get angry before, but these days, I just write. What is the point of boiling my blood? We haven't had police reform in our nation and the police work politically. Think about Hathras. Even after Criminal Law Amendment post Nirbhaya—where we clearly have it that no semen is needed, no penetration is needed—they are looking for semen days after and are giving statements like no rape has happened. And then they are burning the bodies. *So kahan se hoga conviction* (So from where will conviction happen)? A criminal conviction is very difficult in this system. I have studied FIR cases for over 13 years. I talk daily to women who come to file FIR. Every one of them is pressurized—by everyone—from family members to local bodies to police. *Thoda paisa le lo aur khush ho jao. Jis ne bhi FIR likhwaya, ek ka bhi ghar nahin basne diya* (Take some money and be happy. They don't let anyone who has filed an FIR to be in peace). It's not non-compoundable.[133] So FIR is written but then the women are pressurized. *Mahila se likhaya jata hain ke galat faimi mein complain kiya tha* (They make the women write that she complained because of misunderstanding). Today I tell them not to file a FIR. I repeatedly warn them, especially if they don't have family or maternal family backing. *I tell them FIR likhayoge phir withdraw kar loge. Usse 50 per cent cases false hain jaisi statistics aayegi. Acche se soch lo, muskil raasta hain* (You will register a FIR and then withdraw. That will give 50 per cent cases are false kind of statistics. Think hard, it's a tough road).

—Renuka Pamecha, Activist, Rajasthan

Pamecha added that just in 2019, she had 700 cases (between sexual and other assaults including domestic violence), and she sent them all away from registering an FIR. 'It's a waste of our time and theirs.' She says. 'We can help them better differently.'

---

132 https://papers.ssrn.com/sol3/papers.cfm?abstract_id=1531148
133 https://www.lawhousekolkata.com/2019/03/09/what-is-a-compoundable-and-non-compoundable-offence-in-india/

Both Renuka Pamecha and Kamini Shukla repeated to me that even when it's registered, it is mostly impossible to get an FIR to stand, let alone proceed to court and conviction, even when the women have visible signs of violence all over them. Others added that when it goes to court, witnesses change statements, evidence disappears and, in high-profile cases, judges get changed. I couldn't disagree based on what I now know of the Bhanwari Devi and Gujarat riot cases. 'But what about when accused don't have power or political backing?' I had asked.

'The women have even lesser power and confidence. How can people not see that?' Pamecha's voice had trailed into a sad silence, just like Reicha Tanwar's had when I had asked her about the women in the committees formed under POSH who, according to her, came to the defence of the accused men before even listening to the woman.

The point on conviction rates then, at least for India, I hope is settled. I urge those who have trouble believing to just go to a few local non-profits working with the criminal justice system, meet the volunteers or workers, and go over their notes (I did the same with some volunteers at ASFI—it is a day's work at most, travel time included). Then, if time permits, ask the officials to walk you through some of the FIRs, get the contacts of the women and go visit their homes. In doing so, I was able to corroborate what Pamecha and others said to me. As mentioned, I wrote back to everyone who had emailed me, offering to share what I had learned. I also offered to put them in touch with the organizations and volunteers. To some, I asked if I could have them included here—in this chapter—with their voices captured as is. I assured them that I will send final drafts to them before publishing. As I said, I never heard back affirmative on any of my asks.

This is androcentrism, or, in a broader sense, biased thinking—feeling threatened and having a mindset coming on of being the victim, believing the system to be rigged and shutting down when invited into a discussion. It's having a belief and then looking selectively for information that confirms the belief. Because we don't want our beliefs to be disproved. I found this to be a general behavioural trend in some people, men or women. For example, many people in the USA do not believe that the native people of the Americas were mass annihilated. They search for and find on the Internet only information that supports their belief and ignore the plethora of counter-evidence. There's a Netflix documentary *The Social Dilemma* (2020) that tackles this issue from another angle. Ex-employees of the major companies discussed in this documentary how fake news and conspiracy theories, in the age of the Internet and social media, can be driven by designed algorithms to take up the space that facts use to previously occupy. Meaning, if I want 'men are going to die' and keep searching 'men are going to die', the Internet will give me only 'men are going to die' until I figure it out and do a different search.

AVFM and SIFF site articles that I scouted through demonstrate these phenomena with many of their articles, doing a disservice to the real issues that men face. SIFF's articles on the opposition of the criminalization of marital rape are materials that a neutral reader (man or woman) should go through if they have the time in hand.

Another tenet of androcentrism is the refusal to involve. Many men feel that issues such as gender violence, rape and prostitution concern women and, therefore, are not worth their time. I spoke with politician Margaret Alva,[134] who stressed the importance of having men and women involved in policymaking for gender equality and societal progress. But while women are mostly eager to have a voice, she expressed that many men in the Parliament choose to excuse themselves at the first chance on issues they feel concern women.

> I was in a session, and the men said, '*Prostitution? Yeh to mahilayon ka mamla hain, aap log dekhiye*' (Prostitution? It's a women's issue, you all look into it). And they stood up to leave. I stood up too. I said, 'Sit down and listen. If it was not for you

134 https://en.wikipedia.org/wiki/Margaret_Alva

men, the matter wouldn't have existed. There would have been no "issue" in the first place.'

—Margaret Alva, Politician, India

It should be obvious that prostitution is not a woman's issue. But men, the primary demographic availing the services of prostitutes, believe that rehabilitation and well-being of the prostitutes and their offspring, or even prevention of prostitution (it's a crime in India), is a woman's issue because most prostitutes are women or transgender. This was noted by Renuka Pamecha too, who said that she was in the previous administration's women's committee and is also in the committee set up by Amit Shah.[135]

Aap log kijiye, aap mahilayen hain, NGO hain (You do this work, you are women, you are the NGOs). They say. I say to them, '*hum to kar hi rahien hain, aap karne dete kahan ho?*' (We are doing it, but do you let us?) *Committees banna chahiye offices mein POSH monitoring ke liye. POSH committees bana di par ek bhi monitoring ki meeting nahin huyi. Abhi Amit Shah ke neeche committee hain, ussme bhi main hoon par ek bhi meeting uski bhi nahin huyi. Criminal banana chahiye bolte hain. Arrey, civil law ko criminal kyun banayun? Woh to already hain ... the workplace needs to be safeguarded and saved* (Committees should be made in offices for monitoring POSH. They made POSH committees but not a single meeting for monitoring has happened. 'Now there's a committee under Amit Shah, I am in that too but not a single meeting of that too has happened.' Make this criminal matter they say, why should we make a civil law criminal? That's already there ... the workplace needs to be safeguarded and saved).

—Renuka Pamecha, Activist, October 2020

So we have a problem of disengagement, from an understanding of women's issues to participation in the solution space until it starts affecting (or seem to start affecting) men's (read personal) interests. We have biased thinking laying the foundation and incorrect and incomplete knowledge finishing the building.

---

135 https://thewire.in/women/metoo-congress-amit-shah-gom

The last example is on the prevalence of dowry deaths and reporting of domestic violence cases in India and false accusations.[136] We have discussed previously the misuse of Section 498A; we are not discounting or discoursing that here. However, dowry death and domestic violence are still matters of extremely high occurrence in India. Statistics from the same National Crime Records Bureau[137] from which the numbers and snapshots get sent to me and the Law Commission of India show facts like the following.

- Since 2008, more than 8,000 women are killed by their husbands for dowry every year (this excludes women murdered by their husbands for reasons other than dowry (Section 302, murder) or women driven to suicide (Section 306, abetment to suicide).

- Despite popularized belief, conviction rates under Section 304B (dowry deaths) are relatively high (35%).[138]

- Studies of reported judgments reveal that Section 498A complaint was not filed previously for most Section 304B deaths (meaning, these deaths are additional dowry cruelty statistics additive to Section 498A complaints).

Also, researchers note that police officials refuse to register complaints of domestic violence if dowry harassment allegation is not added, perpetuating the myth that Section 498A is applicable only if dowry is involved. Mere cruelty to a woman doesn't matter. Forcing this addition of a matter of dowry to non-dowry abuse and cruelty complaints contributes to the problem of misuse. The police–lawyer nexus causes law-enforcement agencies to mostly ignore or send back poor women (even with visible grievous injuries) without registering domestic violence complaints.

As Flavia Agnes writes,

---

136 http://majlislaw.com/file/2015_06_06_Section_498A__Marital_Rape_ and_Adverse_Propaganda_EPW_Jun _2015.pdf
137 https://ncrb.gov.in/
138 2012 Law Commission of India report.

There is also an economic motive for the police not to register cases of domestic violence of women from the lower class, as there is nothing to be gained from registering such complaints. On the other hand, if a woman from the middle or affluent class approaches them, registering the complaints becomes a lucrative business, as the police can immediately alert the husband and provide contacts of a criminal lawyer for filing for anticipatory bail, all for a hefty fee. The police–lawyer nexus within the criminal law is well established and the blame for it cannot be attributed to section 498A. When a victim of domestic violence approaches lawyers for a protection order, maintenance and child support, or even divorce, they rush to the police station with a written complaint, which includes dowry demands, and assure her that it is a shortcut to solve all her other problems as her husband will soon fall in line once a complaint is registered. But ironically, the problems only get compounded. It is not as though the woman was not subjected to domestic violence, but this aspect gets relegated to the background.[139]

The last one I witnessed first-hand was with one of our maids, who, after multiple refusals by the police, ended up dead along with her children. Her husband killed himself after killing the family. Visuals on the local news channel of her shanty, with sarees my mother had given her hanging as curtains as the reporters moved in and out of a house where three murders had happened, remain as clear in my memory over a decade later as the bruises on her which she used to hide.

The issue of ignoring what goes on in the heartlands and the socio-economically disadvantaged sections of the society by men's rights groups is definitely a matter. This makes the movements quite classist—with mostly urban, upper (to lower-middle at most) class men crowding the agenda with concerns of loss of reputation, loss of employment and loss of wealth. Yes, that, some

139 http://majlislaw.com/file/2015_06_06_Section_498A__Marital_Rape_and_Adverse_Propaganda_EPW_Jun _2015.pdf

might say is an issue with #MeToo too, and we have talked about it. But movements like MeToo, as discussed in the other chapters, take us beyond the apartment lights. If the MRMs (in India and the world) start focusing on reforms needed for the poor and their socio-economic problems in addition to their current charter of debunking rape statistics and ending #MeToo, I will take back this segment. But till then, let me just summarize through my interview of Anugraha Kumar Sharma, an activist and co-founder of Child Free India,[140] whom I particularly sought out for a perspective on this matter. Anugraha lives a city life in Bengaluru and works with and around technology professionals, but he also spends most of his time with Dalit NGOs and village-focused non-profits. He is also a father to a daughter and an upper-caste man by birth. I had spoken to Anugraha quite a few times, asking for his views on multiple matters covered in this manuscript. When I got him on call on an October evening after a few days back and forth on WhatsApp, he had just gotten into a cab.

'How is Child Free India doing?' I asked for starters (I am always curious about Child Free India—for reasons completely different from the matter in hand here).

'It is going great, Tanu. A lot of people have started following us on social media since the pandemic, so I am now making memes.' He laughed his usual laugh.

I told him why I was calling, explaining what I was messaging him.

> It seems like there's a split Anugraha. On the one hand, there are these men—mostly city dwellers and prolific on the Internet— who believe that men are being victimized, rape statistics are being overblown and there's no issue, definitely not to the extent women make it seem. On the other hand, there are piles and piles of examples the other side puts forward—men and women working in the fields. What goes on it seems is in the villages,

---

140 http://childfreeindia.org/

with the panchayats in power, and even in the fringes of the hubs and just the outskirts....

'I agree with the second group. Not the first,' Anugraha cut me off. 'Women are still getting a raw deal. In scores.' For example, my daughter, when she turned 18, got into some trouble with the men in her life. I introduced her to the police system. I work with NGOs who work with that system—so I told her to not expect justice and explained to her that the police system is still quite patriarchal. But I wanted her to experience the system first-hand. The police, right here in Bengaluru, asked her why she was wearing jeans and a T-shirt. She tried to argue with the police with her brand of feminism. Now, her brand of feminism, mind it, is a bit skewed. Because she is not class conscious. She understands misogyny but not the class or caste nuances. But anyway ... I work with Dalit groups and villagers all the time—'the real India is not for women. Still.'

I told him in detail what I learned about the statistics, FIRs and conviction rates. I also shared some of the material quoted in the MRM site articles, and what some of the men I interviewed (some of which I have quoted) had expressed. Anugraha interrupted me again and said it better than I could.

'Men in urban spaces are coming for an elitist mindset. They are absolutely clueless about class and caste.' Working with Dalit NGOs, Dalit women are double oppressed, but this is not even seen by the Dalit men. The women are much more aware in this regard. So, coming back, in the villages, or the slums, what these men are talking about will sound like fairy tales. The atheist feminists as we call them—very elitist. I believe in the Marxist brand of feminism, which is class and caste conscious, and pretty woke.

Anugraha and I continued to talk for some time on what feminism is and should be. But he had already made the point I was slowly arriving at.

When I had started studying MRMs, men's grievances and issues affecting men (from diving into websites, conference papers and research studies to reaching out to men on the Internet and calling family and friends), I had started with an open mind, with almost a slight bias towards the MRMs. As I have said, I did find several issues concerning men needing highlighting and active mitigation. We have discussed them already. But as I have been summarizing in this segment, the most important finding I arrived at is regarding the MRMs. I found the popular men's rights sites, and, therefore, most of the popular opinion that gets published on men (to either appear woke and balanced or for click-bait value) online, to be mostly misogynist, ill-informed (potentially deliberately) and lacking in intention towards the society.

These sites and articles are not protesting abuse or fighting for redefinition of rape laws or protection of male children in churches or Pakistan. They are looking to end feminism and #MeToo. They are not demanding sponsorship of studies. They are demanding a change of laws that they perceive to be in favour of women through public outcry, without the willingness to go deep into the numbers. They don't want to understand the issues women face and the nuances of caste, class or race. They want a unified front with a single enemy. I found some of them (e.g., AVFM and SIFF) to be calling out hegemonic masculinity. For example, SIFF website has material that calls out the generalization of all men and protests alpha-male and hegemonic masculine behaviours extrapolated to all. Yet they post images on their sites derogating women, calling them a burden (Figure 8.1). And no, they don't feel the need to call out only 'feminist' or 'women who are of a certain kind' while doing so.

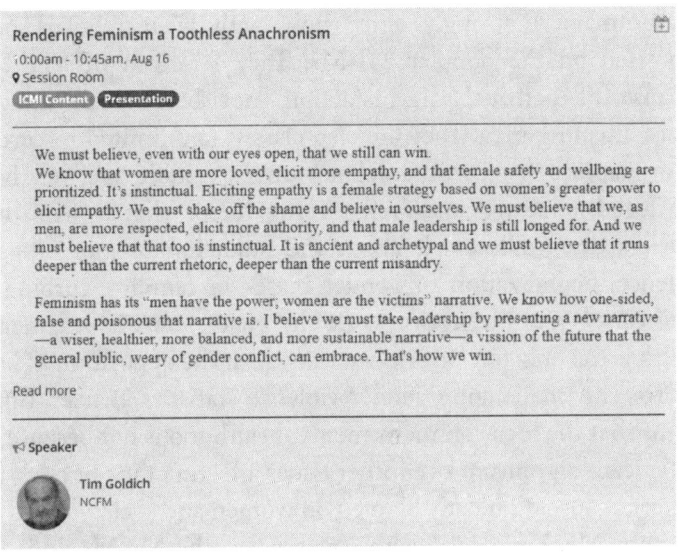

Source: http://icmi2019.icmi.info/

Figure 8.1: Snapshot from Conference Agenda, International Conference on Men's Issues, 2019

On searching for what prompts men to become anti-feminists, I came across articles on Paul Elam—the founder of modern MRM and most prolific of men's rights activists whom we have mentioned above. There is a lot published on his behaviour with his daughter, his refusal to support his children post divorce and his childhood (in which he is noted to have blamed his mother for the ill-treatment and aggressive actions of his father). I will not divulge into details or agree with such implications here, for I don't want to fall into the trap of going ad hominem (and that is why I am not including those publications as references here). However, there are studies, especially on men and their adverse behaviour towards women, that show personality traits and personal experiences to be playing a significant role in the perception of the other gender. The fallacy here is that often the interpretation of the experience itself is shaped by societal gender expectations and, therefore, becomes a circular and perpetuating trap. This is not different for women either.

In summary, I strongly agree now with what scholars have expressed on the popular MRMs: They arise out of fear[141] or because of personal dissatisfaction, not because of broader issues affecting men. They are also classist and limited to certain demographics (e.g., middle-class fathers; middle-age, relatively privileged, educated and well-earning men). That is why their charters don't talk much about the reduction of gun or gang violence, neuralization of gender biases in families, curbing of drug cartels and illegal drugs. Of the major men's issues, mental health is the only one prioritized outside of the opposition of legal reform and challenging gender violence statistics charter. But it seems that the focus on men's mental health too is not because it's statistically significant over other issues affecting men or boys, but rather because it's mostly blamed on women and society in MRM charters. Men's mental health concerns, as the MRMs do it, are not presented from a physiological or data-driven point of view. It's tackled with individual examples blaming women and liberal media for 'stress' on men. Otherwise, corporate performance and work–life balance policy reforms would have been a higher priority, not debunking rape statistics.

As I have concluded earlier, misuse, malicious and erroneous prosecution and victimization of men happen and need to be considered in both policymaking and popular discussion. That, however, is not an excuse for not understanding the socio-economic indexes that show the severity of oppression of women and the ground realities which might be different from one's immediate sphere of experience. Loopholes and biases exist, but the measures do serve valid purposes. So the baby shouldn't be thrown out with the bathwater, which can happen when fires are flamed with misinformed opinion. Let's end with a thousand-foot view, leaving the details aside. How many grievous incidents against women have we heard of, say

---

141 https://idronline.org/need-talk-men/

just in India and just in September–October 2020), that are currently dominating the headlines? Is it possible that the same amount of grievous harm has happened to men, caused by women, over the last month but nothing has come out in the news? However, quotes like the one below can be found abound on the Internet from educated individuals. The excerpt is from an online article.[142]

Sadhukhan joined the MRM five years ago when a sticky divorce left him in search of brotherhood. It was then, he said, like many others at the conference, that he found the men's rights movement and woke up to the 'condition of men in India.' Sadhukhan, who runs a popular MRA blog, calls himself a 'human rights activist,' and he stays away from dowry-law debates. Instead, he devotes himself to other pet causes, including one cherished by MRAs the world over— debunking rape statistics. **'These things,' Sadhukhan said in reference to the fatal 2012 Delhi gang rape of a 23-year-old physiotherapy student, 'they don't happen. It was a very one-off case.'**

THE POINT

Why does any of this matter? Of course, we are not talking about dismissing men's issues—we have made our point on why they matter tremendously if we indeed want to mitigate women's issues. But why does that drive MRMs matter? If, indeed, MRMs and other online propaganda are backlashes, so what?

Well first, it's not just bark, we get bitten too. Legal changes to Section 498A primarily driven through MRMs are arguably steps in the right direction. But many activists argue that it will cause

142 https://www.vice.com/en/article/9b8akp/why-indias-mens-rights-movement-is-thriving; emphasis added.

real harm to the reduction of domestic violence and dowry death. Marital rape, which should be criminalized, will potentially not be anytime soon. Most dangerously, there could be significant reversals of laws and provisions. This is not just an Indian concern, of course (we have discussed the impact on family law and custodial judgments in the USA, Canada and Australia). But for India, where women's safety and development lag quite behind, this will be particularly harmful.

Second (and more importantly), in the age of social media, the battle techniques have changed. Facts can be manufactured, and public opinions can be flamed. One example (again) is the case of three different Central government organizations getting behind the 'pin Rhea (and then Deepika) down' cause in face of other issues of much higher national significance in the fall of 2020.[143] Conspiracy theories and fake news are not in the fringes anymore, and it is getting harder to isolate ounces of truth from manufactured narratives. These movements, if misled, have serious potentials of misleading. It is quite easy to have a significant chunk of the population—male and female—believe that women's rights will mitigate men's rights and, therefore, charters of direct opposition can be established. On the other hand, men's rights activists will benefit and gain legitimization from deep dive into social problems and a broader socio-economic understanding of men–women issues if driven by the right cause of social justice. Laws and measures, after all, can only take us so far and, if reversed under misinformation, they cause more damage than progress.

> Many students expect that a law course will teach them 'the rules' and so they experience considerable frustration when they find—especially in an area of law such as family law that is riddled with discretion and indeterminacy—that the boundaries

---

143 https://www.nationalheraldindia.com/opinion/the-witch-hunt-and-fall-of-rhea-chakraborty

between law and society, law and morality, law and politics and law and other disciplines are not always discernible.... 'Law is not a neutral set of norms, but rather a site of struggle over social meanings ... gendered power relations influence both the ways in which statistics and social science studies are invoked in law reform processes and the direction of law reform itself.'[144]

144 Boyd, 20 Windsor Yearbook of Access to Justice, 2001; emphasis added.

CHAPTER 9

THE PATH FORWARD

In this exploration of MeToo, we went from MeToo to gender rights and are now back home. It became quite a journey for me too. From experiences to statistics and from laws to opinions, I looked deep inside my birth nation and the nation I now call home. I looked back and forward again and again in my attempt to understand women, homes, workplaces, nations and, lastly, men. Now, before I wrap all of this up, let's revisit what we learned.

Feminism, women's rights movement, gender progress—whatever we want to call it—has had its patterns of developments. While in the USA and the West, post the 1960s, progress came in clusters but was continuous, in India, gender has come to the limelight mostly when triggered by incidents. Such protests (which can be called movements themselves), albeit often segregated by class, caste, urban vs rural and regional goals, have caused India to have a plethora of gender laws but the societal change didn't quite come about. In Chapters 1–5, through a review of contemporary cases and study of historical events in India and beyond, we established that:

- 'Societal tolerance is the biggest barrier to women's safety.'

- Such tolerance happens because of what societies have been taught, what human behaviours define (trusting positions of authority and staying together as units: families, communities) and how gender has been manipulated in nations.

- Gender as a cause suffers because gender becomes a sub-identity (to caste, class, political ideology, race, etc.). 'This is unfortunate, inevitable and universal.'

- MeToo, with it's potential to serve as a wide-reaching experience, has done the job of taking a good (and visible) part of the world over a hump, towards a culture of belief. This is because of its relatively general problem statement (sexual harassment and abuse) and easier methodology (callout/name and shame). Its biggest potential continues to be in the creation of a 'such things happening so much is unacceptable' global conscience.

In other words, a culture of seeing evil as evil is needed above and beyond anything else. That is why, as we quoted in the Introduction itself, MeToo being anarchic is a good thing.

In addition, in Chapter 2, we also reached the realization that before and after discussions around MeToo need to be nuanced and fluid, and the same applies to 'awareness', 'inspiration' and 'unification'. The world has struggled to see gender as a problem statement. Gender safety (or equality), as a social argument, has not been convincing. And counter-arguments of family, community, honour, class and caste—whatever really—have trumped it again and again. In Chapter 3, therefore, we presented the economic case for gender.

In Chapter 4, we explored gender violence against women in wartime vs in peace, the legacy of gender subjugation, manipulation of intersectional divides by use of gender and how all of this comes together when it comes to seeing the other sex as equal. Especially for designing a solution space for India, the learnings from this segment are key:

- Gender has been designed into all spaces—from national identity to culture and language in India with specific goals. Therefore, much of what seems eternal and forever, and is celebrated as heritage, is by design and can be traced down to a time in history (from medieval to colonial to postcolonial and modern).

- This is so because gender has been used as a mechanism of control. It is an instrument for maintaining societal hierarchies and curbing oppositions. Specifically, aggravated gender violence has been used as an effective tool in conflict.

- There can be genuine struggles and concerns with understanding the granularities of men and women interactions that can lead to unfair victimization of men and unwanted harm to women (which we have captured in Chapters 6–8), but India's problem with consent runs deeper and is 'the' ingredient of societal tolerance. 'Consent is not a concept that is considered important in India, thanks to the designing of women as lesser and objects (lesser objects).'

- Historical design and entitled (androcentric) thinking are worsened through the perpetuation of incorrect information, stereotypes and harmful, hegemonic gender roles.

Although all of this is largely agnostic to any sect, nation or ideology (atrocities can be attributed universally), specifically in the context of India, understanding the origins becomes quite important, especially in an era of increasing nationalism and polarization. This is to make sure that we don't confuse opinions with virtues and degradation or devaluation of other humans with culture. Legalization and granting of impunity to atrocities against women in times of war and conflict contribute tremendously to violence against women—in everyday life and under aggravated circumstances.

Chapters 4–8 also helped establish the root cause(s), which, as promised, I want to detangle and simplify. 'Sexual harassment is not an isolated problem statement, but if we are talking just sexual harassment, it has two primary causes: sociocultural conditioning that leads to viewing of women as lesser and desire vs deprivation.' The two can be interconnected and interdependent, feeding on each other and manifesting in harmony, but I have reached the belief that the latter, by itself, wouldn't cause actions, while the former can very well be a self-sufficient modulator for gender violence and harassment. In other words, opportunity and sexual deprivation do play a role; however, that's a smaller chunk to target and can be dealt with if the foundational issues are fixed. Because it's a co-factor, not a sole cause.

For example, in the Church scandal, it is obvious that John G. Geoghan had a physiological problem causing him to be constantly preying to satisfy his urges. Several of his physicians wrote about this and noted that his disorder was not curable. But without a blanket disregard and dehumanization of the boys he preyed upon, he couldn't have done what he did. Now, could that be a part of his disorder too? Sociopathy or narcissism and not really conditioning? Maybe. But the goal here is to simplify (and yes, generalize) to make sure that we address what can give us maximum return.

In Chapter 8, we established that, globally, women are still getting the raw-er deal by scores, dispositioning the concerns raised by men's rights groups and movements. This doesn't mean that societies as systems shouldn't understand and mitigate some of the valid concerns (of men) in this space. On the contrary, doing so will greatly serve the cause of women's rights and this should be done. On the same note, MRMs should focus on issues plaguing all men, taking an honest look at their current charters which are largely misguided and segmented. What comes out of most vocal of the men's rights groups are quite elitist and removed from ground realities, especially for India.

I established this with statistics and reports earlier, but here I want to do so with something I heard of in the context of privilege. I found it to be quite profound and could relate to it immediately, which led me to look up the TED talk[1] this was attributed to. But I will try to summarize this in my own words.

---

1 TED talks by Michael Kimmel, who incidentally speaks about why gender equality is good for men too.

In a conference I was attending, a black woman speaker said this to the white woman moderator:

> When I look into a mirror, I see a black woman. You tell me that when you look into the mirror, you see just a woman. Not a white woman. You tell me that it is so because you don't see race. I am telling you that is because that is what privilege is. You not having to think of being white comes from your life experiences. Me seeing race comes from mine. When you walk into Nordstrom, you are left alone or assisted. When I walk into Nordstrom, I am followed with suspicion. Your experience not needing to be defined by your race is what makes you not see race.

I keep thinking about this in almost every context that comes about these days. I remember my discussions with R. Prasad, in which she said that she was conscious of her caste ever since she found out that she had a caste—from when she went to Indian events to when she was in an Indian restaurant in the USA—for she now knows what the next questions will be after the server asks in a friendly tone if they are Dubeys from UP. I remember how I never had to see caste—in India or in the USA. I remember this reading comments on social media of another woman, upper class and caste all her life, who chastises people for bringing up 'archaic' concepts like caste in today's India, where she says, 'There's no one who cares about such things.' I remember this thinking of Muslim hairdressers in India working in Hindu-owned salons.

Most of all, I think about this as I think of gender, of what some men, especially in urban areas say, 'It doesn't matter if you are a man or a woman. Men have it hard too—harder at times.'

Well, when I get into a crowded bus, or walk into an empty street, or try to decide if I should be stepping out of home in certain clothes, I see a woman. I see gender. If you (I am addressing men here) don't have to see your gender when you walk into a space, it's a privilege—not equality.

Coming back to our recapitulation, through the reviews of the legal cases, tabulation of the laws and legalities, and comparison of name and shame vs due process, we saw that most nations have:

- Civil or criminal (or both) provisions against sexual harassment
- Criminal provisions against violence against women

However, criminal proceedings are difficult to initiate and to take to completion while civil measures suffer from bias and conflict of interest (e.g., committees for POSH). Independent outside bodies like EEOC in the USA come with some benefit but will have challenges, especially where there isn't appropriate infrastructure for monitoring (e.g., in the USA, most cases from inside of corporations don't make it to the EEOC for it's considered quite an extreme step). We also saw how laws are not without flaws, are riddled with discretion and indeterminacy and are swayed often by public opinion (from the reversal of gender-neutral definition of rape in India to family law reforms in the USA and Canada). And then, of course, there is the matter of gaps and lacks in the laws. 'Legal changes (good or bad) are easier once public perception is changed. But legal changes don't guarantee that the latter will follow.'

I kept on picking nuggets—as I spoke to experts and stared at articles—of possible solutions. Below is some of what I captured.

- 'Panchayat action is key for village-level societal overhaul and village-level prevention of gender atrocities.' Renuka Pamecha is of the opinion that panchayats, which are elected bodies, need to be forcefully held accountable with the help of monitoring committees.

- Pamecha also stressed 'investing in "monitoring infra-structure"' in place of investment into new laws and analyses committee. From village panchayats to POSH in medium- and small-size employers (where we saw there is a gap in what is outlined), she wants cross-organization monitoring committees in place, who would publish regular reports on progress.

- 'Training of men' is not only being preached but also being practised by Kamini Shukla, who, as we saw, with multiple sclerosis diagnoses and wheelchair-bound, continues to train men and boys. This was also stressed by Gloria Feldt. Sensitivity training, implicit bias training and 'gender bilingual communication' are core charters of her organization.

- Gloria had also put forward something very important in one of our conversations: The only way she had been able to have success with men seeing the value of learning the language of women was with fathers of daughters. She believes that 'the daughters (women) need to take responsibility, therefore, get convinced themselves and own convincing others, that gender rights are human rights.'

- 'The is a need to talk men too', but with comprehensive data and on the right things.

- Another important nugget we came across was the recommendation that 'harassment policies need to be based on values: Values transcend local laws, culture and other expectations.'

- Flavia Agnes writes in her papers that 'moving to victim based from conviction based approach is key.'[2]

The last two (below) are my own and are of everyone I have spoken to.

- **The community of women and women supporting women:** We need to unslice gender and the gender problem statement spaces. Whether it's rape or lack of access to resources, whether it's a black woman—disfranchised and disillusioned—or someone with a privileged experience, gender rights is a singular cause.

- **Equal representation by women, at all levels, in all institutions, in all nations:** That is voice, empathy, understanding, implementation and eventual change of the language.

---

2 http://majlislaw.com/file/The_fatal_flaw_in_the_antirape_campaign_Tehelka.pdf

I do not claim to be a gender expert, only an activist. But I took upon myself the task of writing on this problem statement which would be incomplete without a path forward. What I believe is that the path forward is comprised of what I gathered on this journey. I am merely lining up the needles I picked out of the haystack and, for that, my approach is simple: identify the root cause, understand the risks, add the missing motivator—the economic argument—and then find the lowest calorie–highest impact mechanism to put all of this together. Trying to split hairs about the intangible is not the best path anymore. Out of the factors reviewed, how women and women's issues are viewed and why remain the dominating matters.

So the root cause can be noted as 'gender not seen as a single, or important problem statement (neither by men nor by women)'. And that's because of

- Societal tolerance
- The belief that women are lesser
- Other identities and causes becoming more important
  - **Experiences are worse:** Black women, lower-caste women and poor women, for example, find it hard to solidarize with women whose experiences they know to be better than what they experience and, therefore, solidarize with the cause of their sect or class instead.
  - **Experiences are not so bad:** White women in the USA have been known to support a certain party or a president, for example, despite bad behaviour because they didn't have the life experience to understand what a bit of 'inconvenience' or bad talk could do in terms of setting the stage for gender. I have heard from women who have led quite a protected life (from various nations) saying the same.

What are the risks then?

- Nationalism/fear of Westernization preventing reforms (in the USA or some other nations, this shows up as fear of losing a way of life or of disobeying Catholic dictums)

- MRMs (or counter-movements) leading to misinformed backlash and men and women joining in—worse, laws and efforts getting reversed
- Sexual harassment turning into sexual discrimination with men (and women) discriminating against women
- Slicing of the gender space because of increased polarization because of the surfacing of long-festering grievances (race, caste) or divides
- Exhaustion and insufficient bandwidth against a myriad of issues—COVID, economy, war, natural disasters, etc.

This brings us back to where we started from: Social movements that can raise awareness will go (and have gone) much further than targeted actions through prosecutions, policies or penal codes. Therefore, the best action to supplement and support is to continue spreading awareness in a targeted, collected way. The ways (or rather the way) to tackle the cause and the risks is, therefore, singular and simple.

- Training of society (panchayat, institutions, corporations)
- Training of men
- Training of women and the creation of communities of support (cohorts)

'What gets designed into the training, however, is more important than the training itself.' It needs to have the why: the history, reality and benefits (economics again). It needs to have the how: consent, position of neutrality and monitoring. The why and how need to support the what—gender rights and equality—not overshadow it. For India specifically, we need to de-Indianize honour and culture. Most importantly, training women is often trivialized. There are sound bites around this too that sound like the right thing but aren't. For example, again and again, I hear in women's conferences (mostly from male speakers), something like this: 'Well, it's women's leadership training but it's not the women who need to be trained—it's the men.' And the auditoriums, mostly of women, burst into applause. But the point is that women need to be trained too and, on some points, need to be trained more than the men. They need to be trained to prioritize gender. They need to know the history of women's rights to understand what unification can do and the cost of not being united. They need to know why they can't take a stance of not working or, in broader terms, can't have a choice of not being economically independent. They need to know that giving up their responsibility to work can take away the right from someone else tomorrow. They need to be trained to be not guilted with the family first or community first arguments. They need to know what a regression can do and that where we came from is not too long back. They need to know the statistics, laws and gaps. They need to know what one false accusation or malicious act can do to years of efforts by women (and men). Women, men and societies need to know the economic benefits of having a gender-equal world and the risks: Gender violence isn't too far away from gender inequality. It's not just the GDP growth (which leads to better economies of course). The money saved can go to infrastructure and development of a better world for children (male and female) and families we care so much about.

Such training needs to be on social media—shared by government and corporate handles, dispersed through non-profits and development arms of governments, and talked about in schools and families. All the other solution nuggets listed above can be lined up and placed to follow this via the right agencies. But accurate, efficient and widespread training needs to be done first—like we'd do propaganda when needed. 'Gender needs to be fought for not because terrible incidents shock our conscience. It's because there's no other way to live well.'

In 2019, when I started, gender was still on the forefront (coming off the heels of MeToo) in the USA and the UK (which arguably had an earlier onset of MeToo than India) but was already fatigued in India. Now, the point that India had had a major overhaul in gender safety following a movement of its own (Delhi gang rape

2012, IPC modification 2013) a few years back could have been responsible for its earlier fatigue with MeToo. In 2020, as I was finishing up, the USA arguably had gender fatigue—and had moved its focus to broader inclusion with race on the forefront. India, on the other hand, was getting ravaged with one gender incident after another which was showing the nation that its gender problem was left festering under surface, slowly corroding the nation's veins. Because basking in legal victory, India had forgotten that the society hadn't been convinced. No movement can give us a legacy, only constant efforts can. Therefore, as I end this book—mother of a daughter who I was pregnant with during the 2012 gang rape—I do so with the words of my mother.

I used to ask my mother, who, being a working mother in the 1980s India, used to be blamed for everything, why she needed to work. My father earned well after all, and no other women in the family worked. From my vantage point, most of the other kids at school had their mothers ready to pick them up with after-school snacks in hand while I stared at them wistfully from the school bus window. My mother used to be always tired from trying to cook all family meals and shuffle us to activities while holding a full-time job. She used to lose her temper often and chose to pick up fights that exhausted her further. For example, fighting for women's right to paternal businesses and equal property shares for brothers and sisters.

In a paediatrician's office, one time when my sister had a fever, I heard the paediatrician—a man in his 60s—tell my mother the following in response to why my sister played too much with water during bath time: 'What else do you expect mom? Children need attention and this is what happens to children of working mothers. *Nari-sadhinata* (women's independence) is a great thing … but it is destroying the families.'

I had asked my mother, therefore, in a teenage fit, why was she so selfish? Why did she need to work?

'If I stop being a mother, no one will take that right away from you or anyone else,' she had said, 'but if I stop working, someone might take that right away from you someday. Or there might not be a place where you will be able to work, for it will be all men.'

ABOUT THE AUTHOR

Tanushree Ghosh (PhD, Cornell University; alumna, IIT Kanpur and Presidency College, Kolkata) works in the technology sector in the USA. She is also a social activist and author. Her blog posts, op-eds, poems and stories are in effort to provoke thoughts, especially towards issues concerning women and social justice. She is a contributor (past and present) to several publications, including The Huffington Post, USA; The Logical Indian; Youth Ki Awaaz; *The Tribune*, India; Women's Web; Thrive Global; and Cafe Dissensus (where she hosted her own segment on social satire titled 'Black Light'). Her literary resume includes poems and stories featured in national and international magazines (Words, Pauses and Noises—UK; *Tuck*; *The Pangolin Review*; and *Glimmer Train*'s Honorable Mention) as well as inclusion in nine anthologies such as *Defiant Dreams* (Oprah 2016 reading list placeholder) and *The Best Asian Short Stories, 2017* (Kitaab, Singapore). Her first single-author work is *From An-Other Land* (December 2018, Readomania Publishing). She is the founder and director of Her Rights Inc., a 501(3)c non-profit committed to furthering the cause of gender equality. She frequently speaks on gender rights, social justice, and diversity and inclusion in corporate and non-profit events. She is a member of corporate diversity equity and inclusion management committees and an advisory board member of organizations representing minority voices.